THE DIARY OF
A DUDE-WRANGLER

BY

STRUTHERS BURT

SASTRUGI PRESS CLASSICS

Jackson, WY

Sastrugi Press Classics edition of *Diary of a Dude Wrangler* © 2019

Foreword © 2019 Katherine Wonson
Notes, updated images © 2019 Sastrugi Press
Cover images permission © Chris Burt
Modern images © 2019 Aaron Linsdau

Diary of a Dude Wrangler by Struthers Burt

For permission requests, write to the publisher, addressed
"Attention: Permissions Coordinator"
Sastrugi Press
P.O. Box 1297
Jackson, WY 83001, United States.

www.sastrugipress.com
CIP Data available
Burt, Struthers
Diary of a Dude Wrangler / Struthers Burt—Reprint 1st United States edition
p. cm.
1. Wyoming 2. Cowboy 3. History
Summary: The beginning of the dude ranch history in Jackson Hole is explored by the author through his own ranching experience.

ISBN-13: 978-1-944986-43-8 (paperback)
ISBN-13: 978-1-944986-44-5 (hardback)
920-dc22

Sastrugi Press Classics
00133
Printed in the United States of America when purchased in the United States

Diary of a Dude Wrangler was first published in 1924

Cover image (left to right, date unknown): Struthers Burt, Katharine Newlin Burt, Dr. Horace Carncross.
Back image: The Bar BC ranch as it looked in 2018.

10 9 8 7 6 5 4 3 2

TO ALL THE
DUDES, COW-PUNCHERS, RANCHERS, AND
HORSES I HAVE MET

CONTENTS

PUBLISHING NOTE

The text of the original book has been left as was in the first print-
ing. Some words and spellings have since changed, hyphenated, com-
bined, or otherwise gone out of use during the ensuing century in
the American English language. We hope you enjoy the experience.

FOREWORD

"The desire to succeed and the desire to be left alone are antagonistic."
— Struthers Burt

Struthers Burt was a restless Princeton graduate with an inexplicable lifelong pull westward in 1904. This western orientation finally landed Burt in the Tetons as a partner in the JY Ranch, Jackson Hole's first dude ranch, or guest ranch for those wishing to vacation by stepping into the life of Western cattle rancher. After that partnership dissolved in 1911, Burt joined the JY's resident doctor, and fellow Philadelphian, Dr. Horace Carncross, to found the Bar BC Dude Ranch in 1912.

Jackson in the first decade of the twentieth century had seventeen permanent town structures, no bridges crossing the valley's formidable rivers, sixty families and no stable economy. A man could experience solitude in abundance, but success, or financial success at least, was elusive. Jackson stood as the last remnant of the frontier into the 1880s for good reason. The growing season is less than ninety days long; the cobbled soil is poor for cultivation; there was no access to the market to sell goods, and grazing was difficult on the Homestead Act and the Desert Lands Act's limited land allowances.

A natural entrepreneur, Burt flipped the equation by exploiting the valley's seeming liabilities to become its greatest assets. In Burt's view, it was precisely the isolation, ruggedness, inhospitable climate, colorful bachelors and lack of access to population centers that made Jackson Hole the dude rancher's paradise and therefore a good investment. The Bar BC Dude Ranch represents a simple business proposition: It is more profitable to wrangle dudes than wrangle cattle in Jackson Hole.

To build a successful dude ranch business in the spring of 1912 meant erecting nine cabins, two bunkhouses, a shop and saddle shed, a laundry, 1,120 rods of fence, a well, a bridge, and an irrigation system to accommodate the "tiny village" of fifteen dudes, accompanying staff and the owners. Two teams of unskilled laborers accomplished all this over the two-month mud season with unreliable access to building materials. By 1913, the ranch would expand to accommodate forty guests with an additional fifty supporting staff, creating the conflicting relationship between the desire for success and solitude. As Burt writes, "You must do your best, even on a place where from fifty to over a hundred people are gathered together, not to destroy the impression of wildness and isolation."

Struthers Burt and Katharine Newlin Burt espoused the virtues of the Wild West, isolation and rugged individualism through their popular books (namely *Diary of a Dude Wrangler*), films and magazine articles, enticing urban easterners to patronize their ranch. These dudes, or "strangers to a country," once baptized to the dude ranch life would often, in turn, buy land and start their own dude ranches, continuing the successive pattern of eastern settlement. By 1925, dude ranching had become such a staple of the local economy that there were 600 dudes visiting the valley at a time when there were only 400 local residents. Bar BC Dude Ranch was among the leading employers in the valley.

Dude ranching was a welcomed arrival in Post-WWI-Jackson following the collapse of the cattle market. However, the valley's tourism boom posed a new problem. As Jackson left its frontier past behind, signs of overdevelopment and exploitation of its natural resources emerged. In 1919, the Bureau of Reclamation proposed a dam on

Jenny Lake, spurring forward-thinking business owners like Burt to reconsider their position against the National Park idea to conserve the Teton Range and glacial lakes.

Burt's conflicting desire for success and solitude came to a head in the 1920s as the growth of tourism seemed limitless and the land's capacity to support private development clearly limited. Ultimately, Burt chose the desire to create space for solitude and walked away from the desire for continued success when he put his conservation values into action. In 1930 Burt sold his beloved Bar BC Ranch with the intent for it to become part of Grand Teton National Park. Burt writes, "since it was part of the dude-man's job to protect game and preserve beauty, in other words, to use foresight, he was regarded as a reactionary and an impediment to progress... And, as a matter of fact, the dude-wranglers were the first men to realize as a class the potential values of the Far West, partly from clear-sighted selfishness."

I like to think that the Burts satisfied the desire for both solitude and success when they used the proceeds of the sale of the Bar BC to build the Three Rivers Ranch in Moran, WY. As an invite-only writers retreat, the throngs of guest and obligations of running a dude ranch were safely behind them, offering them opportunities for being "left alone." Success certainly found them as the couple, and later their author son, Nathaniel Burt, enjoyed prolific literary careers while writing at the ranch.

In 2017, over three million people visited Grand Teton National Park. Burt's dude ranching economy was the seed that matured into today's tourism industry. Modern Jackson residents struggle with the paradox of success and solitude just as Burt did. For many of us, success depends on growing the tourism economy that brings more people here, though many of us came to the valley for the same romanticized ideals of solitude that Burt did.

In a bit of poetic justice, the Bar BC is now a great place to go to "be left alone." After the life lease attached to the 1930 sale of the ranch was terminated in 1986, Grand Teton National Park stopped maintaining the buildings. By the early 2000s, the structures were in poor condition and in-the-know park visitors or locals would seek out the ranch to explore the ranch as an architectural ruin. Burt's vision of Grand Teton National Park as "a museum on the hoof" where visitors would experience the western cultural landscape was finally realized.

In 2018, the park and the Grand Teton National Park Foundation entered into a partnership to stabilize two core buildings, the Main Cabin and Corse Cabin, making a commitment to start preserving the important story of the Bar BC. With the republication of *Diary of a Dude Wrangler,* we are similarly committing to the preservation of the Bar BC Dude Ranch. It is the synthesis of the logs and nails and Burt's firsthand accounts of building the ranch that makes its history come alive. Too frequently in this valley, we are left with only the pictorial or written history and not the actual physical historical object. I am proud to have been a part of keeping both the story and the building alive.

Katherine Wonson
President of the Teton County Historic Preservation Board

THE DIARY OF
A DUDE-WRANGLER

"From the mountains on every side, rivulets descended that filled all the valleys with verdure and fertility. . .

"The sides of the mountain were covered with trees, the banks of the brooks were diversified with flowers. . . . All the diversities of the World were brought together, the blessings of Nature were collected, and its evils extracted and excluded."

—RASSELAS.

(*To wrangle:* to herd or conduct something: i.e., *horse-wrangler*, a man employed on ranches to look after horses, to take them out on the range, bring them in, etc. Hence, *dude-wrangler*, a man who herds and takes care of 'dudes,' or strangers to a country. Facetiously, *boot-wrangler*, applied to the valets of the elegant 'dudes' who have such things; *girl-wrangler*, equivalent to the Eastern parlor-snake or sheik. Curiously enough, where live-stock is concerned, the verb can be applied only to horses. There is no such thing as wrangling cows, which can only be herded, or 'punched,' or driven.)

I
The Making of a Westerner

LIKE a great many other Americans I have always had the West in my blood. I cannot remember the time when, at the back of my head, the most fundamental dream of all, there has not been a vision of a small log-house set deep in a pine forest, the sunlight falling in tawny patches through the motionless trees. You left the shimmering miles of buffalo-grass, or sage-brush, and going up a narrow trail, the entrance to which was not too obvious, rode into the cathedral-like solemnity of the evening trees until you came at last to a clearing and a little house and, as time went on, the dream being amplified, a young woman standing on the porch . . . a young woman beautiful and laughingly earnest.

We would eat supper, the kind of supper you long for and never get; steak, fried potatoes, crisp and golden brown; coffee, with rich little islands of cream floating in it; and afterwards sit out in the dusk, where I would smoke a pipe and in the pine woods the love-making of the thrushes would die away into the silence of the forest and the rising moon. . . .

That was my dream; I still have it; it will never be fulfilled.

A solitary log-house set deep in pine woods is possible only to the young or the ambitionless. A man seeks seclusion but pretty soon he is surrounded by numerous others of his kind. The most difficult thing in the world to maintain, if you are interested in anything else, is a home in loneliness. I went West partly because I was in love with isolation; for the past seventeen years I have spent my summers in the company of a hundred or more of my fellow human beings and I have been responsible for bringing into my chosen country almost a score of permanent settlers. The desire to succeed and the desire to be left alone are antagonistic. We parcel our hearts out into building lots.

. . . Over a mantelpiece in the house I knew best during the winters of my youth, a Philadelphia house, exceedingly reserved, brick with white marble trimmings, was a full-length portrait of an elderly man in the high white stock and narrow shouldered, broad collared coat of the early 'thirties'; evidently a successful merchant or ship-owner. A small, fine-featured, high-colored man, with a splendid forehead, gray piercing eyes, and a hawk-like nose. Back of the table where he sat, a sweeping curtain of blue silk was drawn aside to show the lighter blue of a cloudless sky. The portrait, I think, was by Nagel and the man was my great-grandfather. My great-grandfather had been born an Irishman and somewhere in the late seventeen-hundreds, indulging in revolution and ruction of sorts, as Irishmen will, had been forced, to use a Western expression, to leave Ireland 'between sundown and sunup,' a younger brother, remaining sensibly but not very heroically loyal, inheriting whatever property there was.

My family do not like this story, but I am proud of it. Most God-fearing young men are revolutionary one way or another, and I like to think of this sedate and hawk-eyed and successful merchant being a firebrand in his youth. At all events, this young Irishman, this revolutionist, came to America and started life anew as a fur-trader.

There are misty traditions of marvelous adventures; grizzly bears, Indians, buffaloes, the swart fur-capped hunting men who poured down from the French-Canadian north and left traces of their words and customs as far south as the Kansas and Oklahoma lines. There are also passes signed by General Harrison— 'Old Tippicanoe'; a few letters. I wish I knew more about this. Possibly, no, assuredly, my great-grandfather knew Jim Bridger and Coulter and Astor and young Fremont; and shook hands with the survivors of an even earlier generation. Immense solitudes, plains from horizon to horizon sleeping under a cloudless sky, the distant mirage of antelope or Indians, great masses of buffalo like sluggish lakes, and then, faint, startling, unbelievable, mistaken for clouds, the rims of snow mountains! Sometimes I think I would even accept what by now would have happened to me – death, to have seen all this. But you can imagine the impression such an inheritance made upon a small boy's mind.

And there were similar impressions as well.

An uncle went West after graduating from Princeton in the 'eighties' and became a cattleman first in Arizona and then in California just outside Santa Barbara. Quaint; think of it; a cow ranch just outside what are now the suburbs of that Pacific Coast resort. But in my uncle's day, and that was only thirty years or so ago, Santa Barbara was a sleepy Spanish village, its old mission dominating the town, its streets filled with jingling silver covered vacqueros. Adobe houses with gorgeously flowering patios were the rule and every one played the guitar. Now no one plays the guitar and every one lives in curious imitations of English and French country houses, and the remaining Spaniards are a marooned people, a lost look in their eyes. They have their revenge, however —their conquerors are out of place and always will be; it is a Spanish country, the coloring is Spanish, burnt umber and mauve, when it isn't a fierce orange, and violet hills that seem to put their heads together and weep softly at dusk. Against such a background a black-haired nation is demanded, and the brilliance of red tiled roofs, and the scarlet of serapes and saddle blankets.

I have seen what is left of my uncle's ranch; a few whitewashed barns and houses, a meadow or two; remnants to which you come by means of a paved road. And just around the corner are countless little bungalows where, in the cool of the evening, shirt-sleeved young clerks turn the hose on tiny grass plots before the admiring eyes of their wives and too numerous progeny. Well, I suppose that is progress of a kind.

Twice while I was a little boy my uncle came East to spend the summer with us at my grandfather's place in the hills of Lancaster County among the Pennsylvania Dutch . . . . The old house slept in the coolness of Revolutionary walls and Venetian blinds. From outside came the smell of honeysuckle and the warm mingled perfumes of a garden to the south. A tall clock ticked in the hall. On Wednesdays and Saturdays a man came by in a two-wheeled cart and sold for pennies delicious round gingerbread, dusted with flour, like powder on a handsome octoroon's face, and sugar cakes sparkling like Christmas cards. And all around the house, stretching for miles under the August sun, were shimmering fields of yellow grain, broken here and there by the dark green of wooded rises, or the light green of meadows where streams ran bordered by mint. To the north faint blue hills arose, in the hot afternoons shadowed by thunder-clouds. Here lived, or had lived, a recondite robber by the name of Abe Buzzard. Splendid name for a robber—Buzzard! And the little Pennsylvania hills! How enormous they looked at the time!*

The house was filled with young aunts and their guests; laughing, mysterious, singing people, godlike, the women dressed in delightful starchy things the like of which have never since been seen. At the moment the popular songs were, I think, 'Annie Rooney,' and 'A Bicycle Built for Two,' and 'Mrs. 'Enery 'Awkins,' not to mention such sentimental ballads as 'The Spanish Cavalier' and 'Juanita.' It takes about thirty years to build romance; I daresay even now our own humdrum behavior is building future romance for youthful minds. And amongst all these figures, exotic and tanned, more charming than any, moved, during those two summers, the lithe figure of my uncle. My uncle had a closely clipped brown beard and humorous gray eyes, and he was tall and graceful, and he had been a famous half-back at Princeton. One of his minor accomplishments was the playing of chords on the piano to accompany a delightful adventurous baritone voice. I remember a little California cowboy song he sang, the words of which were something like this. I have never heard but one other person sing it:

> "She's as sweet as the breath of the fountain,
> She's as fresh as a flower wet with dew,
> She's as cool as the breeze from the mountain,
> Is my Eva the girl-vacquero.

> She can rope a broncho so sprightly,
> She can stick him you bet your life, too,
> She can throw her riata so lightly,
> Can my Eva the girl-vacquero."

Along with this went a lilting melody like the lope of a horse towards mountains early in the morning—or late in the afternoon.

In the dappled shade of an August orchard my uncle showed me how to throw a rope; how to hold the loop and send it through the air; and I never forgot the trick, nor the memory of the tawny length coiling like a sun-flecked serpent under the thick leaves. This is curious, too, and bears out the assertion that what you learn before the age of ten you learn better than at any other time, for later on—when I had to use them—I found myself notoriously bad at remembering other things to do with a rope; knots, for instance. Each year I had to learn again the 'Theodora' and I never could learn the 'Turk's-head,' and I even had to think a long while before I could recollect the single-diamond in packing.

Undoubtedly these early lessons in rope-throwing were good for my sense of rhythm. I would like to see a course in rope-throwing instituted at each of our universities. There is nothing more Greek, more accurate, more dexterous. Even now I would go miles to see an expert roper, when I would hardly stir a foot to witness the dull and unintellectual feat of riding a bucking horse. . . . It isn't what a man knows that matters, anyhow, but how near to a straight line he can drive the processes of his mind; how near to a lean and useful muscle he can make that mind; how near, in other words, he can come to lassoing a truth or a method. No man should be judged by what he doesn't know, he should be judged only by how quickly and sensibly he assumes new duties.

In all of this I am not speaking of fancy roping—a childish pursuit, never heard of until fifteen years or so ago. Fancy roping has nothing to do with actual range work. . . the pursuit of a horse or a cow, the loop falling over the neck, the throwing and hog-tying the dainty steps of the cow-pony, wise and alert as the rider himself. One of the best fancy ropers I've ever seen could barely ride a horse, and there is a famous instance where the art was learned entirely on the stage of a New York theatre.

My uncle also had a wealth of stories, but I remember only one of them, a story having to do with the contempt of the Westerner for 'the parlor' or anything but 'a man's size gun.' It seems that one day on an overland train the porter, while cleaning out the smoking compartment, stooped over and dropped a derringer from his hind pocket. My uncle, darting upon it, had traded a ten-dollar bill for the privilege of throwing the filthy thing out of the window. This tradition concerning 'the parlor gun' still persists. To the Far Westerner there is nothing so humiliating as to be threatened with or shot by a small caliber revolver; although it was lucky for the West that the .22 Police Positive was invented only comparatively recently, for it is an accurate gun, and most bar-room shooting in 'the good old days' was anything but accurate.

I nearly became a Californian. My uncle wanted to adopt me and would have done so had not my two brothers died within a short time of each other. Here was another turn of fate. As you grow older you look back and see the many things that might have happened to you. Undoubtedly a man is what he is, also, undoubtedly, he is not, and I am glad I am not a psychologist or a sociologist whose business it is to attempt to read this puzzle, since it can't be read. The same chance that prevented me from being a Californian prevented me from going to a boarding-school; I went to a city day-school instead. City day-schools are an abomination before the Lord. To bring a small boy up in the city is to make him walk through hell. He is lucky if he comes through unscathed.

After these two visits my uncle went away and did not come back any more until the last tragic time, but every Christmas for many years we children received tiny mince pies, about the size of a fifty-cent piece, baked by his Chinese cook. We never ate them, we preserved them carefully until they became mummies of little mince pies.

I wish lovely, lithe, sunburned young men did not die. I wish charming, adventurous, baritone voices were not stilled. The mountain trails and desert ways of the West must by now be filled with the shadows of such figures and the echoes of such voices.

* Abe Buzzard has just been released—May, 1924—from the penitentiary, after serving forty of his seventy-two years in State institutions. He is now giong to spend the rest of his life in preaching to the convicts upon the follies of crime.

II
THE TROUBLESOME TWENTIES

THERE were a good many years in between, for two of which I was a newspaperman—a very young newspaperman . . . . sixteen and seventeen years old, walking with curious innocence among other newspapermen and fires and murders and suicides. And those were the days when newspapermen weren't considered good news-papermen unless they got drunk. The era of 'fake news,' moreover, was at its height. As schools for sensational fiction-writing there has never been anything invented the equal of the daily newspapers of twenty-five years ago.

I remember one city editor, trained in the latest New York fash-ion of journalism, who informed his staff, of which I was the most youthful member, that he expected 'a beat' (or 'scoop') from each man at least once a week, otherwise a job as reporter could not be held. This, of course, was an impossible demand and the result was extraordinary. For over two months the columns of what had been a conservative journal blossomed with the most gorgeous lies the hu-man mind could invent. Two of the more adventurous spirits forced at the point of a pistol a false confession of murder from a half-witted boy who had already been acquitted in a sensational trial, and the shipping-news reporter, a great friend of mine, introduced to the world of science an entirely new animal brought from the jungles of Brazil by a Portuguese ship. I drew the picture for the woodcut. This story was copied from one end of the country to the other and any number of inquiries came from zoological gardens and learned societies.

It was fortunate, I think, for the salvation of my soul that after my newspaper experience I entered Princeton University and came under the influence of the honor-system and the benign traditions of that venerable institution. And it was still further fortunate for my soul that, after graduating from Princeton, I went for a while to a German university and then to Merton College, Oxford. Hindsight is not fair sight, but I am sure that even then I distinctly knew that the American and English undergraduates were decent fellows and good sportsmen and that the German undergraduate was neither the one nor the other. National generalizations are frequently absurd, but this generalization is true. And I also began to perceive dimly what I now feel strongly and that is that the wickedest thing ever introduced into American education was the German influence introduced fifty odd years ago.

English education develops a man as an individual; German education develops him as a unit of a multitude. That is why the English are thinkers and the Germans students and soldiers. The Englishman believes that even a wrong thought, arrived at by using the mind, is better than a right thought accepted second-hand. The English universities teach you to think; the German and American universities to repeat. And, paradoxically enough, the English universities achieve this result by a somewhat circumscribed course of study. Yet it isn't really paradoxical since thought is the result of exercise not system. The Englishman draws a circle and then tells you to strengthen your mind by pushing against that circle as hard as you can. Subjugation and discipline are not the same thing. All great minds are disciplined; no great mind is subjugated. It is well to think about this, for the gravest danger to which a democracy is liable is that the very initial freedom it grants will in the end result in the complete subjugation of the individual and the intellect. . . .

I did not know exactly what I was doing; I doubt if most young men between fifteen and twenty-five do; and I certainly did not know that half my restlessness came from the fact that my great-grandfather had been a fur-trader and my uncle a cattleman; came from the portrait in the house in Philadelphia and the tawny rope flying through the shade of an August orchard. I knew this afterwards, but youth is not, as a rule, intelligently self-conscious. I only knew that I wanted to live in the West and that I wanted to write.

For a while several things held me back from the West and from writing. For one thing, I was exceedingly avid of life, and that took up a good deal of my time, and for another, having been brought up a Philadelphian of the dark ages, it was impossible for me not to be vaguely troubled by the thought that, after all, the only 'manly thing' for a man to do was to be a banker, or lawyer, or something like that. I compromised, upon my return from Oxford, by accepting for a couple of years a position as instructor of English at Princeton, but I must have been a poor instructor for I loved the writing of English far too well to be able to teach it properly.

. . . The sweet clipped syllables of English; the tender, stubborn unmalleability of it, and the fussy, silly things you have to do, if you teach or criticise, unless you happen to be a great teacher or a great critic.

But I had a living to make and couldn't go on looking about forever. Some way or other I had to settle down, and it seemed to me I had one of two choices; either to go to New York and announce myself 'a writer' and earn my keep by some subsidiary job until I *was* 'a writer'; or else to go West and be a rancher until I was 'a writer.' A mature essayist and poet, a man thoughtful in his generation, finally decided me by wisely saying that, in the beginning 'writing was an excellent walking-stick but a mighty poor staff.' So it is. It is the one self-taught profession there is and the material out of which it is made is life, and I can imagine no place where there is less material of life than in the average literary circle of New York.

I might add that there was a girl connected with my choice; there usually is in the choices of men in the early twenties. She was a very lovely girl, and as I look back upon her now, from not such a frightful lot of years, I see that she was very patient as well. How she could have stood me as long as she did, I don't know. In the end she didn't, and for her it was fortunate. By no manner of means could she have been the 'simple, smilingly earnest young woman' of my dreams, although for several years I tried by every known disagreeable method possible to the mind of a youth in love to force her to be. She escaped.

At all events this—at the time—tragedy added a new element of fierceness to my desires, and I finally settled in the West an exceedingly fierce young man. And that was good, for the frontier has in the main been settled by fierce young men; fierce because they have been disappointed in love, or by their families, or by some untoward stroke of fortune. After a while the fierceness of the country irons their own fierceness out of them.

III
British Columbia And Elsewhere

BUT long before this I had been going West with fair regularity and, in fact, had acquired an interest in some Wyoming land a couple of summers earlier, and for awhile had tried the unprofitable task of running two jobs at once; teaching at Princeton in the winter, ranching in Wyoming in the summer. I say 'had acquired an interest'; I had done nothing of the sort, for I hadn't a cent of capital. What I had done was to obtain an option on a half interest in a ranch, and it took all my summer earnings and part of my winter salary to keep my option alive. It was very fortunate that I had merely an option and had not purchased an actual interest.

A man looks back upon his extreme youth with a sort of horrified admiration. It is a mistake, I think, to assume, as most people do, that youth is more courageous than maturity or old age, but it is infinitely more audacious; it will take chances that no sensible man past thirty would think of taking.

From the time I was seventeen I had, by hook or crook, been stealing, during my holidays, up to the Rocky Mountains and beyond—in those days even Illinois and Nebraska seemed the West and exciting; and twice I had managed to consummate as expensive a trip as a man can make; I had gone sheep-hunting in British Columbia. I don't know how I did this; I don't know how I convinced elderly and rich relatives that it was imperative that I should undertake these costly expeditions. I should have been a bell-boy in a summer hotel, adding to my always inadequate university funds. And it was equally quaint that I, comparatively the greenest of tenderfeet, should have chosen to hunt, as my first big-game animal, the elusive big-horn, the shooting of which admits a man at once to the innermost circle of sportsmen.

Perhaps it was in just punishment for my fool-hardiness that I got no sheep. And I never have shot a ram, although I have shot almost all other American big-game animals. Now I no longer want to shoot one. Only last September on top of the Continental Divide, I was within a hundred yards of the finest bunch of rams I have ever seen; nine of them, and all but one excellent heads, and the leader a great old black fellow with a curl to his horns that made you gasp. And a night later I was on a ridge just above ten other sheep bedding down for the night. Yet I had not the slightest desire to shoot. I have reached the point—I am giving the impression that I am well on in years—I am not in the least well on in years, but it is difficult not to seem so when writing reminiscences—that many hunters of big game reach when it seems to them a stupid thing to kill unnecessarily. It is rather silly, when you come to think of it, to feel that you have done anything especial because for a fraction of a second you've held true a high-power rifle, carefully tested, particularly if you use round-sights, although I should be the last person in the world to say so as I still belong to a firm, part of whose business is the outfitting of hunting parties. One has to be pretty bad, however, to miss, and I hate to see a large wheezy business man, who would be lost in five minutes if he didn't have someone to look after him, knock down a creature he couldn't possibly reconstruct, and so much more beautiful than himself. But the tracking of animals, the outwitting of them, the watching and studying and photographing of them, is magnificent sport.

I hunted sheep in British Columbia perhaps sixty days in all, putting them end to end, in the company of Siwash Indians, and I saw scores of sheep, but mostly ewes and lambs. Once, returning to camp over a divide in the dusty red glare of a northern sunset, I dropped around a shoulder of rock onto a dozen or so sheep lying down. They were just as surprised as I was. They were all about me; I touched them; the dusk was full of flying shadows. Down a canyon went the diminishing rattle of stones and then, as suddenly as the silence had been broken, came silence again. But a wildness had gripped my heart I never got rid of.

A few nights later a similar wildness gripped it when I was riding along a fir-clad crest and, to the north, deep in a wilderness of forest and jagged ravines, a single shaft of flame shot up into the air.

Now I knew that this was a forest-fire, the result of spontaneous combustion, or lightning, or of trees rubbing together, but I cannot convey to you the queer effect this shaft of flame, symbol of the most intimate and primary act of man, had upon me. I felt that this was no forest-fire but the council-flame of some gathering of huge and silent gods.

And there it is! Men are either born with an assurance that Pan exists, or else they are born with a complete lack of knowledge of the subject. Most frontiersmen and prospectors and cow-punchers and woodsmen are Pantheists although most of them have never even heard the term. They are born, that is, with a fluttering wild thing in their hearts that stirs chokingly over incidents that engage the rest of the world with only a mild curiosity, ignorant or scientific.

British Columbia when I first saw it must have been a good deal like California of the earlier gold-days. Physically it is much the same sort of country—rushing mountain streams cutting their way through narrow steep valleys; shaggy forests; small plateaus high above the rivers where straggling towns cling. How can it be summed up in a word? There was an extraordinary misty, smoky romance about it; a feeling of isolated men and isolated canyons. Not in the least like our own West—outside of the coast West. In the United States the mountains spread out fan-wise like the fingers of an open hand. You go through one mountain range and cross a desert, and then you go through another mountain range, and cross another desert, and so on, and even in the mountain ranges the valleys are wide and filled with sun-light. But in Canada the fingers of the hand draw together and you are locked in valleys where the sun sets at four o'clock . . . . I wish I could find the word to express British Columbia. The sentence that would give the flavor of it as you catch the flavor of wine. Perhaps it was like a purple grape with the faint bloom of the coast fog upon it.

There were no cowpunchers there at the time; no cattle life at all. The people were the earliest types of frontiersmen; gold miners, prospectors, packers, stage-coach drivers, gamblers, squaw-men. Bearded men, mostly, with high laced boots or moccasins. Not picturesque to look at, not half so picturesque as swaying buckaroo, but exceedingly picturesque inside.

I remember distinctly three pleasant Scotch-Canadian engineers, because one day they set out in a small row-boat from a gold dredge in the middle of the Fraser River and, the boat upsetting, all three landed at the same moment on a sand pit further down; and one of them could swim and two of them couldn't. They were very much astonished. Their eyes were full of a watery amazement. The Fraser is like a brown avalanche. It roars with a grinding of big boulders tossed about in its depths. Swimming is not of much use; like an avalanche, it depends upon whether, in the titanic mirth of the waters, you happen to be tossed up or down.

For twelve years I have lived upon the banks of one of the worst rivers in flood in the West—the Snake—so I have had a chance to study mountain water. The force of it is unbelievable. A horse will take you through if you refrain from neck-reining him, and, if you have to interfere with his head at all, you pull with only the gentlest pressure upon his mouth, or, if he g begins to sink under you, you slide off and grab a saddle string or his tail. Don't be afraid; he can't kick you in the water. But look out if you upset him, or let go of him. A horse gets into panic in the latter instance and will come straight for you and trample you under. Most men drowned while swimming horses have been drowned in this way.

In my years of dude-wrangling, however, I recall one startling experience where the wife of a member of one of the greatest banking houses in the world performed an unparalleled feat. We were leading some horses around the edge of a lake and, the bank becoming too steep for further progress, I was forced to go out around a point of rock and found myself almost immediately in swimming water. I called out to the lady in question to stay where she was, but in her excitement she mounted and, picking up both reins on the same side of her horse, proceeded to guide him out across half a mile or so of the coldest water in America. I tried to overtake her, but couldn't catch up with her, and then suddenly, with swan-like ease, she stood up in her saddle, made a perfect dive, and beat her horse to shore. I have never seen it done before or since; I am not sure that I want to see it done again. The expertness of panic is as astonishing as the bravery of ignorance. How the lady even arose to her diving position in her heavy riding clothes and poised so gracefully upon a submerged, swaying saddle is beyond me . . . .

There was in British Columbia a charming hunch-backed butcher who, fortified against the dampness by Scotch whiskey, all one day on a four-horse stage that skirted the precipices of the Fraser when it wasn't running through the half-tropical luxuriance of the coast forests, sang over and over again, the dozen or so verses of 'The Picture Turned towards the Wall.' Later on this same butcher introduced me to a man who became an excellent friend of mine; a sober, horse-faced

man who ran a bar and road house where two rivers joined. He was
a gravely courteous man with a gentle eye—that could look like a bit
of steel—and a soft voice—that had at times an ugly rasp in it—and
I am afraid he had been forced across the border by a pursuing posse.
What I particularly remember about him was his advice concerning
a young Siwash Indian who was cooking for me.

"Find that asterisk Injun fresh?" he inquired genially.

"At times," I had to admit.

"Well, if he says or does one asterisk thing you don't like, take yer
gun and shoot the asterisk son of an asterisk. The world's full of
Injuns." I could see not the slightest sign of paternal solicitude.

But days afterwards, Joe, the Indian, looking thoughtfully at the
sunset dying behind the mountain range that hid our camp, asked
me if I knew so-and-so. "He's a dandy feller," he said, "and he's sure
fond of me . . . . Do anything for me. Treats me just like his own son."
Which in fact, so they told me afterwards, Joe was.

Two remarkable creatures, a Baron and a game-keeper, huge,
bearded, guttural, were out hunting for a prize offered by the German
Emperor. I met them miles away from anywhere while I was riding
ahead of a pack-train. I had heard the bells of their horses, turned
out for the night, and this had excited me for I had seen no one but
my own outfit for weeks; and then I came through a grove of aspen
trees, silver in the twilight, and saw a camp-fire and an immense
solitary man with a forked beard. As I saluted, he stooped suddenly,
picked up a shot-gun, slipped two shells into the breech, and held
the gun at port. Instinct told me he was an exclusive man who did
not care for company, so I said 'Good evening,' as politely as I knew
how, and rode on. I did not know then what I know now, that all
unreasonable hostility is the result of fear. Strange as it may seem,
this huge bearded man was afraid of me, a slight, unshaven boy.

The man with the forked beard was the game-keeper. A few hundred yards further down the trail, a giant of a man, almost fabulous in the gathering dusk, appeared the Baron. He was swinging along, a Mannlicher rifle in his hand, yodeling at the top of his voice, and behind him came a little, white-haired sixty-year-old Indian whom I knew, carrying a freshly killed fawn. Subsequently I heard the story of that first day's hunt, and it was a quaint story.

The two—the Baron and the Indian—had set out early in the morning to hunt sheep, but after an hour or so of climbing, the Baron had suddenly come to the conclusion that his guide was trying to kill him, and, bringing his cocked rifle to bear upon the latter's wizened figure, had leaped behind a rock. The Indian, thinking naturally that his 'hunter' had become dangerously insane, had done likewise, and in this manner the two had spent the broiling hours of morning, noon, and early afternoon. How they reached an amicable agreement at sundown, I do not know. Eventually the Baron got a magnificent collection of sheep, goat, and bear, none of which he shot himself, for, warned by the initial misunderstanding, he spent his time in camp reading novels in a hammock while the little Indian hunted for him.

I have often wondered who won the Emperor's prize.

This is an absurd story, but it is true, as are a good many other absurd stories I shall tell before I am done. No one sees human nature in queerer aspects than the guide or tourist-man. In the end these two fortunate unfortunate classes realize that there is nothing too grotesque, or fantastic, or out of the way to be beyond the reach of human intention. And I will state, before I go any further, that the guide and the dude-wrangler earn every cent they make—which isn't very much. For, if nothing else happens to them, sooner or later their naturally cheery and optimistic souls become filled with a certain grimly humorous sardonicism.

The belief that a guide is responsible for all the roughnesses some-one once scattered about the Rocky Mountains is by no means as rare as you would imagine. Naturally a guide chooses the safest and easiest way he can find, but many people refuse to think so. Just this summer an intelligent man, prominent politically and financially, out with one of my men suffered from this delusion. Perhaps it is Freudian. Perhaps the fact that you turn yourself over utterly to another person sends you straight back to the nursery—you begin to look upon your guide as a nurse. I know of nothing else to account for such childishness.

To me the real importance of my British Columbia experiences was that I came to know the high mountains of my own continent for the first time. Overlaying the passion that was mine by heredity and tra-dition and childish memory there were now varied remembrances of colors and smells and exultations—the dry pungent smell of lichens and dwarf wild flowers up above the timber-line; the cool smell of stream beds in fir-clad ravines; the smell of glaciers on a hot day; the curiously Oriental smell that comes from the chimneys of log-houses burning wood; the exultation of dawn, and sunset, and a night of mountain stars or moon; of conquering a problem in wood-craft, or trail-craft, or horsemanship; the exultation of coming back, through a dusk acridly sweet with catnip and mint and mountain-meadow dampness, to the tiny glow of a camp-fire; the dizzy exultation that is yours because of the colors of butte and valley and immense moun-tain ranges, far or near.

Here is a fact—in all the world there are no two mountain ranges that have exactly the same coloring. There are no other mountains, for instance, that have the exact opaline quality of the Rockies, not even the Dolomites to which they are frequently compared. Our own, and the Canadian coast mountains, have a misty blue solidity, but the Rockies are translucent—something seems to shine from within them, giving to their faint grays and greens and pinks and crimsons and ultramarines the look of a rose crystal. And, with the exception of the Dolomites, they are the only mountains I have ever seen which retain color after dark.

You come to them excitingly. You have become so inured to the plains—the flat country; settled down to it; hot and wide and filled with mirage, utterly still save for the wind and the shadows of the clouds. And then at dusk, or possibly early in the morning, you see what may be another mirage, except that the hour is too late or too early, or what may possibly be merely heaped-up cumuli. All day long you doze in the heat, or all night long you sleep, and by evening, or morning, you wake up to an entirely different earth; an earth of trees and swift water and swift winds; an earth of constant movement, where only the pines and firs and peaks are immensely immobile.

Once I stood upon the open observation platform of a Canadian Pacific train behind two Englishmen when Mount Sir Donald—I think it was—came into view. It is, if you remember, a sombre earthquake of granite turned upside down. The Englishmen stared at it apparently unmoved through binoculars and then, after a long pause, one of them said:

"Care for swarming?"

"Rather."

"Like to swarm that?"

"Possibly."

Doesn't look half bad for swarming."

"Not so bad."

But that isn't fair, for, under their trained unemotional surface, the English are a passionate race, perhaps the most passionate in the world, and they adore mountains and the land. My irritated companion remarked, however, and not without justice, and sibilantly: "Bees !"

You must search for the loveliness of America; it is not obvious; it is scattered; but when you find it, it touches you and binds you to it like a great secret oath taken in silence. I wish that it were possible for me to see the Rockies once more for the first time.

IV
The Pass

RATHER vaguely and adventitiously; driftingly, in a manner typically Western, after interludes in the State of Washington and New Mexico, where I must have been a very green and useless, if eager, ranch hand, I found my final abode. I was twenty-five years old and I happened on a June day, a tepid dispiriting June day, to be walking along the streets of Philadelphia when I met my friend the doctor. I was disgusted with life in the sharp way possible only to youth. The doctor stopped me. There was a smell of hot asphalt and the languid breeze filled our eyes with dust. What was I doing that summer? Nothing. Would I go West with the doctor and his wife? They were going first to the ranch of a man of whom they had heard and then, later on perhaps, they might hunt antelope. The expedition would cost practically nothing, which was good, for I had just about nothing to spend.

And then and there—we were standing on the corner of Fifteenth and Walnut Streets, if I remember correctly—I became a Far-Westerner, although, at the time, I didn't know it.

The doctor was a delightful adventurous citizen with a drooping yellow mustache and a clear eye and a lean figure, who looked somewhat like a cowpuncher himself, and who had reached his high estate in medicine, from being a country school teacher, by the very combination of audacity and energy that sent him off on long trips to the Far West. But when he reached the Far West he spent his time curiously, as I subsequently learned. He had a passion for carpentering and he did little else but make rustic furniture out of pine poles, hardly moving from the patch of sunlight in front of his cabin until the hunting season opened. He is dead now—another fine dead man.

Death after a while does not so much appal you, or frighten you, or, possibly, even sadden you, as irritate you. It takes out of the world so many charming and colorful people.

For some reason the doctor, an extremely busy man and one fairly absent-minded about the actual details of living, thought we were going to a country eighty miles or so east of the country for which we were actually headed, and I don't think any of us knew the difference until we had left the train and were swaying across the Idaho prairies in a two-horse, white-top wagon towards a great barrier mountain range that barred the rising sun. I am glad the mistake was made, for we found the loveliest mountain country in America, and I have been there ever since.

This is not merely the enthusiasm of a resident. I think most people who know America agree with me. Both Owen Wister and Theodore Roosevelt have said the same thing . . . . That latter great man! I must step aside for a moment to describe the only time I met him. It was shortly before his death, and it was in a crowd, but he held out his hand and said: "Good for you! We're fellow ranchmen . . . you, in the most beautiful country in the world." No wonder people adored him!

Afterwards we talked—as if he had no other interest in the world— about the West and especially about the big game, the elk herds, for which my country is famous. And this extraordinary man knew more about elk and had wiser ideas about their preservation than any one with whom I have ever discussed the subject. A few minutes later he was talking to my wife, who is of Dutch descent, with equal eagerness and knowledge about Dutch nursery rhymes. Subsequently I wrote him a letter saying that when the war was over—we had just entered the war—I would like to take up with him again this matter of the elk and I added that he was the only man in public life in whom the Far West 'thoroughly believed.' He sent me back a charming brief typewritten answer and in his own hand-writing he had inserted, as if the conviction had suddenly come upon him with unexpectedness and force, making it doubly flattering, 'and I believe in you too.' . . .

I must tell another story before I proceed. Black Horse, an Arapahoe Indian policeman, who, incidentally, did not know the ex-President except by the name of 'Teddy,' and who had been trained at a government school to be an expert accountant (extremely useful knowledge for a reservation; almost as useful as being taught to be a pearl-diver), was once sent to Washington on a mission. He was granted an interview with the President and found himself one morning in a long room with a man 'with teeth' sitting at the other end of the room behind a desk. A grave prelate of the Roman Catholic Church was just leaving, and Black Horse paused at the door. And then, suddenly, 'the man with teeth' looked up and seeing the waiting Indian in the distance, raised his hands and made motions with his fingers. He was talking sign-language.

There is no road like a new road and no new road like the new road that has as its end mountains to cross. That first day we left the train at four-thirty in the morning and stepped from the stuffy slumber of our still unawakened fellow-passengers into the cool sleep of a little prairie town. Far off to the east, sixty miles or so away in the direction of our destination, gigantic serrated mountains were just beginning to be touched with light. The air was keen and heady. A mysterious muffled figure, descending from a white-top wagon, met us and, after breakfast, we started on our creaking somnolent journey.

The sun came up. We saw a vast billowing country—Idaho sheep-range—tawny yellow in color, ending like a tawny yellow sea upon the dark coast of the distant mountains. Nowadays the sheep-range has almost disappeared and its place has been taken by dry-farmers, and, much as it is in my blood and training to hate sheep, none the less I regret them in that particular place. The tawny yellow of the untouched land has been changed to the rippling yellow of wheat . . . . Wheat, however, is very beautiful.

The railway, too, has moved nearer; a little branch line has been built. The station is now only forty-five miles away from our ranches—I say 'our' and 'ranches' because now we have become a soulless corporation. But in those days the railway was a hundred and five miles away—a two days' journey if you were lucky and the weather was good, a three to five days' journey if you were unlucky and the weather was bad. And at the end of the flat country you had a mountain pass to cross, eight thousand five hundred feet high.

After that first trip the weather seemed always to be bad, where I was concerned, out on those Idaho prairies. I remember upon occasions changing the wheels of wagons to runners because in some places the terrific winds had swept away the snow and in other places the snow lay deep. Had you touched the runners or the rims of the wheels with bare hands no skin would have been left, the steel was so cold. But after a while, an eternity of gray pitiless hours, you came to the mountains and then everything, as if by a magic wand, grew suddenly white and soft and still; there was no sound but the creaking of the tug-chains and the puffing of the horses except, every now and then, the far-off slithering roar of a snow-slide. A world utterly white, or deep green where the forest clung to the clambering hills; and windless and soft; but as cruel as the gray world you had left behind.

Strange how a dominating physical feature moulds the character of a country. The Pass—it is always spoken of as The Pass—is never very far away from the thoughts of the inhabitants of the valley.

From the middle of September on, even in summer after a heavy rain, the most frequent question you hear or ask is: 'How is The Pass?' Sometimes The Pass kills people. There are certain well-known draws descending into it where snow-slides run and on hot sunny days late in the winter you watch these and hurry by as fast as you can. And almost every spring, when the snows go away, they leave behind the skeleton of a horse or two and a breathless tale of a driver who made his escape just in time or who was carried down but managed to get to the surface. Occasionally drivers fail to get to the surface.

But The Pass can be very lovely, provocative, leading you on; like a Grimm fairy tale or the music of McDowell. I have seen it in June and July when it was a mass of wild flowers and in the autumn when the aspens were like yellow water-lilies in the green pool of the evergreens, and a blue haze hung above the summits. The view from the top is like cold water on your eyes. Far below is the valley and across from you mountain range after mountain range diminishes like the faint rumbling of summer thunder.

Of the present truncated journey from the railway only The Pass is left and over that the Forest Service has built a corkscrew road that, during the open months, is almost as good as the roads in Switzerland. Casual motor-cars make it in an hour or so with no thought of what it really is and no recollection that less than forty years ago it was a horse-trail over which the first mowing-machine ever brought into the country was packed on saw-buck saddles. But in the winter and early spring and late autumn The Pass returns to its own. Motor-trucks are abandoned and the mail is carried for a while in wagons, and then in sleighs, and sometimes, after a big storm, until the road is broken out again, on the backs of snow-shoeing or skiing runners.

Have you ever seen them breaking open a mountain road after a heavy storm? They hitch two horses to a sleigh and start at it foot by foot, the horses plunging and snorting like the sea-horses driven by Nereus. Every few minutes they rest or change teams. No wonder that in countries like mine one of the qualifications most desired in buying a horse is that he be a good 'snow horse.' And it is marvelous fun crossing The Pass in winter when the road is well travelled. You turn the horses loose and glide down in the softest, most exhilarating mist of fine snow. Once I saw a man pitched twenty feet or so from the driving-seat when a runner hit a hidden stump. He landed on his head and for a moment nothing was visible but absurdly kicking heels. Yet he was not hurt. It is difficult to get hurt in soft snow.

V
"Wyoming In The Sweet Bye And Bye"

WARM cloudless weather, the lapping of lake water, the singing of thrushes, canyons slumbering in noon heat, a bewildering variety of wild flowers, the green-gold of pine-trees and firs . . . that is what I saw that first summer. I had no responsibilities; nothing to do but loaf and prospect about. I did not know the country. I saw only its softer side.

The country—somehow I wish to avoid the final revelation of its name, why I do not know—was at that time, only as short a time ago as sixteen years, still a frontier. I knew the first white child born there and when I first met him he was only about twenty-one years old, and the ranches were isolated little holdings, with the exception of the original settlement around the small local town, tucked away up subsidiary streams or nestling like the ranch I was on, in the edges of the great belts of timber that ran along the slopes of the mountains to the east and the west. The Teton Mountains to the west, the Grovont—or Continental Divide—to the east, the Absorakas and the Continental Divide and Yellowstone Park to the north, the Snake River and Gray's River and John O'Day's to the south. A most heaped-up and tumultuous country, with the great blanket of the forests, dark green for the firs and pines, light green for the aspens, smoothing it down. Through the middle of it, from north to south, cutting it in half, heading in the southern mountains of Yellowstone Park and leaving by a deep canyon, runs the Snake River, like a silvery snake in its exaggerated windings, but not named on that account, obvious as this might seem. Snake is a translation of the name of the Indian tribe of Shoshones, a name appropriated in its original by the Cody country to the northeast when it seemed desirable to change the forthright Stinking Waters into something more dignified. And the Arapahoes, who are brigaded with the Shoshones on the Wind River reservation at old Fort Washakie, ninety miles or so east, have still another name for the Snake; they call it 'The Ghost Bald Head,' because once they fought and scalped some Bannocks on its bank, and they call the Tetons, whose summit they can see from the top of their own mountains, 'The Ghost Robbers.'

The Ghost Robbers! A most fitting name for incredible mountains. The farther you get away from them the bigger they look until, over in the Arapahoe country, they rise like huge and misty inverted fragments of a shattered sky. Only Maxfield Parrish could paint them, and he makes his mountains up. By day they are landmarks for hundreds of miles, as they were at the beginning of the nineteenth century for the expeditions of the Hudson Bay Company; by night they are sharp, thin silhouettes making even the moon seem commonplace. They are very young mountains, erosion has done very little to them.

The Indians never actually lived in the valley, there was too much snow in winter for them to feed their stock, and they were somewhat afraid of the place, as they were completely afraid of Yellowstone Park to the north—that haunt of spouting devils—but they used to come in during the summer to hunt, and I have found on my ranch, along the river, many of their tepee-rings—semicircular rings of stones placed so as to keep down the edges of the tepees, and one of the last Indian troubles occurred in the valley thirty years or so ago. Recently I met an Eastern man who had been hunting big game at the time and he described to me how he and his guides had built a little fort at the south end of a lake and had settled down to a siege that never happened. For, like a great many other Indian troubles, this trouble, as far as I can make out, was more in the heads of the white settlers and the Indians than anywhere else. But the settlers were right in their determination to drive the Indians out of the country.

Some Bannocks from the west and some Shoshones from the east had broken their reservation bounds and had entered the valley and were slaughtering game. The settlers flew to arms and the government sent a negro cavalry regiment to quell the disturbance. One Indian was killed—the ribald claim, one squaw—and a harmless battle was fought back of a mountain now called Battle Mountain. They tell a story about a prominent settler who was out scouting and who came upon an Indian, also out scouting, around the corner of a trail. The white man gasped and so did the Indian, then they both said 'Good morning,' the Indian in perfect English, and went back to where they had come from.

But that is all very well. It wasn't so funny at the time. No two races whose psychologies are so different as those of the Indian and the white man find each other funny in crises. I knew an old lady down in Arizona who shuddered every time an owl hooted because that was the signal-cry of Geronimo and his warriors . . . .

During those months of the first summer I was completely ignorant of the fact that I had found my future home—the place where so much was to happen to me. I only knew that I was happy and that the country filled every nook and cranny of my desire. It was more satisfactory than the Canadian Northwest or the State of Washington, or even New Mexico. It was sunnier and more expansive than the first, greener and more beautiful and more hidden than the latter two.

In September we went antelope-hunting, leaving our own valley and dropping over on to the head of Green River where we made camp on a stream called Horse Creek. We had cut straight across the Grovont Mountains by means of high mountain trails, taking four days to the journey. Two years ago I made more or less the same trip after a lapse of fourteen years—a rather heart-breaking trip. There was too much memory. Three of the ten people I had been with that first time were dead. Lonely places retain the impression of personalities longer than crowded places. Mountain echoes repeat and repeat themselves, and seem never to die away.

Sixteen years ago antelope were still numerous on the headwaters of the Green. Almost every morning while you were eating breakfast you would see them, drifting patches of sunlight, on the neighboring rises. Nor could you hunt a day without running into numerous herds of from twenty to fifty individuals. The first shot I ever had at a good-sized buck I was unable to take, although I waited an hour, because he was feeding in the midst of a hundred or more Here-ford cattle. In this respect, the constant sight of the quarry, and in others as well, antelope-shooting is the most exciting sport I know—a combination of every other known sport except water-polo and sometimes even that, when your horse falls, as mine did, in a bog-hole. But do not think because you see them all the time that antelope are easy to shoot. Far from it; you see them usually only at a distance. First you ride until you sight them, then you get off and stalk by whatever method seems at the moment best to human ingenuity. You are always in an open country. There is no cover. Frequently you tear up by the roots huge stalks of sage-brush and, lying on your belly and dragging your rifle after you, creep inch by inch nearer. As a rule, when you get within shooting distance, the antelope are gone, flicking their tails sarcastically at you from a butte a mile or so away. Fools they may be, but they know how to run. They are very inquisitive, however, and it is a fact that before they were hunted too much all you had to do to get one was to lie down and put your hat or handkerchief on a stick. They would come up to see what it was all about, courting death to satisfy their curiosity as many a wiser animal, including man, has done. Their meat is delicious, the finest wild meat I know save that of the mountain-sheep.

When I first saw antelope they were just beginning to go into the trees; you could actually corral them against the side of open timber. They would not go into the shadow of leaves and branches. Poor shining patches of tawny sunlight, with their white rumps! The most typical American animal we have ever had except the buffalo, and now almost in the same case as the buffalo. For years the season on antelope has been closed and yet they have been steadily diminishing. The latest report from the head of Green River and the Red Desert, the country in which they used to winter, places the remnant of the great herd I saw only sixteen years ago at about five hundred, and that is the report of an exceedingly optimistic game-warden. Personally, I believe their number is even less.

Antelope were thick during the summer, for instance, in my valley three or four years before I came there, but in my time there have been none at all, except that last summer a solitary female—several people saw her—drifted about the foot-hills of the mountains to the east. How she got there or why she was by herself, no one knew.

The membership of that antelope-shooting expedition to the headwaters of the Green River was interesting; it consisted of the doctor and his wife, myself and my sister, the bride of the man who owned the ranch where we were staying, an old ex-storekeeper among the Sioux, a tall thin ex-cowpuncher I shall call 'Nate,' a bearded ex-miner, a young Mormon horse-wrangler, and the man who owned the ranch where we were staying. All these people subsequently, with the exception of the young Mormon, who was killed by a railway-train, were intimately connected with my life. Some of them became, and still are, my very good friends; the man who owned the ranch where we were staying was my partner for four years.

I think it was the doctor who first put the idea of this partnership into my head. I was restless; I did not want to continue to be a teacher. 'So-and-So's looking for a partner,' suggested the doctor, 'he wants some one to buy a half-interest in his ranch—or rather, ranches; the one we are on and the one down in the valley.' The one we were on consisted of a hundred and sixty acres of timbered land lying along a lake at the base of the Tetons and was absolutely useless for ranching purposes—even the sparse grass that grew under the trees was pine-grass and would not feed horses—but it had, and still has, one of the most superb views in the Rockies, a view that even my juvenile instincts told me some day might be worth a fortune; while the lower ranch was a lovely place of smooth meadows and scattered forest, with a stream running through it, and could be made into an actual ranch. So-and-So, with the odd combination of shrewdness and real love of beauty and loneliness that distinguished him, had got hold of these places and, with the patience that also distinguished him, was waiting to make money out of them.

Fired by the doctor's advice, I went to So-and-So and asked him to sell me a half-interest in his ranches. I didn't have any money, I suggested that I take an option on the half-interest, becoming a partner, and having the privilege, within five years, of buying the option. So-and-So was clever. He pretended he did not much care whether he sold or not. Being young I believed him and tried to persuade him with a fervor of argument that must have amused him greatly. I would not have been so eager had I ever seen him, as I did later on, sell horses. Finally, however, what seemed like a satisfactory arrangement was made and I went back to teach another winter at Princeton.

Just as I had been ignorant in Philadelphia at the corner of Walnut and Fifteenth Streets that I was to become a citizen of Wyoming, so now I was ignorant that I had taken the first steps towards becoming a dude-wrangler. I thought I was going into mixed ranching with a decided emphasis upon the cattle end of it, allowing, perhaps, as a source of added money, a few friends to come out each summer as So-and-So had allowed the doctor and his wife and my sister and myself to come. But my partner had a clearer idea of the possibilities. He was well aware of the value of his view of mountain and lake in combination with a university man and a man bred in the East, much as he despised for practical purposes the college graduate. He had every intention of going into the dude-business.

There is an old cowboy song; the oldest there is, 'The Old Chisholm Trail,' the chorus of one version of which is:

"O ki, yi, yip, and a ki, yi, yi,
Ki, yi, yip and a ki, yi, yi,
Git along little dogies, don't you cry,
We'll be in Wyoming in th' sweet bye and bye."

We'll be in Wyoming in th' sweet bye and bye! Dogie, incidentally, being a cattle term the meaning of which is not always understood to be the same, but which you can be fairly safe in assuming means an orphaned calf, or, as one cowpuncher friend put it, 'a calf whose mama is dead and whose papa has run off with another lady cow.' Not an unusual thing for the papa of a calf to do.

'The Old Chisholm Trail' was composed somewhere during the dim history of the original Texas cattle drives, those rivers that began and ended just the opposite from actual rivers, for flowing from the great southwestern ranches in a broad stream they diverged into smaller streams, some of which led to shipping-points and others to the great, and at that time, un-occupied grass-lands of Wyoming and Montana. And it was composed by many people and over a long period of years, and it is an epic; an epic of the miseries and grim humors that beset a cowboy engaged in pushing cattle across country. It is, moreover, an authentic song, which most cowboy songs are not, since the average cowboy, like everyone else, has always sung the popular songs of the moment. A great deal of nonsense has been written about cowboy songs. Although, to be sure, it was rather a shock to me in face of 'The Old Chisholm Trail,' and 'The Mormon Wife,' and 'Bury Me out on the Lone Prair-ree,' and 'Wrap Me up in My Old Yellow Slicker,' to have the daughter of an old-time Westerner tell me last summer that they sang a splendid cowboy song at her university called 'Rag-Time Cowboy Joe.'. . . 'Rag-Time Cowboy Joe' was written in Tin-Pan Alley, New York, seven or eight years ago, and is about as authentic as 'Cheyenne' or 'Wyoming in the Gloaming.'

But to get back to my point and explain why I introduced 'The Old Chisholm Trail.'

I never think of it without thinking of my own entrance into Wyoming, as casual and wide-eyed as the entrance of the long-horned steers. And yet now it seems as if I had always wanted to get to Wyoming and that everything else had been but a preparation to that end. Perhaps it was so, perhaps the name had somewhere dropped into my consciousness and remained there. At all events, I feel as if for some reason Wyoming had always appealed to me as the most typical and romantic and beautiful of Far Western States. But there is no need of comparison.

Montana, Wyoming, Idaho, Oregon, Washington, Utah, Nevada, Colorado—the choice is difficult; they are all beautiful. And what a list of names! Like the rolling of an Indian drum, or the crashing of Spanish spurs, or the falling of heaped-up waters !

'The Old Chisholm Trail '—I hate to leave it—has a wonderful tune, 'Turkey in the Straw,' to ride to, the rhythm being the exact rhythm of the cowboy jog-trot, and it is a sophisticated epic, it has a basis of philosophy. I will quote four verses—not all, al-though the temptation is great. There are seventy-six known verses and heaven knows how many of which there is no record.

"O a hoss threw me off at th' creek, called Mud,
A horse threw me off with th' Two-U herd,
Th' last time I saw him he was runnin' cross th' level,
A-kickin' up his heels and a-raisin' of th' devil."

You will notice the artistic spareness with which the whole unfortunate episode is indicated.
And:

"O we hit Caldwell and we hit her on the fly,
We bedded down th' cattle on the hill close by;
No chaps, no slicker, and it's pouring down rain,
And I swear, by God, I'll never night-herd again."

One can hardly blame him, although, like all cowboys, he surely did night-herd again.

Finally there are two verses showing, as the first one does, the gift of ironic observation so characteristic of the Far Westerner, and, as the second one does, the peculiar naive egotism that almost invariably accompanies the otherwise deep maturity of the outdoor man, an egotism, however, invariably prone to laugh at itself.

"O old Ben Bolt was a fine ol' boss,
Rode to see th' girls on a sore-backed hoss;
Old Ben Bolt was fond of his liquor,
Had a little bottle in th' pocket of his slicker."

And:

"Foot in th' stirrup and a hand on th' horn,
  Best damned cowboy ever was born;
  Foot in th' stirrup and a seat in th' sky,
  Best damned cowboy ever rode by."

I like "The Old Chisholm Trail"; I like it even better than my other favorite:

"My Uncle he lives on th' Platte,
  And th' banner he waves is a broad-brimmed hat,
  Th' bronchos he rides, they churns him up so,
  He swears he will ride no more bucking bronc-hos,"

and the chorus of which contains these tender sentiments:

"Hush-a-bye-baby,
  Punch-a-buckeroo,
  Daddy'll be home
  When th' round-up is through."

VI
The Methods And Genesis Of Dude-Wrangling

I HAVE come to the dude-business slowly; I have done so deliberately because, as a rule, you come to the dude-business slowly in actual life and you come to it usually by chance, just as I did. Up to the present it has been a fortuitous business, not one in the majority of cases deliberately chosen. You start something else and then find yourself in the dude-business. For sixteen years I have been starting other things, only to find myself always in the dude-business. And the dude-business has grown like a mushroom in wet weather.

The whole State of Wyoming is finding itself in the same position as myself, so are the other Rocky Mountain States. Actually the dude-business is about thirty years old, but it wasn't until fifteen years ago that it amounted to anything at all, and it wasn't until about five years ago that it really came into its own, or that you could write the words dude, or dude-wrangler, or dude-business without quotation-marks. Pretty soon you will be able to write them as single words, in the same way cowpuncher or cattleman or sheepman are written, for the dude-business—the tourist business in general—is becoming perhaps the most important business of all in the States in question.

In the beginning the dude-wrangler was looked upon with suspicion, there was a tendency to laugh at his products—Easterners—and his motives were questioned. It didn't seem a real business to the cattleman, or sheepman, or even that lowly creature, the dry-farmer, and, since it was part of the dude-man's job to protect game and preserve beauty, in other words, to use foresight, he was regarded as a reactionary and an impediment to progress—Progress being written with a large P and the sole possession of citizens who call themselves 'boosters.' And, as a matter of fact, the dude-wranglers were the first men to realize as a class the potential values of the Far West, partly from clear-sighted selfishness, partly because most of them are educated men, in the majority of cases Easterners to begin with. I know of but one or two successful dude-ranches in which there is not one Easterner at least who is a very important spoke in the wheel, for with all his virtues, the native son does not as a rule know what an Easterner or Middle Westerner wants, or why he wants it. On the whole the best type of dude-wrangler is an educated Eastern man with a great deal of Western experience, or—but this is a rare combination—an educated Western man with a great deal of Eastern experience. And it is because of this, because most dude-wranglers are men of this class, or rather because most dude-ranches have a man of this class high up in their councils, that the dude-wrangler has consistently stood for intelligent legislation and intelligent conservation.

The crooked water-power man, the crooked land-development man, hate him; the poacher and the game-hog hate him. He is largely responsible for the increasing interest in Far Western things and their survival. He says to the cowpuncher, not actually but by his methods: "Look here! You're still a cowpuncher. To all intents and purposes you lead exactly the same life that your father and grandfather led before you and your son is going to lead after you. Your father's and grandfather's customs and clothes were the result of long experience and much selection. They are practical and picturesque. Keep on following them and using them." And then he adds, with just a hint of the lowering of an eyelid necessary to a dude-wrangler: "Moreover, they will make you money; people will come a long way to see them." And what a beautiful and romantic dress the cowboy costume is at that! Spanish in derivation, American in adaptation . . . big spurs, high-heeled boots, covered with fancy stitching, 'chaps' of leather or angora wool, flannel shirt, neck handkerchief, and sombrero. The one national costume we have.

There you have it. The dude-wrangler knows a dude-ranch is not a cow-ranch; he knows that when Eastern damsels put on overalls and wear egregious scarfs they don't look in the least like cowgirls, but he encourages them to do these things because it is good for their souls and because it adds color to a business that is not imitative but just as autochthonous as the cattle business itself. In other words, if you wish to sum up the dude-business in a sentence, it consists in giving people home-made bedsteads but forty-pound mattresses.

And the desires and predictions of the dude-wrangler have been fulfilled, or, at least, are on the way towards being fulfilled, and, from being a somewhat despised adventurer, he has become one of the most influential, and certainly one of the most solvent, of Far-Western citizens. Beauty has been proven to be a business asset, game need never disappear, neither need an intelligently controlled and restricted wilderness, and tourists have been shown to be the biggest future the high sections of the Rocky Mountain States have; and Fate, playing its curious hand, has helped the dude-wrangler. The proud barons of the war and the year after, the cattleman and sheepman, have become very humble persons indeed, heavily in debt, impossibly mortgaged, many of them on the edge of bankruptcy. The dude-man, meanwhile, has gone serenely on his way, making no great fortune, to be sure, but keeping his affairs well in hand and with the prospect of a growing future.

So far I have taken it for granted that every one knows just what a dude-ranch is. Fifteen years ago I wouldn't have taken this for granted, for those were the days when young women asked, with a complete lack of interest in their usually eager eyes, if 'Wyoming wasn't somewhere up near the Canadian border?' Well, it is, but there's a large State, Montana, in between. Since then, however, the cowpuncher has become an international figure and there are more people who have seen the West than those who haven't. The Rocky Mountains are overlaid with the echoes of the blithe accents of strangely dressed Eastern youth and there is hardly a cowpony—except the bad ones—who has not at one time or another felt the grave burden of the older generation. Yet, as there may be some people who still do not know what a dude-ranch is, I suppose that here and now I should describe one.

A dude-ranch is not a summer hotel, nor is it a summer boarding-house, much as it may seem like one or the other to the ignorant. Physically it is an ordinary ranch amplified, in some sections of the country the buildings made out of logs, in others, out of adobe, or frame, or even brick. There is usually a large central ranch-house containing sitting-rooms, a dining-room, kitchens, storehouses, and so on, and, scattered about the grounds, smaller cabins or houses, holding from one to four people, used as sleeping-quarters. There is also invariably a great variety of other buildings, ice-houses, saddle-sheds, blacksmith-shops, camp store-houses, frequently a store and post-office, and almost always an extra large cabin that can be used for dancing. And as a rule, unless the ranch is an old ranch turned into a dude-ranch, the dude-wrangler has picked his location for its beauty and, if he is a wise dude-wrangler, has so disposed his buildings through the trees that there is no effect of crowding or of size. You must do your best, even on a place where from fifty to over a hundred people are gathered together, not to destroy the impression of wildness and isolation.

And spiritually as well a dude-ranch is very far removed from either a summer hotel or a summer boarding-house. Unaware as dudes may be of this fact, there is a social and moral and actual responsibility unlike any responsibility attached to the job of being a hotel-keeper. That is what, in some ways, makes the dude-business a very pleasant business and, in other ways, a very trying one. You have, you see, upon your hands a number of people most of whom are in an entirely new and rather bewildering environment. It is not sufficient merely to give them rooms and baths and then turn them loose; it is necessary to entertain them, or see that they are entertained, and to instruct them in a strange and wild and, if not properly handled, fairly dangerous country. You give them horses and teach them to ride, you beg and argue with them not to over-ride, you outfit them and send them out on pack-trips, you flirt occasionally, if you have to, with some of the younger, or, as you get older, youngish ones, and you try to prevent some of the still younger ones from breaking up discipline by flirting with your cowboys, you tell innumerable stories, so that at times your voice becomes hoarse and your mind wanders, and you answer an infinite number of questions.

It is a large patriarchal life in which at moments you feel you are the father of an unruly family and, at other moments, especially when you are asked, as you are every hour or so, about the weather, that some one has mistaken you for a minor deity.

As to discipline, we fluctuate, as do most dude-ranches, between beautiful young cowpunchers who attract the eye and whom we keep until they become thoroughly useless and 'trashy,' and by no means beautiful old men, losing with the latter atmosphere and putting up with being told just what to do, for the sake of work accomplished. The happiest combination, perhaps, is a beautiful young cowpuncher with a young and jealous wife. I am speaking, of course, only of certain positions; others require by their very nature mature men. On the whole our discipline, however, especially lately, has been excellent, and the summers recently have been busy and cheery ones devoid for the most part of the added duty of chaperonage.

Yet this chaperonage, even when needed, was never such a serious task. The younger generation of the East is abundantly well able to take care of itself and the average cowpuncher is on the whole a pretty upstanding fellow, with a fundamental decency and a vast amount of common sense. Of all sections of the country, mothers need be least afraid of the Far West. Moreover, one of the charming qualities of the Far Westerner is his sense of loyalty—a feudal sense—to the outfit he happens at the moment to be working for. He is extremely jealous, even to the point of fighting, of its honor and dignity and good name. He foregoes even the, on the whole, innocent pleasures of flirtation if he thinks it is injuring "his outfit's" reputation.

That this loyalty is transferred immediately in case a man leaves one ranch to the next where he gets a job makes it even more interesting. It is the result of isolation and a close-knit communal life.

But you can see that dude-wrangling is somewhat like a gigantic game of chess and that the dude-wrangler must be on the alert from the moment his guests open their eyes in the morning to the sleepy twittering of birds to the moment they close them at any odd hour of the night.

He must cajole the obstreperous, encourage the shy, restrain the too active, propel the lazy, and, at times, gently snub the impertinent. He must know just what each person is doing on that particular day, whether he or she is going fishing or shooting or mountain climbing or just riding, and if he finds a person, or a group of people, at loose ends he must insinuate into the bored mind, or minds, the idea of a new and delightful trip or occupation. Also he must be a solvent between antagonistic personalities.

Try as you may, careful as you may be in your selection, you cannot hope to get together fifty or more people of all ages and characteristics from all corners of the country, even from all corners of the globe, and expect them to adore each other universally. But the dude-wrangler must see that they are at least polite to each other, for they are in a peculiar position, they—out of their usual surroundings, against a new background—are caught together in a little eddy of lonely life, and they are more or less dependent upon each other. And lonely eddies of life, although they are the pleasantest spots in the world, can also be very dangerous if gossip is not looked after.

Nor do the dude-wrangler's duties end, as I have already indicated, when most other honest men's labors cease—except the dairy farmer's—and that is at night. Again and again when he is tired from riding all day, or from manual work, or when he is wet from rain, or sleepy, he must conquer his natural instincts and 'be about.' He has to listen to a great deal. Something about high altitudes, something about dislocation of environment, the patriarchal position a dude-wrangler possesses, makes his guests confidential and him a father confessor. People, ladies especially, tell him things they wouldn't tell ordinarily. The greatest personal dangers that the dude-wrangler incurs are the dangers of becoming at too early an age gently world-weary and, at too early an age, anecdotal.

Furthermore—and here is the inner secret of it all—the dude-wrangler must do these things—'wrangle' his dudes in all their bewildering complexity—without letting them for a moment know that he is doing so. A salient characteristic of the human mind, and very naturally, seems to be a dislike of being herded, with an unconscious desire none the less to have it done; people hate to be directed, but they get excessively angry if they aren't. The best way to direct them, therefore, either in dude-wrangling or the ordinary relations of life, is to let them think each new idea is their own. A fellow dude-wrangler, a magnificent specimen physically, told me he lost about thirty pounds a summer directing people without letting them know he was doing it.

I have been describing the perfect dude-wrangler, and there is, of course, no such creature; but there are rather a lot of them who are qualifying for some sort of busy and executive and story-telling sort of saint-hood.

On the top of these multifarious social and spiritual duties the dude-wrangler has the ordinary duties of the man who undertakes to feed and bed a number of his fellow human beings, feeding and bedding them in an isolated country, far from the railway, where, as a rule, nothing grows in profusion, not even eggs, and no delicate thing grows at all, and where most of his outfit—except in outdoor matters—is to begin with un-trained. The dude-wrangler is a ranch-owner, a cow-man, a horseman, a guide, a wholesale chamber-maid, a cook, and storekeeper rolled into one. In most well-organized dude outfits these duties, to be sure, are divided between several partners. There is, for instance, one partner, chosen for his peculiar characteristics and training, who does nothing but wrangle dudes, another—the business man of the organization—who looks after the books and the buying of supplies and the stores, and a third who takes charge of the actual ranching, for as a rule dude outfits consist of several ranches on some of which stock is raised and wintered and out of which is made what money can be made in the at present uncertain state of the sheep and cattle and horse industries. And wherever it is necessary to come into actual contact with the labor employed there are foremen, for it is an old ranch tradition, and an excellent one, that the owners shall not do the actual hiring, firing, or giving of orders; even an owner as ingenious as the one in Mexico who used to sit all day long on the top of a hill in the middle of his ranchero, armed with a .22 rifle and field-glasses, so that he could shoot dangerously near to any of his peons whom he saw taking out too many minutes of rest.

The very liabilities, however, as I have said, that make the dude-business trying also make it dignified.

You may have the bothers of a universal father, but you also have a father's prerogatives. You can disinherit any of your children if they become too annoying. I know of no self-respecting dude-ranch that does not retain the privilege of dismissing an over-importunate guest, and I know of one that kept a supply of time-tables on hand to present without comment in the face of unnecessary complaints. But that is going too far. The dude-wrangler has, as a matter of fact, very little trouble with importunate guests. Most people who come to dude-ranches are self-selected, pleasant, adventurous folk who wouldn't come at all unless they knew fairly well what they were doing. More-over, since most dude-ranches limit their numbers and require references, it is possible to make choices and to make fairly certain what people are like before they arrive. After a while the dude-wrangler even acquires an uncanny ability to judge character by letters. He predicts personalities before he sees them. It is a tribute to the type of person who wants to come West and the life led there that, in fifteen years, I have only had to request one man to leave the ranch.

In the early days, food was the cause of more worry perhaps than anything else. Eggs, as Sherwood Anderson has pointed out, can sometimes be the source of drama. Once upon a time, in the prehistoric period when, after the first of August, eggs became as scarce as the teeth of their mothers, we had a famous author staying with us, and the famous author, whenever he fell ill, which was about once in every five weeks, developed a mania for eggs. During such times eggs became a passion with him; he brooded upon them; he could think of nothing else. Anticipating one of these periodic illnesses, I had ridden from one end of the country to the other and had begged my neighbors to save an egg for me whenever a reluctant hen laid one by mistake. The fruits of this painstaking search were to be concentrated at a ranch five miles up country, and on a certain day I was to call for them.

The day arrived—a crisp and lovely day in September—and I saddled my horse and departed. The eggs were waiting for me, two dozen of them, wrapped in newspaper and fitted into a shining five-pound lard pail. I had a long talk with my fellow rancher who had kept the collection for me and it was not until dusk that I started home. My way lay along a road and then took a trail that dipped down into the valley of a little stream. The dusk grew thicker and a brilliant sunset flamed in the west. It was this sunset that proved my undoing, for as I was watching it, and as I came to the edge of the descent into the stream, the rays of the sun caught the lard pail and flashed a heliograph into the eyes of my horse. He awaited no further invitation but threw down his head and pitched with me down the slope. The eggs flew up like a geyser. When we reached the stream I managed to pull up my inflamed "insect's" head and dismounted, and whether you believe it or not, and despite the frozen ground, not an egg was broken. Very much cheered, I gathered them up carefully, put them back into the lard pail, and prepared to remount. But by this time my horse was fore-warned and before I could even throw my leg over the cantle, he jumped away from me. This time six of the eggs were broken.

Aware at last of what was causing the trouble, I hid the lard pail under my coat, caught my horse, and tried once more to mount him. I don't know what especial form of necromancy he was using by now, but so long as I had those eggs with me, conceal them where I would, he would not let me get into the saddle. In the series of struggles that followed all but two of the eggs were broken. Finally my steed, by now thoroughly determined, jerked the reins out of my hand and, as if he had enough of such foolishness, set off home by himself. In a paroxysm of rage I hurled the two remaining eggs after him and walked three miles in his tracks. I am glad to say that one of the eggs hit him in the head, but the explanation of the tragedy was a difficult one to make to the suffering author.

He saw no humor at all in what had happened, although ordinarily he has an excellent sense of humor. He merely turned his face to the wall and groaned.

Howard Eaton started the dude-business and invented the word dude. That was about thirty-five years ago. The word has none of the slurring connotations attached to the term tenderfoot. It does not imply ignorance or softness, it simply means some one, usually a person not resident in the country, who hires some one else to guide him or cook for him, or who pays money to stay on a ranch. The governor of Wyoming can be a dude if he hires guides when he goes hunting, so can the oldest and toughest cattleman in the world. I know a Cherokee Indian who for several years was a dude. His homestead in Oklahoma contained oil and he used to come into our country after elk. Amusingly enough, his guides told me that he was a poor hunter, too easily lost, and what we describe as 'an ornery dude'—hard to please. And often nowadays I, a dude-wrangler, am a dude by deliberate choice—that is, I take guides and cooks with me into the hills. It's splendid fun to do all the work in camp, until—for many years—you've done it. Then it's the grimmest kind of hard work, unless there are no more than two, or, at the outside, three persons. To be a dude is a perfectly honest avocation.

Howard Eaton, if I have not heard the story incorrectly, became, like most of his followers, a dude-wrangler by chance. He was an extremely popular man, originally from Pittsburgh, and with his two brothers had a horse ranch in South Dakota. Like most popular men who have a ranch, he was overwhelmed with guests, and after a while discovered that what he was making on his horses he was losing on entertaining. At first his idea was to make his friends pay merely their share of the expenses, but as they continued to come in increasing numbers, he saw a business opportunity and took it. Eventually he moved his outfit to Wolf, Wyoming, and there it is today, a most interesting village, already historic.

I do not understand about Howard Eaton. He died about a year ago and nobody outside of his large circle of friends seemed to have realized that one of the great figures of the West had passed. Certainly the newspapers didn't, and yet here was a man who, at least to my thinking, was a more engaging and important person than Buffalo Bill. A man who had been West since the early 'seventies, who had seen five decades of Western life, who had participated in everything the West had to offer, who had had the originality to invent a new business, and who was as well that most charming and indigenous of Americans, a gentleman who is also a frontiersman. I would like to see him buried, as William Cody was, on top of one of the mountains he loved so well.

The last time but one that I came across this lover of hills and trails was on top of the Continental Divide. I had stopped for the night at a deserted ranch where I knew he was making his headquarters. About sun-down he came in, after hunting all day, with his cook and his foreman. A big, burly, gray man, with absent-minded blue eyes that missed nothing and could be as sharp as knives, and with a bad limp in one leg. Half the bones in his body had been broken by falls from horses and by other accidents, yet he walked faster than almost any man I have ever seen. We sat up half the night listening to him talk about Indians, about the old West, about big game and hunting.

He was over seventy at the moment and yet here was his programme for the coming year.

He had just finished guiding a three-weeks hunting party and now, his hunters having departed, he was hunting on his own account for a few days. After that he would go back to his ranch—two hundred and fifty miles away—and take a carload of elk East to plant in West Virginia, making rear-platform speeches about the preservation of game wherever the train stopped. Having disposed of these charges, he would go on his annual two months' tour of the athletic clubs of the Atlantic seaboard, perhaps the hardest part physically of his entire routine, although it was a necessary part of a carefully thought-out campaign of advertising. During these visits he went to bed at any hour, told innumerable stories, saw countless friends, and was entertained on every side. This over, it would be time to take his usual trip, with forty tourists or so through the Southwest, and that would bring him to another scheduled trip, also with tourists, up to British Columbia for the spring finishing. It was in the summer, however, that he did his real work, for it was then that he made his two famous and gigantic annual expeditions into Yellowstone and Glacier National Parks. . . . And—after that—once more hunting.

Rather a strenuous programme for a man over seventy. I am glad that Yellowstone Park, with the good sense and tact that has distinguished the National Parks Service of the Interior Department in the last few years, has named its new horse trail that parallels throughout the motor-road the Howard Eaton Trail. I was on it this summer, and one could feel the old man's ghost, debonair and smiling, riding by one's side.

Some one told me that he ran into the father of the dude-business and his seventy-five or so mixed dudes up in Yellowstone Park a few years ago. Of course the father of the dude-business couldn't know all his dudes, but he did his best. His real introduction was to get out every morning at the head of the company street and shave. After breakfast he and his following lined up beside their horses. There was a moment's pause and then the grizzled leader called out: "Every he take a she and fly at it!"—and they all got on their horses and two by two ambled down the road, Eaton at their head. My own business started in much the same way as Howard Eaton's. The first summer of my option four or five Princeton men, hearing I was connected with a ranch, expressed a desire to come out to see me. We built a couple of little log-cabins and told them to come. The next summer fifteen people wanted to follow their lead. The following summer, the third and last, we had forty people—our limit—and turned some away. I had had wished upon me a Frankenstein monster, although a very interesting Frankenstein monster, and when I split off from my original partner and took another, the monster went with me. Again we intended to take only a few tourists and concentrate upon cattle. We were more lucky than we knew. Once more we had to concentrate upon dudes and run cattle as a side issue.

But I have been building log-cabins for so many years! . . . It seems to me that I have been building log-cabins ever since I was a child.

VII
So Much To Experience

I HAD taken to myself a strange partner and I found myself in a strange position, just how strange it took me a couple of years fully to realize.

I can best sum up this partner by describing him as a sort of financial Blue Beard who inveigled others into intimate business relations and then, when he had derived all the benefit he could from them, got rid of them with infinite subtlety. After I left him he had several more of my kind until he achieved the moderate success which was his goal.

A fascinating man, my partner—I know of no one today with whom I would rather sit down and talk. A long, powerful, graceful, long-nosed, ugly man, with humorous, unreadable ironic eyes. He had been born an Easterner, but when he was eighteen years old he had emigrated to a big Spanish-American ranch in the Southwest, where he had worked as a cowboy and from which subsequently he had drifted all over the country, sometimes a cowboy, sometimes a fore-man, a forest-ranger, a cook, a guide, and, at intervals, a professional gambler. In regard to the last, when I knew him he always avoided playing cards if he could, but if by any chance he was over-persuaded, it was interesting and a little terrific to watch him. Card-playing seems a curious madness to those, who, like myself, have no trace of the germ in their blood. A slow, passionate, heady fever. I remember my partner remarking upon the virtues of a tilted cracker-box as a seat in a game where the other players were strangers. 'Then you can always fall over backwards without a moment's hesitation in case any one starts to shoot.'

But outside of the cracker-box and a few practical details of living such as that, my partner believed in nothing, least of all human nature. He assumed that all men were dishonest and met them on that basis. I am not sure, thinking it over, that he wasn't rather a tonic for too idealistic youth. At least, in his company, too idealistic youth either expired or else discovered the iron in its composition. As is the case with most skeptics, however, there were odd crevices of superstition and fear in this iconoclast's make-up. He believed in a vague way in Nemesis, and like so many lonely outdoor men, given to solitary expeditions through the hills and forests, was aware of some haunting and following presence. He told me that he was sure one of these days he would fall unseeingly over a cliff—down into the misty iridescence of great depths. It was somewhat eerie, as if he expected a shadowy hand to push him over. He was marvelous hunter and must have been a top cow-puncher, for, although his right arm had been broken in a railway accident and never properly set, he was still a cunning man with a rope. I have already said that socially he had few equals. He had a fund of experience, he had been in countless queer places, and all this was illuminated by a dry humor and a slightly wicked turn of mind. And when he wanted to convince any one he could assume an unbelievable ingenuousness of look and recital.

I think the two most interesting stories he told me were these. I asked him once what had been his most unpleasant experience—and a man who had led his sort of life must have had many—and he replied it had been a night he had once spent in what, until eight o'clock, had been a solitary camp in the mountains of Nevada. Then at eight o'clock, or thereabouts, a man had stepped out of nowhere, out of the loneliness and the star-emphasized darkness, and had come up to the tiny camp-fire, where he had stood warming his hands. Just so, silently, without a word of greeting. My partner had asked him if he wanted anything to eat and the man had answered 'Yes.' Just so again, a monosyllable and nothing else.

After the meal the stranger had sat with his back against a tree and had stared thoughtfully and without blinking across the fire. And so the two had spent the night until the stars had begun to dim. In the gray-ness, the man had got up and had disappeared as silently as he had come.

"Did you sleep at all?" I asked my partner.

He smiled. "Good God, no . . . . I reached back for my gun and sat on it."

The other story took place in Montana.

My partner, drifting about from State to State, from the Southwest to the Northwest, as cowpunchers do, had reached southern Montana and had been made a round-up foreman. He claimed it was because he was a Southwesterner and therefore an infinitely better cowman than any Northwesterner possibly could be. Perhaps he spoke the truth. I don't know. It is an old argument, and an amusing one. At all events, he was made a foreman and was ordered to take his crew down to the range just north of the Wyoming line. At the last moment the regular cook could not go, so an entire stranger, an unshaven desperate-looking person who packed two guns, had to be hired instead, but the stranger said he was "a son-of-a-gun of a cook. Yes, sir," and more or less lived up to this declaration. Once on the round-up, however, the rest of the outfit began to notice his queer habits and eventually these began to get on the outfit's nerves. Whenever anyone appeared over a neighboring butte or rise the cook would drop whatever he was doing and stand with his hands on his hips, just above his twin guns, until the newcomer had come into camp and made known his business. The psychology of men in an isolated situation is curious; several times my partner nearly had a strike on his hands. His outfit didn't like the strange cook; very justly they decided that he had a guilty conscience. He had.

Later on he was discovered to be one of the fifty Texas gunmen whose lives had been spared, a few weeks earlier, just over the Wyoming line, on condition that they would leave Wyoming and never come back; one of the fifty gunmen, that is, who had been mixed up in the T. A. war; the Big and Little Cattlemen's War. Communication in those days not being what it is now this innocent Montana outfit, engaged upon a round-up, did not hear until much later of the troubles disturbing the State to the south.

What was the T. A. war? Well, it happened in the early 'nineties and was due to the fact that the little 'nesters' who had homesteaded in Johnson County in the north of Wyoming took it into their heads that the easiest way to obtain herds of their own was to steal them from the big outfits whose headquarters were in Cheyenne and who came north every summer to the grass-lands. As most of these 'nesters' had originally been cowpunchers for the big outfits, until they had seen what a sweet country northern Wyoming was, they knew their way about. After a while the big owners in Cheyenne grew weary and sent Tom Horn, the famous cattle detective, into Johnson County. Tom Horn's method was to locate a troublesome 'rustler,' and then to shoot him at dusk, usually in his corral or some other out-of-the-way place, and to put two stones under his head. The two stones were a sign to the men in Cheyenne that Tom Horn had done the job, and in due course a check was sent. By this evasion all letters or other incriminating documents were avoided.

But even Tom Horn could not stop the 'rustling' in Johnson County, and so the big owners finally grew desperate and called a meeting. They decided upon open war; they decided to hire fifty or so of the worst gunmen in Texas and send them north with wagons and cooks and even a doctor. It was one of the most dramatic and foolish decisions ever arrived at in the history of this country, and it was as epoch-marking as Don Quixote, for it was the last stand of the old feudal cattle barons.

The expedition arrived unheralded and fell upon the ranch of a notorious 'rustler.' For twelve hours they besieged it and in the end killed the owner. This man kept a diary—minute by minute of that day—all the while he was shooting from his windows and the cracks of his log-cabin.

So far all had gone well, but the invading forces had overlooked the fact that a couple of freighters had been guests of the murdered man and had made their escape early in the morning. By nightfall Johnson County was aroused and there were five hundred galloping men. Word of this came to the besiegers and they in their turn galloped to their nearest headquarters—the T. A. ranch. There they themselves were besieged. At the end of three days, just as extremely earnest efforts were being made to burn the ranch-house and all its inmates, a cavalry regiment sent by the President of the United States arrived from Fort Sheridan and put a stop to the grim and futile warfare.

But no wonder the cook up in Montana was suspicious of strangers.

Cooks are queer creatures, anyway, especially round-up cooks and camp cooks. They are masters of the situation and they exercise their privileges and their temperaments. Personally, I believe that no man willingly becomes a cook unless he is slightly insane. I once knew a cook who when he had burned his hand or something had gone wrong, silently piled into a heap—boxes, saddles, and so on—anything movable, and then, climbing to the top of the heap, shook his fist at the sky and expressed his opinion of providence in no uncertain terms. This over, he would climb down again and quietly resume his duties.

The man who was lieutenant-governor during the T. A. was an acquaintance of mine, a very famous little doctor. You can read all about him in Owen Wister's 'Lin McLean.' When the war broke out, the governor was out of the State, and this young doctor, only four years away from the University of Pennsylvania and elected lieutenant-governor by the merest chance—furthermore an Easterner to begin with—found himself in full charge. He met the situation admirably, telegraphing to the President for troops; he also rescued a fellow member of the medical profession. I have heard the story from his own lips.

This fellow member, himself at the time a very young man, now a widely known doctor, happened to be in Cheyenne when the big cattlemen held their conference and thought it would be interesting to join as medical adviser the expedition into Johnson County. It was interesting but it became too much so, for, when the war was over, Johnson County, being a full-fledged county and having the necessary legal machinery in its hands, proceeded to try to hang the ringleaders of the excursion that had so disturbed its peace. The Texas gunmen and other "innocent victims" of predatory interests were allowed to leave but the doctor was imprisoned. The lieutenant-governor, hearing of his friend's predicament, met this further complication with his accustomed readiness. He sent a sheriff up with a forged warrant, saying that the doctor was wanted for murder in Cheyenne and that Johnson County might as well spare itself the trouble and expense of hanging him, because he would be hanged anyway. When the doctor arrived in Cheyenne, the lieutenant-governor put him by night on the cowcatcher of a Union Pacific train and told him to get out of Wyoming and stay out.

The echoes of the T. A. War survive, although faintly. I know several men who were involved in it. One old friend of mine was a Johnson County man. He told me that he and another man were riding through a draw in the dusk when he happened to look up and saw, along a neighboring ridge, black silhouetted against the sky, an army of shadows—wagons, horse-men, and spare horses. He did not know what the army was; he had no idea until the next day what it portended; but some instinct told him to seek cover and he did.

It was during these first four years in Wyoming that I met the only ghost I have ever known in the Far West. The Far West, unlike the South and even the East is singularly unmarked by ghost stories; a fact due, I imagine, to the type of man who settled the mountains and the plains, for certainly there have been enough grim stories in the records of both plains sand mountains to make them fertile fields. But outside of Skeleton Springs in Utah and Hanging Woman Ford—where a woman is supposed to come out and warn you if the water is high . . . a most obliging ghost—I have heard of no others. And my ghost has, I am afraid, an obvious if not a simple explanation. I heard it three times, or rather I heard it once, for I was asleep the other two times.

Near the ranch was a canyon called Death Canyon, a huge slit in the granite wall which took you into the heart of the Tetons and came down to the fir and aspen surrounded lake on which the ranch stood. Why it was called Death Canyon I have never been able to find out, although there is a tradition that an English-man fell off a cliff and was killed there while hunting sheep. Just where the stream that feeds the lake leaves the level upper country and pours down in cascades and whirlpools for a couple of thousand feet, there is a narrow mountain meadow, with a few pines scattered about and sheer precipices rising still higher. This is one of the stillest places I have ever been in. The stream, soon to become so turbulent, runs sluggish here, and deep, and ice-cold between rank mountain grasses and heavy moss, and there is the pungent smell of wild carrot and damp evergreens, and the only sounds are the occasional creaking of a small glacier near by and the cawing of camp-robbers. My partner told me that when he had first found this place he had come across an old drift-fence behind which a number of horses had been kept for several months. Evidently some one had lain out there with stolen horses and had laughed at his pursuers, searching for him in the valley far below.

To reach the head of Death Canyon and make it a base for further climbing used to be one of our favorite excursions, and it was no light task to pack fifty pounds or so on one's back all of a breathless day over huge scattered boulders and through the clinging under-brush.

The first occasion on which I unearthed my ghost I had gone up the canyon with my partner, the doctor with whom I had first come to Wyoming, and a setter-dog. We made camp in the little meadow about half past four in the afternoon. It was late in the year, a gray day with 'a spit' of snow upon the ground; I was tired, and fell asleep. I was awakened by footsteps and looked up to see my partner leaving the tepee, a curious look on his face and his hand on his revolver. The dog was barking. In a few minutes my partner came back and shook his head. I asked him what was the matter. He laughed sheepishly and said that he and the doctor had heard some one leave the near-by timber and come up to the tent. But it couldn't have been any one, for there were no footprints in the snow.

Two years later I was camped in Death Canyon again—a brilliant moonlit night with the canyon walls making great shadows across a saffron foreground. Now I happen to be a dangerous man to awaken too suddenly; I react too violently; my more intimate friends know this; I found myself sitting upright in the semi-darkness of the tent, pointing a revolver at a dark shape crawling on hands and knees towards the open flap. "Don't shoot," whispered a voice. "It's I . . . (probably he said 'me') Hal . . . (my camping companion). I heard footsteps circling the tent."

The third time was like the second, at night. I was camped in Death Canyon, myself and two others, and we had finished supper and were sprawled out by the fire. Beyond the circle of flames was a thick darkness. Back of me, hanging to a bush, was my gun. You know the manner in which, when you are frightened, you find yourself, your heart beating wildly, in the midst of an action still half-unaware of what has produced it? That was the way, out of silence and relaxation, I found myself standing upright, my gun in my hand, peering into the shadows . . . . I had heard a horse galloping up the canyon, where no horse had ever been, and directly over me, and the sound of his hoofbeats were dying away in the further reaches of the meadows. I would swear to that.

These are facts, but the explanation, as I have said, is obvious, if not simple. Little is known about acoustics but enough is known to make possible any mystery of echoes when you have clouds and great rock walls as amplifiers. There was a haunted canyon in Arizona— you heard voices and galloping horses—and only recently it was discovered that the sounds came from forty miles away, and in the mountains of North Carolina there is a valley with a similar mystery not as yet explained.

Youth cannot grow without experience, but youth is fortunate if its experience does not cost it too much. Through no intelligence on my part I purchased my experience fairly cheap. The few thousand dollars I had I had invested in a part stock, part apple ranch in the State of Washington, and I have long ago written this off to profit and loss. In Wyoming I was more fortunate. My partner was constantly urging me to buy up my option and I was eager to do so, but a providence more kindly than I deserved saw that I never had enough money for the purpose. Subsequently I realized just what I had escaped, for my partner was playing a game in which he won no matter how the coin fell. He was using me, in other words, to build up his business and then, when the business was sufficiently stable, he had every intention of getting rid of me by his usual subtle and ingenuous methods. One of these methods was to make life so unpleasant for me—an unpleasantness in which his bride played a leading part, as wives always do—that it would have been impossible for me to have stayed with him any longer even had I invested actual money. In the end I would have paid him, had that been necessary, to let me go.

Being a utopian youth it took me a long while to convince myself that my partner was deliberately trying to get rid of me, but the last summer I was with him left me in no doubt. He began to exhibit a marvelous cleverness in putting me in a false position with every one on the ranch from the man who passed around the hot water in the morning to the most easy-going and good-natured of the dudes. As for the fussy and irritable dudes, they hated and despised me. Everything went wrong. None of my plans were fulfilled. There was never any wood for the fireplaces, nothing was done on time, and at intervals there was not even enough to eat. I found myself in a baffling web of intrigue and unpopularity.

Being completely innocent and hard-working I could not at first make out what was going on, but eventually I discovered the truth. My orders were being countermanded and, when the inevitable confusion arose, my partner, abetted by his wife, shrugged his shoulders, smiled wearily, and by a dexterous word or two implied that try as hard as he could it was impossible to overcome the liability my ignorance and inefficiency put upon him. When he knew his guests better he took them aside and told them pathetic stories in which he played the role of the innocent rancher and I that of a not too honest young ne'er-do-well from the East. And the curious part of it was that most of these people believed him.

Two people did not; one, a man who had just been released from the penitentiary and who was working for us, and the other, the ranch doctor, a young neurologist from the East, for in those days there was no doctor in the county and we had to import one annually. I imagine that four years in a penitentiary either ruins your point of view or else gives you a dour clear-sightedness, and neurology, of course, enables you, with what seems almost black magic, to detect the tricks and foibles of mankind. At all events, both these men stood by me and the latter became my partner and remains so today.

VIII
And Considerably More

SCANDAL is like a forest fire, it easily gets beyond control. Events even more dramatic, I think, than my partner intended piled one upon another, and the final months of my partnership certainly dissipated forever from my mind the notion that a dude-ranch is lacking in action. There were a number of fist-fights, a great deal of assorted drunkenness, one of the ranch hands tried to shoot his wife, I was hounded in the most curious manner by a lady whom I believe, at the moment, to have been insane, and the doctor and myself were nearly killed with an axe by a man who was chopping wood. I merely mention the highlights. The background of unpleasantness was broad and constant. I am a peaceable citizen, but before those months were over I came dangerously near to shooting one or two persons myself.

And all the while—as it always is in life—behind this scandalous aggregation of human beings, flung together for a short space, was the calm and lovely picture of the country. The great granite hills, dark green at their feet with fir and pine, lighter green above, where the buck-brush and juniper and mountain ash grew, gray where the rocks showed themselves, soared with heart-stopping perpendicularity into a completely blue sky. There were a hundred little valleys and draws where streams ran and the ground, beneath the shadow of the trees, was purple with fringed gentian, violet with lupin, crimson with Indian paint-brush, faint yellow with columbine, and pink with wild geranium. In the mornings a multitude of birds sang, and the waters of the lake spoke sleepily, and Death Canyon mirrored like a copper plate a shining cloudlessness or the slow darkness of clouds . . . I will come presently to the temporarily insane lady, but first I will describe the incident of the axe because the denouement exhibits a frontier way of thinking.

The doctor and myself had been having trouble with 'the rastabout'—the man on a ranch who chops wood, passes around water, and attends to the other details of living. Nowadays this particular rastabout is a good friend of both the doctor and myself, but at the moment he hated us, due largely to the subtleties of my partner. On a certain snowy day the doctor wanted some wood and went to the wood-pile to get it. The rastabout, appearing around the corner of a building, cursed the doctor and demanded the wood back, whereupon the doctor knocked him down. Unfortunately the rastabout fell where his hand touched an axe and he arose with this terrific weapon balanced for use. I can see the scene now; the quiet whiteness of the snow, the bright morning, the green pines, the smoke curling up from the kitchen, and the shining blade above the doctor's intellectual, slightly bald head.

It is no use to run from an axe, it has a three-foot start on you, so I tried, in the level voice best used in danger—also unconsciously used in fright—to argue the rastabout out of his intention. Meanwhile, from the corner of one eye, I saw the cook—a splendid old blue-eyed, straight-as-an-arrow frontier woman—peering at us from a window of the kitchen and directing by signs her husband to take part in the disturbance. I continued to talk. The husband crept nearer, sprang, and pinioned the axeman's arms from behind. Then his wife appeared. She was furiously angry and for a moment I imagined it was because she was so fond of me and was shaken by the peril I had been in.

"Tom," she said to the rastabout, "you're a damn fool and you deserve to get killed. Doc's got a right to go off and get a gun and shoot you on sight—don't you never raise an axe again so long as you live unless you mean to bring it through."

She was a magnificent woman—this cook, and in her youth she must have been very beautiful. She had a charming way of sitting on the edge of a table and suddenly lifting up her skirt and producing from her stocking a bag of Bull Durham and some papers and rolling herself a cigarette. She had come West on her honeymoon in a covered wagon and once, while her husband was away from camp, had stood off three desperadoes by herself. Later on when she was settled in a country where there was only one other woman, the tradition is, not liking the other woman, she had divided the country in half and given notice that, upon pain of death, the separating river was not to be crossed. The enemy's name was 'Grandma Sam,' and she too carried a gun. There are other traditions—how apocryphal I do not know—one of which was that the cook had married her present husband, the man who had saved the lives of the doctor and myself, at the point of a pistol, having taken a fancy to him while he was courting one of her daughters, and another of which was that she had stopped this second husband from drinking by lining up every man in town at a bar and spending all her marketing money, giving in this manner a tableau of how foolish the average male looks under such circumstances. She was a fearless and splendid creature.

As for the temporarily insane lady, she arrived at the ranch one July night extremely late with her young son—about two o'clock, I think it was, frosty and clear. We had been expecting her for four days, but she had been lost, as she herself expressed it, 'on the prairies of Idaho.' Six days earlier we had sent a white-top wagon out to meet her driven by a man nicknamed 'Maria' because he had such a drooping mustache and such a melancholy disposition. 'Maria' was utterly mad by the time he finally arrived with his charge; melancholia had become active insanity. I found him walking up and down moodily in the darkness, and he asked me three times in half an hour where he could pasture his horses, although he knew the place well and knew that at that moment he was standing in a pasture of many acres. The next morning, when he was calmer, he related his trip to me and gloomily predicted that we might look for trouble. "I think," he confided, "the lady is a lemon."

It seems that he had waited two days for the lady and had finally abandoned her in despair, but she, arriving fifty hours after she was due and by an afternoon train instead of the early morning one, had caught him by telephone, twenty miles on his way home, and had brought him back to the starting-point, and, once there, had insisted upon leaving immediately for the ranch, although it was by now seven o'clock in the evening and the nearest stopping-place was a little town sixty miles east in the shadow of the Tetons. This would mean, as you see, a hundred-mile drive for 'Maria's' team. Having little character and being easily bewildered, 'Maria' consented. By four o'clock that morning the caravan was definitely lost.

'Maria' insisted that this was all the fault of the lady, who had taken entire charge of the expedition, stating that she was an expert in astronomy, and had begun to steer by the North Star. She forgot, however, the error of calculation in the case of horses who are animals and who, regardless of the North Star, are likely to stray here and there in search of grass when they are tired and hungry. After many weary hours a light was seen in a distant cabin and the wagon was headed in that direction. Why a rancher should have been up at that time of night I don't know. The whole thing sounds like Alice in Wonderland anyhow. The lady said she would get out and ask the way. She walked up to the cabin and knocked on the door and said—at least, 'Maria' swears she said—"Kind sir, I am a lone woman lost on the plains with a child"—and at once, of course, the light went out and the bolt was shot. Whatever nefarious preoccupation was keeping the rancher up so late, he was still sufficiently detached mentally to bar his door to what, very naturally, he considered to be a dangerous lunatic.

The journey was resumed. At four o'clock the following afternoon the caravan limped into the little town that was its first stopping-place. By that time 'Maria' was no longer a man, merely an automatic obeyer of absurd injunctions. One of his team was foundered, but despite this fact he was given one hour in which to find another horse, feed his team, and proceed. Night came upon the weary travelers crossing The Pass. 'Maria' said that even there he was considerably delayed by the lady, who by this time claimed that she was a writer, and who insisted upon stopping at almost every ranch-house to ask questions, mostly insulting ones. Fortunately there is only one ranch—a half-way house—once you really get into the hills.

When The Pass was finally negotiated, 'Maria' headed north. He was now less than twenty miles from his destination, but he was so thoroughly lost he would have kept straight on to Yellowstone Park, almost a hundred miles away, if our lower ranch had not barred his path. I don't think that at any moment he was on the road except when he zigzagged across it. Afterwards I followed his tracks and they plunged into gullies, ascended rocks, and did not even turn aside for clumps of aspens. He was suffering a total nervous collapse.

In a moment of lucidity, however, he recognized the dark outlines of the lower ranch, and awakened the ex-storekeeper amongst the Sioux, who lived there alone, and whom I have already mentioned and asked this alert old gentleman to guide him back and west to where he belonged. The ex-storekeeper was wearing a white nightgown and the lady, in order to complete her perfect record, having seen the nightgown crossing a window asked eagerly, 'who the woman was the ex-storekeeper had with him,' and when he indignantly denied any woman at all, would not believe him. Four o'clock of a frosty morning is no time for insinuating remarks.

'Maria' was right, trouble was in the air, but it was to be exclusively my trouble, for my partner recognized in the newcomer a weapon forged to his hand. I cannot go into the details—I will simply say that, being still fairly innocent and having said to my partner and his wife a week or so after the lady's arrival, in what I thought was a business meeting, that I thought the lady was a nuisance and that we ought to suggest delicately to her a trip north, my partner immediately sent down his wife to repeat to the object of them my opinions.

The lady had been more than a nuisance— two nights earlier she had rushed to her cabin door, a rifle in her hand, and had shot over a neighboring cabin inhabited by an elderly woman, explaining afterwards that she thought she had 'heard a wolf,' whatever that may have meant.

From the time my partner's wife told the lady what I had said, misfortune was my bedfellow, and even if I had not already decided to dissolve my partnership, I would have done so then. The lady persecuted me. She used to send me notes at six o'clock in the morning. Once she sent me a note requesting me to answer a list of questions and sign my name to them immediately, because her lawyer in the East had written her that if she obtained a signed statement from me she would be able to sue me. I was innocent and young, but that struck even me as funny. Finally I packed a horse and departed for a hidden place in the hills. Nobody but the doctor knew where I was going and he had an engagement to come up and visit me in three days. While he was riding along the road, miles north of the ranch, he overtook a small hot figure trudging valiantly through the dust. It was the lady; she was on my tracks. The doctor reasoned with her and finally persuaded her to return to the ranch before nightfall, but she sent me by his hand a very disagreeable letter.

The climax followed shortly afterwards.

When I returned to the ranch, the lady and myself indulged in what I thought was a complete reconciliation, promoted by her. She confessed that she had been in the wrong, and I confessed that I had been in the wrong—although I hadn't been—and, during the two weeks before her final departure, we were noticeably attentive to each other. The day she left, early in the morning, she leaned out of the wagon and handed me a bulky envelope. "Don't read this," she said coquettishly, "until I get out of sight." I was a trifle embarrassed because I thought, as youth will think, that perhaps she was confessing a deeper emotion for me than she could permit herself to explain in my presence.

I waited until she was gone; then I opened the letter.

It was four pages of the most bitter abuse to which any one has ever been subjected. . . .

Possibly the most lasting effect my former partner had upon my disposition and future was what might be termed a 'reverse English' effect. It was largely my anger and disgust with that last summer that determined me to stay in the country and show what I could do. That autumn I formally dissolved my partnership and, the doctor expressing a wish to go into ranching, he and I formed a partnership instead.

There is nothing so productive of effort as a good old-fashioned hatred.

IX
A New Partnership

WE had an infinitesimal capital, the doctor and myself—a couple of thousand dollars each, my share of it borrowed, and he was almost totally ignorant of conditions, while I, although not so ignorant, was handicapped by the frequently disastrous impetuousness of youth. Or is it disastrous? I don't know. Sometimes it is necessary. Without it youth would frequently get nowhere. Had the doctor and I appreciated what we were doing, perhaps we would have done nothing at all. And that would have been a pity, for we would have missed a considerable amount of success, a vast amount of happiness, and an experience which has been invaluable. As it was, we set out in the most nonchalant manner possible to burden ourselves with debt, depending on the business of the following summer for recompense. What would have happened had no tourist appeared I shudder to think.

By the time I had finally decided that my former partnership was on the point of dissolution and the doctor had decided to abandon the East and become a Westerner, the year was approaching its fall and we had only about two and a half months in which to make our plans and look about us. We appreciated the necessity for continuity in the business. It would not do to allow a season to lapse, not only for the psychological value of not going into abeyance for any length of time but also because having so little capital, it was imperative, as I have said, to take in some returns as speedily as possible.

But this meant that with the best of luck—an early spring, and all the materials on hand, and labor easy to obtain and hold, in a country where material is always scarce and labor always hard to obtain and hold—we would only have two months, May and June, to get ready in. In that time, out of sage-brush and deadfall, we would have to create a home for fifteen Eastern people and the five or six Westerners needed to take care of them, and not only a home for the former but a comfortable and artistic one as well, a very different matter from starting an ordinary ranch. Moreover, having taken care of the interiors of our guests and the interiors of our cabins, we would have to turn our attention to the outside world and see that there were cows to milk and horses to ride and other horses to do the hauling and farm work. In short, we had to build a small town in the wilderness, complete and self-sustaining in every detail.

Such a task might seem impossible unless you bear in mind the astonishingly short time it takes experts to build a log-house and the genius of the Westerner for turning his hand to anything. Our fireplaces were built by a man who had never built a fireplace before in his life and the rocks with which he had to work were the worst that can be imagined—slippery cobblestones and unshaped granite. The same man who one day is laying logs, the next can manufacture the pleasantest kind of an easy chair or a dining-room table.

We made excellent chairs out of two by two lumber and elk hides and are using them still; we made chairs and beds out of willows and alder and stripped aspens and pine poles. And the most beautiful furniture in the world, of course, is home-made, as the most beautiful houses in the world are, on the whole, unless really great architects are employed, those built from necessity not artifice. Nothing is lovelier and fits more perfectly into the background from which it came than a Western log-cabin, and nothing is more comfortable. In the summer it is cool, in the winter it is warm. Its walls inside are restful to the eye, taking on a mellow ruddy patina as they get older. Moreover, they form the best of settings for anything you choose to put upon them. There is something of magic about the inevitable correctness of simplicity and usefulness.

In regard to the things we could not make, I conceived the brilliant idea, if I say it myself, of reading from beginning to end the huge catalogues of two of the largest mail-order houses . . . 'Western Bibles,' the irreverent call them . . . and checking off what we needed from adzes to zithers. In this way nothing was overlooked, although possibly a good deal was ordered we did not really need. These catalogues are ingenious. Little pictures accompany the text. And as a result you get into the habit of sending for various objects just to see if they are as useful and as pretty as the pictures make them out to be. By the time the winter was over I could repeat those catalogues backward. . . .

As a matter of fact, we never did use a zither on the ranch or order one, although we have had imported from tune to time plenty of ukuleles and guitars and have always had down in the bunk-house a plethora of mouth-organs, that most typical of cowboy musical instruments. . . .

But, to return to the task on hand, here, specifically, was what we had to build and assemble by July 1 of the following summer. . . . We had decided that we would take only fifteen people and for some reason, why I don't know, it never occurred to us for a moment that we wouldn't have those fifteen people, although it was not until the last few weeks before they actually arrived that we were sure of any one of them. . . . We would have to have at least seven small sleeping-cabins, fourteen by sixteen, with fireplaces, four bunk-houses, a couple of storehouses, a meat-house, corrals and necessary fencing, a well, and a large central cabin, the last with a kitchen, a dining room, a sitting room, and two or more smaller rooms for writing and card-playing. Those were not the days of bridge, but even then we had to make some provision for people who can find nothing better to do at night but follow suit. Nowadays with bridge and the added complication of Mah-Jong—an extraordinarily spreading game—we use every unoccupied cabin on the ranch and probably eventually will have to put up a mess-tent somewhere out in the sage brush.

We built for fifteen people—we have been enlarging ever since. This is what we have to-day: forty-five buildings, ranging from single room and double room sleeping-cabins through cabins designed for all kinds of use, to the central cabin with its two dining rooms, its kitchen, its two big sitting-rooms and its two smaller rooms, a cabin ninety feet long one way and sixty feet long the other way. We have a blacksmith shop, a garage, a saddle-shed, a granary, a camp storehouse, three ordinary storehouses, a root-cellar, an office, an ice-house, an outfit dining-room, five bunk-houses, a store, a laundry, four houses in which live the partners and the upper ranch foreman, and a dance-hall, or recreation-hall, or whatever you choose to call it. We have eighty saddle-ponies, two work teams, ten cows, sixty saddles with their paraphernalia of bridles, blankets, and so on, complete camping outfits for about twenty people, a motor-bus, a smaller car, and an incredible amount of diversified supplies. We must be in a position to replace anything at a moment's notice. I cannot tell you how many sheets and blankets and quilts and things like that are stored away. These, I am glad to say, are in charge of a person delegated to keep track of them.

Furthermore, to this Indian village of an upper ranch, we have added recently two more ranches, a lower ranch which is a stock-ranch and which has an outfit and life of its own, and another ranch which we use as a boys' camp and as headquarters for pack-trips for boys.

These additional ranches have added two more partners, two more foremen, about twenty more employees, half a hundred more buildings, considerably over a thousand acres, and more than a hundred horses, counting saddle and pack and work horses. It is interesting to reflect that the whole thing started twelve years ago from practically no capital and directly—with the exception of the stock-ranch—from sage-brush. The dude-business is the only business I know of in the world, certainly the only business in the West, where such a thing would be possible, and even at that we would have gone along considerably quicker and have made a net profit considerably earlier had we had sufficient capital to begin with. As it was, for years we put back into the business every cent we made and, having often to build hastily, lost money by this haste and by having to amplify and rebuild at our leisure.

We did not know in the beginning that the dude-business is something like the old-fashioned game of 'idiot's delight,' you no sooner get one thumb on top than you have to get the other on top of it. We found that fifteen tourists were not enough—the over-head charges ate up the profits. We tried twenty-five, thirty, forty, eventually we discovered that you could run fifty people with just about the same outfit with which you could run thirty, and we also discovered the simple fact that a dude-ranch that takes only five tourists can be made profitable because you can run it as an ordinary ranch and make little extra provision, but that from five up to fifty tourists there is no stopping.

Having once discovered these facts, we seemed never to be able to build quickly enough to keep up with the demand. I have nightmarish recollections of trying to get the builders out of a cabin just before its first occupants were due to appear over the bench. And the oddness of human nature was never better exemplified than by our difficulty in meeting the demand. Whatever limit we set we had always more applications than we could handle, the surplus showing a surprising evenness of ratio to the limit. Any place that limits its capacity seems to be the one place to which most people want to go.

The doctor and I utilized the last two months of that final summer at the lake ranch hunting for a ranch of our own. It would have been easy enough to buy a ranch, but there was no site already occupied that exactly suited our purposes. We decided eventually that we would have to take up government land. Almost every day we would get on our horses and ride until sundown, exploring out-of-the-way corners of the valley. We argued and fought endlessly. We have done that ever since, but always with infinite mutual respect and forbearance. The doctor is a conservative man and sees the worst side of things first; I am just the other way about. Sometimes we have fought for days over a five-foot jog in a fence. But this combination of opposing qualities makes for a good partnership. Frequently in the end our final half-and-half conclusion is not so far from being right. While we were hunting for a ranch our respective characteristics were uppermost. We would no sooner find a likely spot than one or the other would discover a dozen objections.

There are so many more things to be taken into consideration when you are choosing a dude-ranch than when you are merely choosing an ordinary ranch—and heaven knows, even with an ordinary ranch there are a score of factors that require the use of experience and common sense—soil, the lay of the land, prevailing winds, timber for winter shelter of stock, nearness to range, water rights, nearness to building material, neighbors, five or six other considerations, but with a dude-ranch all these factors have to be governed by and adjusted to the factors of beauty of situation, a certain amount of isolation, opportunities for fishing and shooting and other sports, and the close proximity to points of interest. Even mosquitoes have to be considered. A ranch along a stream where a river wind blows is much less likely to be troubled by mosquitoes than a ranch back from a stream or in thick woods.

At last, after many weeks of search, of delighted discovery and ultimate disappointment, the doctor and I found the place we were looking for. It was not perfect, but as nearly so for our purpose as any piece of land could be. It lay on three benches sloping down to the river; the first bench had no agricultural value at all; the second not very much; and the final flat beside the river, although it contained rich soil, was so stony and cut up with numerous little draws that irrigating would be peculiarly difficult. All this was emphasized later on. The whole place, moreover, was covered with sage-brush—supposed to be a good sign of its growing capacity but a dreadful thing to clear off—and on the lowest flat, where we would want to put our houses, the sage-brush was of the giant variety that reaches up to a man's neck, and there was dead-fall piled like jackstraws. A grim task was ahead of us.

Yet, on the other hand, aspens and pine-trees grew in a half-moon at the base of a bench and were beautifully parked out in the open, and to the south were the beginnings of a meadow, and to the west was a magnificent view of the Tetons, not over two miles away. While further off to the south, blue in the distance, closing the valley, was a gorgeous horizon of rolling mountains, and to the east, fifteen miles or so distant, the green containing walls of the Grovont Range. The whole landscape, except to the north, spread out before you. On your left hand, bounding the flat on that side, was the Snake River, very useful in the fishing season, and along the Tetons, within riding distance, was a series of forested sapphire lakes. Ducks and geese were plentiful, the latter along the river and the former both on the river and in some near-by sloughs. But there was no water on the place except at its southern end; we would have to dig a well and bring our irrigation ditch over three miles. All in all, though, a lovely hidden spot.

The doctor and I, after we had made up our minds, used to ride up two or three times a week to what was to be our ranch and dismounting on one of the upper benches, lie on our stomachs in the warm sunlight and roll cigarettes and dream of what we were going to do.

Strange, I can still feel the warmth on the back of my neck, and I have no sense of time. I might have been doing this yesterday. It is odd when you look back and place yourself in a situation that happened twelve years ago. The site we had chosen was eight miles north of the ranch we were then on, in what, until we built, was totally unsettled country, and as we looked down on this untroubled stretch of sage-brush, we did not know how many feet before long were to cross it, and we had no idea how many things—some of them tragic—were to happen to us there.

Pretty soon, however, the opportunity for dreaming ended, for the autumn came and on top of it a record winter.

The winter started, I remember, the second day of November. I recollect the date well because, unfortunately, it was the date on which I had arranged to go out to the nearest good-sized town in order to see a lawyer and definitely wind up my affairs with my former partner. Usually in our country the winter does not really settle down until around the middle of December, and I recall one Christmas Day when our guests rode up to the ranch on horses, but the year of which I speak the snow started the day I left, and it continued to snow for a week, and the snow never again left the ground until the spring. I was outside several days and by the time I was ready to come back The Pass was blocked and we were the first team to start breaking it open. Following this initial storm came weeks of iron-cold weather. The elk poured down from the hills to their all-too-scant winter feeding-grounds just north of the nearest town a month or two before they were due, and the world seemed suspended in a glimmering gray net of frigidity where the only color was the blood-red of the sunsets.

The doctor was waiting for me at the little ranch of an old bachelor friend twenty miles up the river. He was as anxious as I to get started, for there were a number of preliminaries to be got through with that would take us at least two months before we dared go East to hunt out and pin down to the promises we might extract from them the extremely necessary dudes of the following summer. Before we left the valley we would have to see that everything we could arrange for at the time was lined up so that we could begin work at the earliest opportunity in the spring. There were logs to be contracted for, lumber to be ordered, teamsters and builders and ranch-hands to be engaged, and all the supplies we would need from nails to food had to be ordered in advance so that they would surely be laid down at the freight-station one hundred and five miles away by the time we needed them. Our credit was extended mightily. We wrote business-like and haughty letters to various firms demanding wholesale terms and ordering what we wanted.

I had left a saddle-horse at a ranch near the foot of The Pass, so now when I returned from Idaho I had to take him up-country where he belonged. The journey, usually accomplished in four hours, occupied two and a half days. Although the snow was not so deep, except in places, it was crusted, and I had to walk ahead, breaking trail for my horse, who plunged and snorted after me. One night I was nearly lost in a blizzard that came up suddenly and raged until the following morning. I remember my relief when I stumbled across a wire fence and followed it until I saw the dim glare of a house. I do not like wire fences but they have occasionally saved a man's life—although they have also killed a great many horses and cattle.

To be lost in a blizzard is a baffling, weird, uncanny experience. You feel as if you were in the presence of a real demon. You alternate between hot gusts of anger at your own helplessness and the cold dreariness of despair.

On the morning of the third day I saw far off in the white expanse of the snow a black speck coming toward me on snow-shoes and the black speck turned out to be the doctor armed with a huge and rusty .45 Colt, which he had borrowed from our bachelor friend. He was worried about my lateness especially since he knew I had to stop at my former ranch on the way and the memory of the stormy events that had recently taken place there was still fresh in his mind. He had set out to rescue me. . . . That is another one of the doctor's heart-warming characteristics. He will set out to rescue a friend at any hour of the day or night, and if he can't borrow a rusty .45 he will pick up a stone or go empty-handed. Although like all brave men—with imagination—he thinks himself a coward, he is utterly fearless where his duty or affections are engaged, and that is a trait you cannot overlook. After you've lived in a fairly adventurous country for a time you begin to separate the world into two classes: those, a tiny number, who will stand by you through thick and thin, and those, the rest, who won't. I have a foreman who belongs to the former class, and that is why I love him far better than a brother and why, at present, he is not only a foreman but a partner as well.

A loyal man finds it hard to starve to death and if he adds to his loyalty even a modicum of talent he is practically certain to be a successful man as well. And yet loyalty is the rarest and least cultivated of traits. Before we found this foreman the doctor and I had turned over man after man in an attempt to discover some degree of faithfulness.

The week we spent with our old bachelor friend before going down to town ranks in my recollection as one of the most amusing in my history. I am very fond of this old bachelor; an interesting man, a tall, gaunt, fine-eyed old fellow who once punched cows on the Kansas trail—a good, frank, outspoken man. To my great regret he has now left the country, although across the river still lives, I am glad to say, his younger brother, the bearded ex-miner whom I have mentioned as one of the party who had gone antelope-hunting four years before. I have never met two men I would rather talk to than this ex-cowpuncher and this ex-prospector—they read diligently through the winter months and their ideas on important subjects are wiser than the ideas of the average half-dozen city dwellers put together. I wish some of our politicians and philosophers could meet these brothers. But even the most charming of bachelors have their own way of doing things and not many of them can stand guests for more than a few days at a time. I don't blame them. And I realized that we were getting on the nerves of this particular bachelor and that it was about time to go when, hunting around for some handle to his growing annoyance, he began to focus more and more upon the doctor's waxed mustache. The doctor left his window open at night with the thermometer at forty degrees below zero and appeared at breakfast with his hirsute adornment frozen and drooping. This annoyed our host. "I like fresh air as well as anyone," he said, "but that is danged silly."

The climax came on a particularly cold morning. Our host was cooking hot cakes on his stove and the doctor and I, in rocking-chairs, were watching him. Our host looked over his shoulder to where, through the rime-covered window the bulbous white shapes of bush and tree covered with hoar frost were dimly visible.

"Days like these when I was punching cows we used plenty of grease," he remarked reminiscently.

"Inside or outside?" inquired the doctor.

Our host paused and glared balefully at the questioner, the handle of the frying-pan suspended in his hand.

"What d'you mean?"

"I mean, did you eat it—bacon and stuff like that—or did you rub it on yourself?"

The quiet kitchen, warm and cosey, smelling of coffee, a hot-water kettle purring, was stirred with sudden passion. Our host brought the frying-pan down on the stove with such force that the batter flew in all directions.

"Nobody," he roared in a choked voice, "but a damned fool with a spiked mustache would ask such a question—ate it, of course."

The doctor, always gallant, and just as frank as his host, leaped from his chair and, leaning across the stove, faced his assailant.

"And nobody," he retorted, "but a damned obstinate old fool like you but would know that hundreds of people rub grease on themselves to keep off cold. How about channel swimmers?"

For a moment the two continued to glare at each other, and then our host, ladling out some more batter, quietly returned to his task and the doctor sank back into his chair.

The minds of both seemed relieved. They were happy once more. . . . The doctor is a bachelor too.

The psychology of extreme loneliness is a queer thing. When you add cold to it it becomes even queerer. Lock the best of friends up together in a snow-bound ranch-house where they see no one else and before long they will begin to quarrel. I have seen men fight over the most absurd trifles and I have seen women concoct—men also, I hasten to add—the most elaborate disagreements for the mere excitement attendant upon them. Gossip is relished by the best of people for the fillip it gives to monotony. I once came upon the trail of two aged prospectors who had been together for years but had finally quarreled fatally—one killing the other—because there was a suspicion that the murdered man was taking more than his just share of the shrinking supply of sugar.

X

BACHELORS

PERHAPS, after all, the old bachelors you find tucked away up narrow river valleys and in the folds of the hills are the most interesting and the most typical of the dwellers in isolation. At all events, ex-miner, ex-cowpuncher, ex-gambler, they are all marked by the same love of loneliness and the same love of the country. Under their gnarled and frequently thorny surfaces they are the true bards of the mountains. And most of them are mighty hunters before the Lord, and back of the loneliness of the majority are histories you hardly ever hear.

My friend the ex-storekeeper amongst the Sioux is not so reticent as some. I wish he would write his reminiscences. After an adventurous life during which he was one of Sherman's men in the march through Georgia and subsequently, for many years, on an Indian reservation, he settled down—or thought he had settled down—in a prosperous Western town to spend the remaining years of his life. It was not for long. The noise of the city was too much for him and he found himself on the edge of a nervous breakdown. The discovery of this was dramatic. Near his house was a church with an open belfry the bells of which tolled constantly. He could see the bell-ringer and finally he decided that he would have to shoot this innocent hireling in order to stop the infernal racket. One Sunday morning he came to himself on the roof of his house, a rifle trained upon the belfry. He still had sufficient self-command to stagger back down-stairs and summon a doctor. The doctor sent him to the Rockies to die. He is still alive, after twenty years or so, a most alert and active old gentleman. During the winters he lives entirely by himself, surrounded by seven or eight feet of snow.

This ex-storekeeper talks Sioux as well as he does English, which is extremely well, and his stories of Indian warfare are unforgettable.

He was only a few miles away from Wounded Knee, he was on the Custer battle-field shortly after the fight and saw the troopers, stiff and frozen, lying as they had fallen, and during the Red Cloud Rebellion he was told to take his own Sioux tribe—the sole tribe not involved in the uprising—south where their minds would be diverted by hunting. He was the only white man amongst all those lodges. During the day his charges were happy at their hunting but almost every evening there would come over the horizon to the north, breathless and wild-eyed, a rider from the fighting tribes. A council would be called after supper. Like a train of gunpowder to which fire had been held, the rider's words would crackle around the tepee, and the young bucks would leap to their feet and talk war. My friend would wait until all this was over, and then he would arise and tell them what fools they were, a statement seconded by the old chiefs. But if for one moment he had lost control he would have been the first white man to die.

Custer's battle-field is the most dramatic battle-field in the United States. Across the Little Big Horn from where the Indians, hidden up a canyon, poured down upon the regiment cantering past and cut it in two, are long lines of small tombstones like companies of soldiers in formation, and at the very top of the butte to which the white men withdrew and where they made their final stand, is the stone that marks the grave of Custer himself. He was the last man to die, and the story goes that, on his knees, wounded in a dozen places, his yellow curls flying in the wind, he roared with laughter and when the two revolvers he was using were empty flung them in the faces of his enemies. . . .

One of my partners snow-shoed up to a solitary old bachelor's cabin on a winter's night. He heard a great commotion going on inside—several voices arguing and demanding and pleading. He pushed the door open and looked in. The old man, entirely alone, was holding court, taking the roles of judge, prosecuting attorney, defending attorney, witnesses, and even audience.

And then there was 'Uncle Jim,' the best friend possibly I ever had among the old bachelors.

'Uncle Jim' was a little white-bearded ex-prospector crippled with rheumatism, but he still got over the mountains like a troll. Leadville, Thunder Mountain, Yellow Jacket, other magic names dripped from his lips as water drips from an ancient sluice-gate. Like all prospectors 'Uncle Jim' had made great fortunes and lost them, and like all prospectors he had discovered famous mines and practically given them to the men who afterwards made money from them. Prospecting is the most romantic of pursuits, but it is not a lucrative one, for it is the chase not the quarry that is of importance. 'Uncle Jim's' relatives had at last persuaded him to settle down on a ranch, but they couldn't prevent him from stealing off into the hills each spring, and, besides, he was not much of a success as a rancher, for he could not resist over-feeding his horses. They were huge gross creatures with bulging pleading eyes. He killed three or four of them by this mistaken kindness. Early one summer morning he was found unconscious in a stall in his barn. He had been stricken down in the act of giving a horse an extra quart of oats. The doctor and I were summoned and rode down to his ranch and while the doctor was inside, I stood by the door-sill in the sunshine and listened to the buzzing of the flies.

I can see 'Uncle Jim' now coming towards me and waving the willow branch he used as a whip—a most gentle whip. He would waylay me and tell me in his high cracked voice another marvelous tale of 'a good prospect' just discovered. I think he is still doing this, wherever he may be. And he never failed to claim that the fat, white, insolent mare he rode had just bucked with him. That was another instance of the perpetual glamour in which he lived.

When we left our old bachelor friend of the flap-jacks, the doctor and I went down to town and stayed at the hotel for a couple of months. The weather grew colder and colder. You hated to put your nose out of doors of a morning. Later on in the winter the elk died by the thousands. That was one of the fatal years that come to them every so often. The hotel had no heat except the big wood stoves on the first floor. We slept in our clothes and piled overcoats on top of us. At six o'clock each morning the proprietor paraded through the halls blowing a trombone in order to waken his guests. I remember the doctor emerging from the immense mound of covers that concealed him and blinking at me sleepily. "This damned luxury," he said, "will someday ruin us."

But what the hotel lacked in conveniences it made up for in social life. As winter draws down in a frontier country the principal town becomes the focus of the community. Families move in from their ranches so that their children can be near the high school and stray cowpunchers and ranch-hands, with nothing to do, make it their headquarters. I know of nothing more physically comfortable or more mentally enthralling than to sit about a warm stove all day and at nightfall watch, one by one, the snow-covered stage-drivers and teamsters and riders come in, clouds of cold steaming from them as they push through to the warmth. Most of them have news to tell, the state of the storm, the news from up-country; reports of men who have disappeared and can't be found, or of slides that have run burying a sleigh.

The doctor inaugurated an anti-spitting campaign. The hotel blossomed with signs commanding and petitioning the patrons not to spit. I am afraid these commands were about as effective as are a good many other laws of a similar nature, even some constitutional amendments. I have never been in a gambling hell in the West where there was not, directly over the dealer's head, a notice calling attention to a State regulation forbidding under the severest penalties the every act in which the players were so calmly engaged.

Hardly a day passed without some delightful incident. A crowd of us played stud-poker every afternoon by a window that looked out into the snow banked open space upon which faced the stores and the two hotels. A gentleman from up-country nicknamed 'Beaver Tooth,' because of his incisors, insulted a waitress and a young cowpuncher undertook to avenge the insult. He chased 'Beaver Tooth' across the snow but when he caught up to him, 'Beaver Tooth' flung himself upon his back and said, very justly, 'you can't hit a man when he is down.'

"Get up!" commanded the avenger.

"No."

The infuriated youth, tears of vexation streaming down his cheeks, borrowed a shovel and, amid the cheers of the spectators, proceeded to bury 'Beaver Tooth' and pack the snow around him. When he had finished, he gave the rounded heap a disgusted kick and walked away. After a discreet interval, 'Beaver Tooth' emerged, dusted off his clothes, and, unabashed, went about his business.

On another afternoon a young Englishman—one of the lantern-jawed gangling Englishmen—who claimed that he was a cowpuncher and who was working for the lady who ran the rival hotel, interrupted dramatically our game. The lady who ran the rival hotel was a genius at cooking but in order to enjoy her cooking you had to understand her. She was a half-breed and on the slightest provocation bit, kicked, or hit you. She also used brass knuckles, and the story goes that wishing one day to assault a six-foot-two cowpuncher, she obtained a chair and climbed upon it and struck her victim from behind. Her exit from the country several years later was in keeping with her previous record. She decided that she had too many bills to bother about paying them, so she said she was going out to the station to meet a cousin, and got on the stage and never came back. But before she left she chose for herself a trousseau. The apex of this trousseau was a handsome travelling-bag. She went over to the general mercantile store and said to the proprietor: "Rex, I haven't seen my cousin for a long while and I want to give her a present. What would you suggest?" The proprietor, looking over his stock, suggested the travelling-bag. The next morning he was up when the lady departed and she favored him with a brilliant smile and nodded proudly at her bag. . . . I understand that she is doing very well at present down in southern California.

The young Englishman, hired to chop wood and feed the pigs and draw water, always wore a gun—without anything to hold it to his leg—while performing these tasks. That was funny enough in itself, but it was still funnier when he suddenly appeared, bounding across the snowy square, or plaza, as it would have been called further south, his gun flapping like a rag in the wind and his tiny employer only a foot or two behind him with an uplifted broom. He made our hotel just in time and refused to leave it for several days.

A small mule and a little woman can do a great deal of damage if they have sufficient intelligence.

At the end of a couple of months the doctor and I completed our business in the West and went East to interview prospective clients. While I was East I further complicated an already complicated life by getting myself engaged. At least, it looked at the moment like a further complication, but it wasn't, for it was one of the few completely sensible things I have ever done. When you are first in love your critical faculties are in abeyance, but without knowing it I had found the charming, laughingly earnest young woman of my earlier dreams.

As is the case with all happily married men, I was not complicating my life, I was simplifying it enormously.

XI
Homestead And Desert Claims

AN unrecorded wit has said that 'homesteading consists of the government betting you one hundred and sixty acres against starvation, and the government always winning.'

In the main this is true. Only a very hardy man or a very ignorant one would at present take up government land unless he had some definite object in view or a small independent income. Even twelve years ago when the doctor and I homesteaded and desert-claimed there was little public land left that was worth ranching. Nowadays there is hardly an acre. Scattered throughout the West, to be sure, are hundreds of square miles of unoccupied territory, and some day part of this unoccupied territory will undoubtedly be put under irrigation, but even then the settler had best know exactly what he is doing. . . . I must halt my narrative for a moment to speak about this subject of homesteading and desert-claiming and irrigation projects, for it seems to me a very important subject and my feelings are deep. I believe that there is no more fundamental passion in the breasts of the men of the northern races than their passion for a home, and I believe that one of the wickedest things other men can do is to balk or prey upon this passion. There is most certainly a special hell for such jackals, and the West, like all new countries, has been, naturally, a favorite hunting-ground for them.

And yet they are not entirely to be blamed, for the human race, except in a few instances, will not think synthetically, will not look ahead or around, will not realize that all life consists of a delicate balance easily thrown out of adjustment. If the average man took as much thought to the balance of life as he did to the synchronization of the engine of his motor-car, civilization would go forward overnight. You cannot, for instance, have one country starving to death and not sooner or later run the risk of all countries doing the same; you cannot boom or 'boost' or inflate one interest without harming all the surrounding interests; you cannot do a selfish act, or a stupid act, without, if you have any brains at all, knowing that the ripples of what you are doing will spread out indefinitely. In the end everyone goes down in the universal chaos. The Worldly Wiseman of today is the ancestor of the hunted fool of tomorrow. The self-seeking German and English business men of thirty years ago did not know when they christened their little sons that one day those sons would die because of their fathers' short-sightedness. The rich men of Syria did not take time to think when they cut their forests that they were bequeathing a desert to their descendants. Thought is the one possible salvation of the world—and then . . . more thought.

For years I have been entreating the government to appoint a commission to study the country as a whole and draw, if nothing else, a map that will at least guide and warn prospective settlers. There are certain parts of this country that can never be anything but grazing land, there are certain other parts—such as my own country—that are suited solely for the tourist and for big game. The very factors that make a country a good grazing country are the very factors that make it a poor farming country, and the very factors that make a country a good tourist country—mountains, cold, a properly protected wilderness—are the very factors that make it a poor land for stock.

What are you going to do about it? Are you going to encourage a country, whenever possible, to develop along the lines for which it is best suited and so become prosperous, or are you going to allow things to go along in their usual higgledy-piggledy fashion?—this higgledy-piggledy nonsense being the cause of most of our troubles. What would you say if, instead of talking about a country, you were talking about your son? And yet, next to a man's family, he is supposed to love his country better than anything else. Well, the answer is most men don't. If they did the country would be different. They have no real love for their country at all. They regard it merely as a place in which to live and sleep and eat, and as a captured town to loot and ravage at will. What do most men care if forests are cut down so long as they can buy a limousine with the profits, what do they care if they can sell a man a piece of land what becomes of him and his children? The State will take care of them. Will it? Possibly, but at infinite cost.

The descendants of Ada Take, born in Austria in 1740, a woman of the slums, have been traced. She has had 709 descendants, of whom 142 were beggars, 100 were illegitimate children, 181 were prostitutes, 46 workhouse inmates, 76 criminals, and the remainder more or less habitual drunkards. This one family alone has cost Austria one million two hundred thousand dollars. And no doubt you are familiar with the history of the Juke family in America. It does not do to discourage people or to impoverish them.

But a commission and a map after all would probably do little to prevent land crimes. Human hope is too powerful and human greed too active—especially the latter—and human ignorance is also at work.

There is no appreciation that even a clear-headed selfishness leads one to the point of view that quality is better than quantity. Civilization, agriculturally speaking, is still understood to mean the settling at any cost of a starving 'nester' upon a plot of ground in order that he may encourage other starving 'nesters,' in order that they may in turn encourage still further starving 'nesters'; the encouraging of an untried alien to emigrate, in order that he may raise food to encourage other untried aliens to emigrate, in order that they may raise food, in turn, for other untried aliens. It is a vicious circle. A tin shack is supposed to be of more economic value than a forest. The old tale of localities where there is only fifty dollars in cash and this is passed around from hand to hand at harvest time is not so far-fetched as it may seem.

To begin with, and as a general proposition, except in various favored sections—and of course there are a great many favored sections, but we are not talking about these—new land geologically speaking seems to resist in some mysterious way the attempt to cultivate it. It is as if the savage soil had a personality of its own. This is merely a theory and has not the slightest scientific backing, but to come down to what is known, and to repeat what I have already said, you cannot make money out of farming if you are in a country where the same frost and snow that produces strong range grass upon which cattle thrive is the same frost and snow that prevents your crops from ripening; and you cannot make money out of stock-raising, even if you have strong grass, if you are so high up in the mountains that you have to feed hay to your stock five or six months of the year. In short, if everyone tried to suit himself to the country, as the citizens of older countries have learned to do, instead of trying to suit the country to himself, both the Far-Western stock-raiser and the Far-Western farmer would be in a happier state than they are at present. And, although it is true that the stockman cannot to any extent live in the same country as the farmer, in a land where natural conditions are such as they are here and where there is so much room, there is not the slightest reason why he should. There is nothing more silly than the accepted point of view that stock-raising is historically a more primitive occupation than farming and is bound to pass as the frontier is settled. Wheat and meat are the two primary necessities of the human race and the latter never can be raised in sufficient quantities in any restricted way. In a narrow and homogeneous country such as England the stockman may have been pushed into the sea, but why should he be pushed anywhere in a vast country such as this, where there are immense tracts of land fit for nothing else? On the plains of Hungary there are cattle-ranches hundreds of years old, and even in the tiny country of France, in the Camargue, are cowpunchers not unlike our own.

Until you answer this question you will continue to pay exorbitant prices for meat, the stockman will continue a bankrupt, and, eventually, you will be lucky if you get any meat at all.

In the old days—that is, the old-recent days, ten to twenty years back—when the stockman could turn his herd out in his back yard, so to speak, his expenses and his summer loss were practically nothing. Now he has to send his stock back into the hills, he must employ herders, he loses a certain percentage through poison and wolves and mountain-lions, and weight is lost on the long spring and autumn drives. With the price of labor what it is and the increased cost of living, the stockman can afford no loss whatsoever, but if he had back some of his old range even costly labor and costly living would not prevent him from getting along fairly well. Every time a farmer settles in a range country he increases the cost of meat. Even in a country like my own, which is too high to be anything but a small cattle country, one can witness the process. If the farmer on his part made a living there might be some palliation or room for argument, but he doesn't make a living. The first farmers came into my valley about ten years ago and today they are broken and ruined men.

As a matter of fact, the average American farmer has never been a farmer, he has never been anything but a miner, skimming the top soil and moving on. He has all the restlessness of the miner, and it will take him years of bitter experience before he learns anything else.

Added to this confusion of local ignorance and greed are the more wide-spreading operations of the average irrigation and land-development company. Let me relate an odd story about one of them:

For a number of years the vast flat to the west and north of our upper ranch, a fairly good cattle-range, was withheld from settlement under the Carey Act. The Carey Act is a bill originally introduced into Congress by ex-Governor and ex-Senator Carey of Wyoming granting to a private company, where the government does not wish to act, the right to bring water to and parcel out into homesteads a tract of land too difficult to irrigate by an individual or group of individuals but possible to irrigate if a good deal of capital is expended. When the main ditch and laterals are built, settlers are allowed to come in and take up homesteads under the Homestead Law, but they must pay the company an annual rental for water. On the surface this is an excellent act and was intended as such, but its actual workings have been weird and devious. Ex-Secretary of the Interior Lane said that 99 percent of all private irrigation schemes had to be taken over by the government because they were either fraudulent or inefficient.

This particular flat would grow nothing; I happen to know because, unfortunately, we own some of the best of it. It consists of a thin stratum of soil with cobblestone river-wash underneath. The whole of the valley as a matter of fact was once a lake-bed. High up in the Tetons you find fossil fish and oyster-shells. You could turn a river on to the flat in question and in a few hundred yards the river would disappear. If you persisted in turning the river upon it, in a short time the top soil would be washed away and only cobblestones would be left. You cannot take the stones off this flat, because each time you plough you turn up more stones than there were there to begin with. Even badgers won't dig in it, and that is saying a good deal. To complete this charming picture of agricultural possibilities, the main slope of the land is towards the south but the slope of the countless little draws and depressions is towards the east. Irrigation ditches, therefore, like the mythical angry rattlesnake, would bite themselves in the tail if they tried to cross it. However, the Carey Project Company went calmly ahead with their plans.

Their engineer used to stop with us. He was a nice fellow personally but our gibes at his occupation were so savage that eventually he stopped coming. Here is what his company intended to do. They were going to dam one of the near-by lakes—incidentally ruining the lake, a lake which is as beautiful as any in the world—and when they had run their main ditch from this lake they were going to sell the water to the homesteaders at thirty dollars an acre. Thirty dollars an acre! When you could buy the best land in the valley, fenced, irrigated, built upon, and producing hay at fifty dollars an acre! By the time the homesteader got through with his fencing, building, and the putting of his land into cultivation, the cost per acre, at the very lowest figures, would be at least one hundred dollars, and even at that he would have nothing—only land that badgers wouldn't dig in, land the water on which alone, at that valuation, would be costing him a tax of 30 percent a year per acre. The Carey Project people, however, seemed to be quite certain of the feasibility of their preposterous scheme, and there was no reason why they shouldn't have been. Plenty of equally preposterous schemes have proven profitable to their originators. And this especial company had grounds for believing themselves to be even more secure. They were cleverer than most; they proposed to make money coming and going, as was subsequently discovered.

The stream which was the outlet of the doomed lake from which the main ditch was to be built, emptied into a river which already carried impounded water from a dam twenty miles north to an irrigation development hundreds of miles away in Idaho. But this big dam did not supply enough water and therefore our own Carey Project expected to sell its waste water to the farmers down in Idaho and, in time, when the flat was empty of settlers again, all its water, for the men back of the project knew as well as we did that eventually even the most obstinate of their homesteaders would give up in despair. In the meantime, besides their waste water, they would be making a tidy little sum of many thousands of dollars on the side.

Homesteaders would come in, in a year or two they would leave in disgust—well, that was so much in initial payments—other homesteaders would come, and, at last, when everybody was sick of it, the land could be sold back at a round figure to the cattlemen who originally had had the use of it for no more than a nominal annual fee to the Forest Service.

Like so many other logical plans, however, this especial plan went askew, although it took years of desperate effort to defeat it, and perhaps it isn't defeated yet. The men who make money by such means are sleepless and one never knows where they are going to attack next. There is not a valuable future asset in the West to-day, not a lake or a watershed or a forest, the conservation of which is necessary to the health and wealth and security of future generations which is not in danger from forces who do not care a snap of their fingers for future generations so long as they can gut and fell and dam and fill their own pockets. Every once in a while they plan incursions even upon the national parks, as in the recent attempt to dam Yellowstone Lake. In connection with which project, one aesthetic and high-minded politician said that 'a handsome dam at its mouth improved any lake.' It would have been easier to agree with him had he substituted the word 'confrère' for 'lake.'

I am no engineer but if any irrigation engineer can show me where, in ninety-nine cases out of a hundred—I would make it an even hundred—it is necessary to dam a lake for irrigation purposes I will grant that he is a better engineer than an economist. It is, looking at it in its lowest terms, merely ruining one business asset for another, when the latter business asset would be better off somewhere else, for a lake is usually near the headwaters of a stream, and the headwaters of a stream is just the place where you do not want to store water. You will never have enough. You will miss all the subsidiary streams that come in below. But, and here is the catch in the puzzle, you can usually get a lake for nothing from the government, while it costs money to go down a valley and buy up ranches in order to locate your dam.

The great and beautiful lake twenty miles north of our upper ranch is the best example I know, of what I am talking about; an example so good that it is constantly being used as an object-lesson by the enemies of stupid spoliation. Here is one of the most beautiful lakes in the world, eighteen miles long, snow-capped mountains to the west of it, a lake that in a few years, possibly a generation, would have been as famous and profitable as the Italian lakes, and yet it has been ruined forever unless the dam that holds it is broken down or forced to keep its contents at an even level. All around its shores, gaunt trees, millions of feet of them, stand up like skeletons. After a while, of course, these trees will disappear, but the twenty feet or so of evil-smelling mud that marks the recession of the waters will never disappear.

The Swiss, the Canadians, the Norwegians, all wise nations who know the value of scenery, would laugh at us for the fools that we are.

Not long ago I came across another private irrigation enterprise that proposed to make its living by damming two gem-like mountain lakes and then holding up in times of draught a nearby larger enterprise. The small enterprise would be able to charge as much as the large enterprise could stand, but in the end, of course, the farmers would pay the costs. Well, high-jackers live by holding up bootleggers and bootleggers live by holding up the public, and so it goes.

Possibly I seem bitter. I am. Early in my life I learned to be chary of good, kind development companies who were going to make me rich by any other method than my own hard work. I lived through the apple boom in the State of Washington, and it was a salutary lesson, and I was lucky, for I only lost all the money I had. I saw the time when you could walk into practically any club or office in the East and sell apple land 'sight unseen' to people who didn't even know where it was located. And I saw shop windows filled with apples purporting to come from countries where I knew an apple tree hadn't even as yet been planted. Huge co-operative associations were formed that, in five years, if you just left them alone and didn't bother them, would turn over to you five or ten, or whatever it was, acres that would give you a home and keep you in affluence for the rest of your life.

I lived alongside some of these community orchards and saw the puny unhealthy trees die within the first year if they weren't dead when they were planted. All the land surrounding our nearest railway station—twenty miles away—a spit of land deep down in the naked valley of the Columbia River, where the station agent couldn't grow vegetables because the wind blew and covered the seedlings with sand, and where the only inhabitants, except the station agent, were rattle-snakes, was sold as town lots to Chicagoans by a particularly enterprising citizen. The station agent told me that every now and then some one would get off the train looking for his or her town lot. And the seller hadn't even taken the trouble to get a title from the

Great Northern Railway in the first place. Then, in the end, having seen all this, I invested, as I have said, some money myself.

But folly has its uses. In latter years I found my heart exceedingly staunch against the oil prospectuses with which, being an author, and therefore on every 'sucker list' in the country, I was deluged, and nowadays I find myself equally deaf to the more modern appeals that guarantee to make me rarely beautiful or keep me permanently young or endow me with vast personal power.

Fascinating how advertisements and get-rich-quick schemes follow the feel of a period like hounds upon the scent? Years ago when I was in the State of Washington, people had just awakened to the fact—a fact that has since become a stupefying reality—that modern life was growing increasingly bewildering and perplexing. Charles Wagner had written his 'Simple Life,' and every one wanted to get back to the land. The clever gentlemen who keep their ears to the ground immediately offered you fortunes in apples and oranges and grapefruit and wheat. A little later, most people having decided that if you had to live in a city you had to, and the immense new mysterious forces of quick communication and closer international relations stirring in the minds of men, oil was discovered in vast quantities and the clever gentlemen, abandoning their bucolic pursuits, held out to you for practically nothing a chance to share in world power and an opportunity to touch in your feeble way this black genius who worked for you day and night. But in the last three or four years, perspective having been gained concerning the war, and the most of us having become more sophisticated and greatly more weary and individualistic, with a new appreciation of the shortness of life, mere money, even impersonal power, is no good to us any longer unless it brings with it personal satisfaction, and so we have offered us all sorts of panaceas that will do for us what our own brains and hearts and bodies are too lazy to accomplish. A Morgan is no longer the eikon of our hearts but a Valentino. We can become motion-picture stars in a week, famous novelists merely by writing a letter or two, radiantly lovely creatures by swallowing a pill or by creeping into our baths backwards. Some of these remedies are so simple that you have merely to rub them on.

And close to the bottom of the list of those who are chasing the pot of gold at the foot of the rainbow, and amongst the most unfortunate, because of the hardships they must endure, and because their intentions are industrious and honest, are the men who, without knowing what they are doing, settle on government land.

I have seen them come with high hopes and their small belongings, and I have seen them wage the dreariest sort of warfare against poverty and famine. They must beat the devil around the stump. In order to live they must work during the summer months for some wealthier rancher, and if they work during the summer months for some wealthier rancher, they haven't time properly to develop their own holdings. Each summer they earn just enough to feed themselves and their families during the winter.

OUT-OF-DOORS the moon is a guide and a street-lamp and the sun a fire by which you warm your heart, but in the city the moon is a theatrical unnecessary adornment and the sun is something you feel but never see except as a reflected light high up on walls of brick or stone. You do not even know the moon is in the ascendant until unexpectedly you discover it at the end of an avenue or down an alley peering at you with the wide stare of a village girl in whose innocence may lie all manner of chances for misfortune and adventure. About the city moon there is none of the wide and wise and placid maternity of the moon in uninterrupted places.

Weather generally to the farmer or the rancher is a personality in a way not understandable to the man who has too many neighbors; a passion and a source of fierce inward rejoicing or despair. Rain or snow is heavy upon the countryman as lead, and a speck of blue sky sends the blood coursing through his veins. In a high mountain country this preoccupation with the weather becomes a mania, especially as the days grow shorter and the winter sets in. There is always so much left to be done about a ranch that never gets done, and a storm, particularly to a man in camp, may mean more than discomfort; it may come near to meaning actual danger. At all events, a storm late in the year means this—for it is at that time that you are either hunting big game or else rounding up cattle and horses—it means long days of riding over slippery trails or soggy flats, half the time in the face of a gale and often so cold that you are numb in your saddle. And it means that you ride from gray dawn until late into the gray night, and it means that when you do finally come back to your camp or your ranch that you will be so sheathed in a thin armor of ice that for a moment you will hesitate before dismounting in order that you may bring back some circulation to your legs.

That first spring of the doctor's and my partnership the weather seemed even more determined to test the sincerity of our intentions than the United States Government. The government at least had granted our applications for land, but the weather granted us nothing. We came back to the valley early in April to find it still in the grip of frost. The mortality among the elk was increasing daily. Darkening the snow in all directions leading off from the feed-ground to the north of town were pitiful tawny patches that marked where a bull or a cow or a calf had fallen, for it is in the spring that most of the elk die, their ribs so visible that you wonder why they haven't broken through the taut skin. When they have nothing else to eat they eat willow twigs, and although a moose thrives on such diet, to an elk calf near starvation willows frequently supply the final fatal touch. As usual, the government had not provided enough hay to carry through an extra severe winter, and as usual the ranchers had donated what they could out of their own scanty store.

The doctor and I stayed in town for a few days, and then, restless with impatience, went up-country to the cabin of the bearded ex-miner who was the brother of our friend of the flapjacks. His ranch was only a couple of miles west of one of the two mail roads kept open during the winter, the road to the north, so it was to some degree in touch with our nearest base of supplies, the town we had just left—a very inadequate base at the moment, as you will subsequently learn—and it was only three miles south of our final objective. Even if we could not as yet begin work, we could at least cross the river and snow-shoe up to our claims and plan still further what we were going to do with them. Something of a satisfaction, if not a very great one. The one tangible satisfaction—the only one we were to experience for weeks—lay in the neat piles of logs, the upper layers breaking through the snow, the ex-miner had cut for us during the winter. There, at any rate, were the beginnings of a ranch.

The beginnings of a ranch! . . .

In building a house, even as simple a house as a longhouse, everything needed must be on hand, or else you will find yourself in what is called out West a 'jack-pot.' You must have spikes with which to nail your logs together, various-sized nails for roofing and flooring, window-sashes, doors, hinges, and roofing-paper. If one of these essentials is lacking, your house cannot be finished. And we were facing the worst roads and the latest winter the country had known in years. Sometimes when an essential is lacking you can substitute for it, and the frontiersman is excessively clever at substitution, or with doing without, but substitution takes time and we were building for people who would not understand delay. The Mormons built their great temple with wooden pegs and used deerskin, rubbed thin, for window-glass, but then, so far as they knew, they had all eternity to build in, and we had no longer than the Fourth of July. Six people were due to arrive then, my fiancée one of them.

I say we had until the Fourth of July. That is not quite correct. One tourist, a portrait-painter, was due to arrive at any moment. Although he was an intimate friend of the doctor—now an intimate friend of mine as well—his coming preyed upon our minds. We need not have worried, for when he did arrive we discovered what we have proven again and again since then, and that is that the one person the dude-wrangler need never bother about is the artist, the actual working artist or the person with an artistic mind. Wyoming is too beautiful for a person of imagination to be much concerned about anything else.

The artist, moreover, is an adventurer. He wouldn't be an artist, especially in America, unless he had more moral courage than his fellows. If you can give him interest or beauty he will put up with any amount of discomfort. By the same token, when he is back in civilization he demands, if he can pay for it, more nicety of living than any one else.

I do not fear silken people in rough countries—silken men or silken women. What I fear is the big so-called 'regular' fellow; the hundred per center who worships his bathtub and his automobile. I want either one of two classes when I am in a tight or uncomfortable place, the very simple man or woman or the very civilized ones. The tough blade does not break, neither does the rapier.

I don't think this point of view is sufficiently understood by Americans, especially by those Americans whom Mr. Roosevelt described as 'hard-faced and soft-handed.' Sooner or later something will have to be done about it, for raucity is increasing—the feeling that if you shout and push people aside and pound the table, in some way or other you are amplifying your ego. One of the few generalizations I thoroughly believe in, having lived in a lonely country, is that the gentlest are most surely the bravest, and the longer I live the more this notion is confirmed. Some day there will be a revolution on the part of the gentle and they will kill all the table-pounders. Most of the reformers will die in this slaughter.

. . . No, the gentle will not have to kill the table pounders, thus stultifying their own instincts, for the noisy, being bullies, will melt away at the first sight of the army of the soft-spoken.

In the beginning our particular portrait-painter hadn't wanted to come at all—he was coming because he needed a rest. Like a great many other people he imagined the Far West to be a flat land of tin shacks with a brazen cloudless sky over it. When he first saw our clouds—like Italian clouds—he was astonished. He was completely enraptured with the discovery that our skies, far from being brazen, were filled with these great, soft, piling-up, constantly shifting clouds. And he fitted into our absorbed and uncomfortable life without the slightest friction. He ate his bad food contentedly, and slept on the ground, and made friends immediately with all the men working for us, most of whom thought him a sort of super-sign-painter, and he was interested in everything.

And he did have bad food. Nails, spikes, door frames, windows, and roofing-paper were not the only things that did not arrive on time or failed to arrive at all. The hard winter had stripped the shelves of the general stores down in the town, and The Pass was still in too bad condition to admit of much freighting. There wasn't a thing in the country but canned fruits and beans and coffee and carrots. No flour, or sugar, or even canned milk. Eventually it became difficult to look a canned peach or a bean or a carrot in the face. And the fact that canned peaches are ordinarily the most expensive of luxuries did not increase the doctor's or my appetite for them. We suffered both internally and externally.

There were other things to bother about. An indignant resident once described our valley as 'a country where a twelve-inch board shrunk an inch a year for fifteen years,' and twelve years ago this description was not inapt. There were at the time only two saw-mills—the nearer one twenty miles away—and the gentlemen who ran them were more intuitional than practical. You could order lumber as far ahead as you liked, but when the time came for delivery you took what you got and thanked God for it. Also, what you did get was invariably so green that it dripped sap and weighed, thus complicating hauling, about twice as much as it should. What is known as a 'wanie edge' was especially popular. A 'wanie edge' is an edge cut so close to the bark that the bark shows and the end of the board tapers off, or it is an edge that starts at two inches and dwindles to nothing. You can see that to lay boards of this description is difficult, and that even when in place they are not as useful as they might be. When it came to dimension lumber, if you ordered a 2 x 4 or a 2 x 6 you might get anything from a slab to a joist, and such exotic affairs as boards planed and grooved for flooring had to be spoken about with bated breath.

It is a wonder to me that we ever managed to build our cabins at all, let alone furnish them, and put chintz curtains in the windows, and complete them with such final details as candles in little brass candlesticks. And you must remember that all the while we were doing this we were gathering horses and driving recalcitrant and homesick cows from the ranches where we had bought them, and persuading pigs to accompany us, and that we had even constantly to turn aside from the delicate problems of interior decoration to inspect such adventitious creatures as cats or dogs. Our life was very much like that of Noah. To cap the climax, in the midst of our fury of haste, the ferry went out, cutting us off completely for a while from the town.

But I am anticipating. I haven't even yet got rid of the weather . . . .

We stayed three weeks with the bearded ex-miner before we were able to turn a hand. Sometimes there were mornings when the Grand Teton showed above the mists, and the camp-robbers and magpies were alert and gay, and the great blanket of snow was pulled back at its edges an inch or two as if a gigantic hidden form stirred sleepily beneath, but for the most part we watched despairingly gray skies or driving storm.

I remember—I don't know why—one of the mornings of sun when we took off our snow-shoes and ate lunch by the stream that bounds our ranch to the south . . . no ranch then, merely a flat expanse of whiteness with the pine-trees along the bottom of the bench dark green. The recollection lies in the pocket of my memory like a bright coin. The blue shadows of huge leafless cottonwoods fell across the perfect silence. The stream-bed was a miniature land of buttes and hills, where the snow was piled in white mounds over rocks and hidden logs. Only here and there, where the snow had fallen away, could you see the water, black and self-contained. A little mouse came out and looked about him with the wise glance of a farmer who studies the weather. Over all was the bluest and warmest of skies, and the air was warm and soft. Surely spring had come . . . .

By the twelfth of May, almost a month later than usual, the snow had gone sufficiently, except in drifts, to permit the doctor and myself to delude ourselves into the notion that we could at last start work. We sent word to a four-horse team, waiting to bring up our first supplies, to start for the ranch, and we our-selves, with two of our building gang, went up the river and camped. We had one small tent and enough food to last us a couple of days.

That afternoon it started to snow again, a bitter storm from the southwest, and the next morning we heard that the four-horse team was stuck in a drift five miles down-country. We ate supper with our backs to the wind, our fingers stiffened about the handles of our coffee-cups. Had we not been able to joke, it would have been hard to get through those first four days. I'm not especially fond of indecency, but all men have heard it when it sounded extraordinarily like prayer.

Those four days of misery, however, while we were waiting for the team and the rest of the gang of twenty-two men, were not completely wasted; we spent our time inventing a name and a brand for the ranch to be. Eventually we decided upon the name and the brand Bar B C, or, written as a brand, B C; B for my name and C for my partner's name, Carncross, and the bar to make the brand distinctive and pleasantly alliterative. You can imagine that such historically important letters as B C and such an at present historically important word as 'bar' have not been allowed to pass unchallenged without numerous puns and witticisms.

Later on, when we came to register this brand in the State brand book, we were told that a neighboring ranch ran a brand too similar to ours, Bar C, to make ours acceptable. The name of the company, therefore, is Bar B C, but the brand is written B C Bar, or B C. It is still bad taste, in the Far West, even if it were permitted, which it is not, to use a brand that can too easily be transformed into the brand of a neighbor, or vice versa.

In our haste to make camp during the miniature blizzard we had pitched our tent in a hollow, and later on, when the remaining snow melted, water ran down upon us from several angles, but we were always too busy and too tired to move; we shifted our beds as necessity arose. Weeks later I lifted the heavy tarpaulin under mine and found a contented colony of the little black beetles who like dampness. I hope they slept as well as I did, for I slept the sleep of utter exhaustion. Moreover, I had less sleep than the others. When all the rest of the camp was in bed I sat up by a guttering candle and wrote four and five page letters to the girl I was engaged to with the stub of a pencil. They were optimistic letters; I did not dare tell her what was actually happening; I filled many paragraphs with description.

When my fiancée finally arrived, what between lack of food and lack of sleep and worry and too much work, I had broken out into a strange sullen rash that did not leave me for weeks. It shows the magnanimity of my future wife's nature that she allowed the engagement to stand. . . .

I cannot convey the stress of that particular period. The piling up of details will not help. You will have to take my word for it. Youth is not a happy time, for all the sentimentality—a paradoxical, cynical sentimentality—it now showers upon itself. It is a miserable time, unless you are a fat rich youth with a fat shining motor-car. Even then it is miserable.

It is all rather like the fairy-tale of the little girl who was offered poverty up to twenty and riches afterwards, or the other way about. How happy your youth is depends upon how imaginative you are. The young and imaginative suffer. No new saying, but one that cannot be too often repeated.

XIII
INCIDENTAL COMPANIONS

SURELY, however, even if slowly, something was being accomplished. We had divided the builders into two gangs, one to work on the sleeping-cabins and storehouses, and the other to work on the main cabin, and two ranch-hands who were to stay after the builders had gone, and the doctor and myself began to build corrals and fences and clear off the sage-brush and deadfall. The semblance of a ranch was arising. We set fire to one huge old log in front of the main cabin, and it smouldered for a month before it was reduced to ashes. Near our tent we uncovered a bleached buffalo skull. . . . Before long it was June and real summer, the sudden springless summer of high countries, with violets underfoot, and thrushes and meadow-larks singing.

The first cabin we built was a tiny one, twelve by fourteen feet, which we used as a mess-house. We might be able to sleep in water and work in all kinds of weather, but it was necessary to have at least a dry place in which to eat. Here we consumed our canned peaches and our beans in two shifts, as fast as a perspiring cook could supply us. One of our teamsters was a quaint and pleasant little fellow with an enormous appetite. It came to be his tacitly understood privilege to enter with the first shift and stay right through the second, cleaning up, when all had gone, any food that might be left. This same man did not like to drive through high water, but he was courageous and conscientious and did what he was told. In the quiet violet dusks we used to hear the rattle of his wheels and the sound of his voice as he sang at the top of his lungs to keep up his spirits while he was crossing, on his way back to camp, the creek, then in flood, a mile to the south of us.

Another man, by no means so conscientious, never left us to spend Sunday with his family without taking with him some unconsidered trifle. Once we saw him riding calmly off with a couple of rounds of stovepipe under his arm. But we did not remonstrate with him. Good workmen were scarce.

I seldom pass the little mess-house nowadays, the original focus of the ranch, without thinking of the breathless weeks during which we went in and out of its doors. Subsequently it was turned into a sleeping-cabin. It took us days to scrape the soot and grease from the walls, and days to get rid of the smell of food. Afterwards several millionaires slept in it, and are still sleeping in it. I wonder if their dreams are ever disturbed by the vision of grimy men wolfing their food in the silence that is considered etiquette by those who work with their hands?

Our relaxations were simple. One of the men invariably went to bed immediately after supper, and always, for some reason, slept with his bare feet sticking out from under his quilt. We considered it the height of wit to tie a string to his big toe, pass the string over the ridge-pole of the tent, and then, elevating his foot, place a candle near the string, so that the string would eventually burn through. These preparations completed, we would go about our business. After a while we would hear a muffled exclamation, followed by a grunt and renewed snoring. We did this night after night, and the drollery never seemed to lose its savor.

Old Bill Blackburn, who describes himself as 'a Rocky Mountain carpenter,' but is also a miner and practically everything else useful, and who is stone-deaf and speaks in what might be described as a soft roaring whisper, had a way of stopping such nonsense. Once when he was in a road camp some of the younger blades thought it would be amusing to stuff his stovepipe with gunny sacks and watch him build a fire. Bill puffed and blew, and got his eyes full of smoke, and then, without a word, stood up and left the tent. In a moment he reappeared with a gigantic hunting-knife, which he proceeded to whet gently upon the sole of his boot. "Don't want any trouble," he said. "Not looking for it. . . . But if any young son of a he goat thinks he's going to get funny . . ."

Bill, by the way, worked for us while I was still at the lake ranch, and a most excellent workman he is. One night after supper I saw him go down to a flat-bottomed boat, his arms filled with pillows and newspapers, and a lighted lantern and part of a torn sheet hanging from his wrist. He busied himself for a while rigging up a jury-mast and attaching the torn sheet to it. Having adjusted these to his satisfaction, he pushed off from shore, tied the strings of the sail to his foot, put the lantern and the pillows in the stern of the boat, and, lying down luxuriously, began to read his papers. For an hour or two he drifted about in the darkness at the caprice of the gentle winds, like a meditative will-of-the-wisp. "Too much noise," he explained afterwards. "Too many women talking. Can't hear 'em. See their lips move. . . . A man needs a little quiet."

'Johnny Highpockets,' so named because he bought overalls too large for him and then pulled them up until they were painfully tight, was on the whole a good hand, and a nice fellow, but he was cursed with a magnificent and untrained imagination. In happier circumstances he might have been an Oppenheim. Once I told him to build a dog-house. The result was something that was seven feet high and six feet across and looked like a Dissenting chapel. We are still using 'Johnny's' dog-house as a place to store gasoline-tanks.

On another occasion he told us, when we were in a hurry to build fireplaces, that he had been 'a bricklayer all his life.' Possibly he may have been, but he did not know much about slippery cobblestones.

He laid them up in a single layer instead of double or triple layers, and towards dusk called me over and showed me with a proud expression, to my utter astonishment, a chimney, almost completed, that an ordinary man would have taken at least three days to build. I did not want to discourage his zeal, so I walked away. A moment later I heard a dull roar and ran back to find 'Johnny,' a puzzled look in his eyes, standing knee-deep in cobblestones and mortar.

'Johnny,' like so many of his kind—and it is astonishing how many mechanics are neurotics—was a victim of the delusion of persecution. Whenever he did anything wrong, which was not infrequently, he laid the blame on somebody else who had with malice prepense followed him about and wrecked a perfect contrivance. We still have in a cabin a door-jamb upon which he wrote with a carpenter's pencil these cryptic words: "Leave me alone!" Nobody ever knew whether he was referring to the door-jamb or himself.

Curiously enough, I never realized so much the continuity of language as when building in Wyoming. Carpentering is an ancient and honorable trade, and it is interesting to hear frontiersmen, thousands of miles from where the English language began and hundreds of years away in sentiment and point of view from our Saxon and Norman-French ancestors, talking about 'mortises' and 'tendons' and 'valleys,' as if they were twelfth-century Englishmen building a cathedral.

'Johnny' was an authority on skunks—at least he said he was. Later on he worked for us as a 'rastabout,' and I shall never forget a certain summer evening when, enraged at a skunk who lived under one of our cabins, and who had broken the treaty that I supposed existed between us, I chased the offender with a revolver out into a field and shot him, 'Johnny' leaping along a couple of feet behind, pleading with me to stay my revenge.

"Don't shoot!" he yelped. "Don't shoot! His skin is worth three dollars! Catch him from behind! I've caught hundreds of 'em that way."

In passing, however, I will add my testimony to all those who are intimate with the skunk, and say that on the whole he is one of the most courteous of animals. For years we had a skunk or two under every cabin on the ranch, and only twice was there any disagreement. The second disagreement occurred in the middle of the night and right under my cabin. Half asleep and extremely indignant, the brilliant idea came to me to fight my visitor with his own weapons, so I poured a bottle of household ammonia down through the cracks of the floor. In a moment or two I heard a tiny strangled cough, and then another, and then the skunk went away and never came back. I recommend this homoeopathic cure to all those who are troubled in a similar manner.

Labor in common produces intimate temporary friendships that seem at the moment everlasting. The recent war was an example of this. But out of that first spring I did achieve three abiding friendships: with 'Nate,' the lanky ex-cowpuncher of the original antelope-hunting party, who joined us and stayed with us several years until we got well started, with a builder of log-cabins, who became a lifelong friend, and with the boy we engaged to wrangle horses for us and who is now a man and a partner in the company.

All these three were typical products of the West. The cowpuncher had been born in Arizona, the builder in Utah, the boy in Idaho.

The builder was a frustrated poet and a genius, a bright bearded, blue-eyed man who dreamed log houses and fireplaces and bestowed upon them the loving care of an artist. He possessed also the sensitive and difficult temperament of the artist.

The boy was the descendant of one of those especially marked frontier families who have followed the frontier every second generation or so, starting in Virginia when the country was first settled, and migrating to Kentucky, to Ohio and Indiana, to Nebraska and the Dakotas, and finally to the Rocky Mountains. All through the West you will find men and women with this clear, cool strain of adventure and exploration in their veins. They are a distinct breed, filled with candor and cheerfulness and doggedness.

'Nate' had been a cowpuncher all his life and had to the fullest extent that curious baffling Spanish pride that seems to have come over the border with 'chaps and taps and latigo straps.' It makes a man with whom you have camped and slept and talked leave you suddenly without a word of explanation, and it is as sharp as moonlight, and as cold as a knife.

But I must be getting back and getting back immediately, to a concrete ending to those first two months of effort and worry. The doctor had gone to Idaho with 'Nate' to buy horses, and his instructions were to waylay the portrait-painter en route and drag him off the train and delay him as long as possible. But the portrait-painter proved a recalcitrant dude; he insisted upon continuing his journey. And so the doctor left 'Nate' to drive the horses north and returned himself with our first tourist. And then, pretty soon, July came upon us and, one morning, it was the day upon which most of the country sets off firecrackers and overindulges in iced foods.

Once when I was a little boy I went to a Sunday-school picnic, marching in a dusty line and waving a tiny American flag—on my mother's side I am descended from seven generations of Baptist ministers; oh yes, and we still have the saddle-flasks, one to contain brandy and the other to contain whiskey, my clerical ancestors used— and I ended my day with a stomachache and delirium from eating cherries and ice-cream, but now, on this Fourth of July, twenty years later, I celebrated by riding down to the foot of The Pass to meet the girl I was engaged to and the people with her. The girl I was engaged to had travelled four days by train and two by wagon to see my country and my place, and I would have to explain to her that as yet we had only half the roof of the dining-room on.

No Lochinvar ever rode into the face of a sweeter or softer gale. Every now and then there were little scuds of rain that by nightfall turned into a downpour, but that morning there were no more than enough to bring out the almost non-existent scent of the lupine and the wild geranium and the mallow. The aspen-leaves shone like small disks cut from silver-foil, and down-country the meadows were pungent with hay. . . That night our suddenly augmented family ate by candle-light on the dry side of the dining-room, while the rain beat in upon the side that was unprotected, and the pines around the house whispered and clashed together.

My dear wife! All young married people should live for a while on a ranch or in some quiet place until they get over the troublous silly times through which they are bound to go. By so doing they will build up memories too vital and dramatic to tear apart. . . . Two years later my son was born in the middle of a snowstorm, when I was driving a band of forty horses through the whirling madness to their winter feed-grounds, and the doctor, my partner, suddenly shorthanded by reason of an unexpected strike, was chopping wood and hauling water and being a doctor all at the same time.

XIV
Dudes, Dudenes, And Dudelets

THE portrait-painter, sitting on a floor-joist of an unfinished cabin, the sunlight of a July morning falling on his curly black head and Gallic face, said to me:

"You have an interesting place here—more interesting than you realize. It will be a psychological laboratory. This country will have an immense effect upon those who see it."

Well, I don't know. I used to think that when I was younger, and I am afraid that I tried to produce a change in the minds of some of my guests by force majeure, but having been in the dude-business sixteen years, and having in that time seen fifteen hundred or so tourists, I have come to the conclusion that people, once they have passed the formative period, are on the whole pretty much what they are. Let them come West when they are still below the age of seven and I will guarantee that they will be drenched with memories of mountains that will last them a lifetime, or let them come West when they are in their teens or early twenties, and the same thing will happen, although possibly in a more diluted form, to three-fourths of them, but after twenty-five if they go away with some new beauty and freshness in their hearts it is because they have brought beauty and freshness there in the first place.

And this after all is reasonable. Experience, to be effective, must be cumulative. Tragedy scours for a while almost every human heart and so does joy, but before long both are forgotten in the details of living. The man or woman who comes West and actually lives there does, as a rule, experience some change, but it is expecting too much to think that two or three months in the summer, the least distinctive months of all, will greatly affect the mature person.

The human soul is a curious thing, anyway; you have to be a hardy adventurer to continue to try to perform miracles with it.

But whatever the effect of Wyoming may be on others, especially those who stay there only a short while, I know that it has altered me considerably—my point of view; my philosophy; even, I believe, to some extent my bodily structure; and I would not have missed for all the galleys of Tyre what I have learned, or think I have learned, of human nature during my sixteen years of dude-wrangling.

For human nature itself, for the material, I have achieved an immense respect. For the individual man and woman, if not so great a respect, at least some sympathy. For the circumstances that make the average man and woman what he or she is, I have only a profound hatred.

Give the average man and woman plenty of sleep, good air, enough to eat, exercise to keep the blood moving, and a few friends for company, and you have as a rule a pleasant and kindly-intentioned person. Fifty per cent of all the crimes committed I firmly believe are what might be called 'crowd crimes.'

You can see in a simple and articulated form what I mean if you watch a bunch of horses in a corral or a paddock. Give horses a nice big sunny and, in places, shady corral, or a paddock with trees and running water, and they will behave towards each other in the most courteous fashion, but confine them too closely and, like city crowds, their worst instincts will come to the surface. They will not be jostled, except by friends, and they are not particularly amiable even about that.

We have entertained millionaires and poets and artists, business men of every description, spoiled little bobbed-hair flappers and large selfish women who have allowed their minds and bodies to grow fat; angels and those who weren't; people whose homes were in every part of the country from New York to San Francisco; Prohibitionists and Anti-Prohibitionists, Fundamentalists and Modernists, Reactionaries and Radicals, Futurists and Classicists, those who enjoy Ethel Dell and Frank Crane and those who read nothing but D. H. Lawrence and *The Dial*; the bow-legged and fat-legged and spindle-shanked and knock-kneed; the fortunate creatures with legs resembling Venus and Apollo—for, like the street-car conductor, there is one thing at least every dude-wrangler knows, and that is the shape of the lower limbs of the men, women, and children on his place; Englishmen and Frenchmen and Canadians; and with a few exceptions this rule has held good. One Englishman who was brought up to the ranch by a Mormon bishop was announced in this fashion: "The Lord's down in the bushes. What'll I do with him?" And then, as an afterthought: "But that's where the Lord liked to be wasn't it."

Incidentally this Englishman—who had been two years on the Western Front, until he was wounded; a typical British junker; a V. C., a colonel, who had been in the army since he was seventeen and had fought in eight campaigns—said upon one occasion: "War doesn't make men. . . . It's a wonder to me, and a tribute to humanity, that men can go to war and come out human at all."

But to me it is equally a wonder that men and women can endure ordinary life and come out human. This lovely thing of flesh and blood and aspiration, this intricate and delicate adjustment of tears and laughter and evil and heroism, is beaten upon by noise and confusion and ugliness and hatred and endless, senseless killing, like a tree in a storm. Out of its own mind have come, to be sure, the very forces that are its enemies, but like the djin the poor fisherman released, these forces promised happiness only to grow into a cloud of tragedy. With all the brute in it and the monkey and the clown, humanity per se manages to remain astonishingly fine.

If you learn, however, from seeing people on a dude-ranch that most of them are fundamentally charitable, at the same time, paradoxically enough, you perceive their minor and amusing vices with a clearness not possible in more crowded places. A white light beats upon them. You must remember, for one thing, that they are standing before a soaring and lucid background. With the Rocky Mountains bounding them, a man or a woman can look very small indeed. Yet, if you are at all kindly or humorous, you will be inclined to forgive these minor vices, although at times they may prove to be exasperating.

A friend of mine, a translated Easterner, who owns a ranch a few miles below us, brought his family butler out one summer to cook for him. I remembered this man from childhood. He had always been a portentous figure in my childish eyes; something nearly as grave and to be looked up to as a president or a head master of a school or a bishop—a large, red-faced man, as I recollected him. Moreover, he had once been a valet to a duke, and in those days, being a snob as all children are, a duke seemed a more important creature to me than he does now. And then suddenly, years later, I saw this family butler, this ex-valet of a duke, standing in his shirt-sleeves before a log-cabin with a gigantic snow-covered peak back of him . . . a little crimson-faced, soft-armed, deprecatory person in dusty black clothes. So do the mighty fall.

The sequel is amusing. I went in and had lunch. The owner was absent, but several of his young ranch-hands were about. In my honor the ex-valet of a duke revived his former grandeur. He passed me watery boiled potatoes and outrageously tough meat with the air of one who waits upon a banquet. Finally he said: "Will you have dessert, sir, or fruit?"

"Wha-what dessert?" I stuttered in my astonishment.

"Pudding, sir; and it's not very good, for I haven't learned yet to cook upon a wood-stove. And I wouldn't recommend the fruit, sir, either—dried peaches and very old."

Nor was this all, for the 'fruit, sir—dried peaches and very old' having been consumed, I rolled an after-dinner cigarette and saw with horror the ex-valet of a duke, where he stood by his stove, mark my action out of the corner of his eye and strike a match and advance towards me. None of the young ranch-hands had ever witnessed such procedure, and they stared in openmouthed astonishment. Possibly they thought Ruggles of Red Gap was going to set fire to my clothes. I had not a moment to lose if I wished to save my face. I arose hurriedly, brushed aside Ruggles of Red Gap as if I hadn't seen him, and sought the air.

I could tell a thousand tales, most of them pleasant and cheerful, some of them sardonic, a few of them tragic. Were another King Shahriyar to be born I should make an excellent Scheherezade. But unfortunately, unlike Scheherezade, who was blessed with both an Oriental and a feminine candor, my lips are sealed concerning many of my more histrionic memories. Besides, I haven't a thousand and one nights for the telling.

I must not dwell, for instance, upon the attempt of a good friend of mine, a charming woman when she was herself, to shoot me. She had tried to shoot several other people as well. I sat on the edge of her bed and for five minutes or so looked into the wavering end of a .32-caliber revolver before I persuaded her that murder was out of the question. Nor can I repeat what other women, some of them extremely well known, have told me. . . . Most people's lives are curious.

Nor can I linger upon the intimate recitals of demure business men. I cannot even go much into detail concerning the boy, originally sent out to me from the East, who threatened for a couple of years to kill me. Why, I don't know, for I had done him nothing but kindness. And, if I cannot tell you these things, how can I tell you other happenings far more odd and interesting?

But in passing I should like to call attention to the fact that this business of people threatening to kill you is a strange affair. It is a peculiarly American threat, and you cannot live long in any sparsely settled country, and be busy about anything, without threats of the kind being made. Sparsely settled countries or otherwise, however, nowhere does life consist so much of minding your own business as in trying to prevent others from minding it for you. The most peaceable man in the world cannot always avoid trouble if he stands up for his rights, although as a rule he can avoid serious trouble if he makes his stand and remains there and goes no farther. Most of the people who from time to time have threatened to kill me in various parts of the United States haven't bothered me very much; indeed, the majority of them are good friends of mine to-day. A certain type of man, if he lives in a lonely country, is likely to speak that way in moments of anger, and since the majority of these particular men happened to be courageous they were not deadly. Moreover, it is seldom the man who says he is going to kill you who does so; the man you should watch is the enemy who says nothing.

But in the case of the boy who threatened me I was actually troubled, for he was of the type that in good company is a good citizen and in bad company becomes the material out of which a bad man is made. In the wrong sort of company he might very well have killed a man just to show that he could do it. Moreover, he complicated matters by taking to himself a wife who agreed with his threats, and on the whole murder is more a feminine vice than a masculine one. . . I don't mean homicide, I mean murder. Women are more violent than men, they are aware of a physical inferiority, and they are also aware that punishment is less likely where they are concerned than it is in the case of a husband or brother or son.

There was a thick fringe of timber bordering the place where this boy and his wife lived, and for a while at dusk it wasn't an especially pleasant place for me to pass, although I had to do so frequently. Finally a threat more outrageous than the rest reached my ears, so the doctor and my foreman and myself rode down to see what it was all about. We rode up to the boy's cabin and dismounted and knocked upon the door. We had been told that if we set foot upon his place we would be shot at sight. His wife met us, gulped, and then, with magnificent calmness, welcomed us in.

"You're just in time for dinner," she said. Throughout our visit nothing but the highest courtesy was observed.

XV
"Horses Again!"

BUT little as mature people change, Wyoming, taken in large doses, can still sometimes do much for them, especially, perhaps, the pathetic rich. I have one good friend who came to the ranch with eight wardrobe trunks, a French maid, and an incipient nervous breakdown. If it hadn't been that the French maid hated the country more than her mistress, her mistress would have left at once, but since the French maid was so unpleasant, the mistress decided to send her home and stay herself. The splendid rule of human perversity was at work. The eight wardrobe trunks couldn't be got into any cabin, and for a week they remained out in the weather, spilling mysterious white things onto the sage-brush. That was nine years ago; to-day this same victim of an incipient nervous breakdown is a hunter of big game and has a ranch of her own. Whatever else Wyoming may have done for her, it has most certainly prolonged her life many years. She presents an interesting case, and not an isolated one.

And it is the habit, or necessity rather, the dude-wrangler has of observing individuals closely that leads him into the further habit of classifying them into groups.

The business man, the executive, the prominent professional man are amongst the most interesting types we get. Perhaps the most amusing thing about them is their universal passion to return to their boyhood, or young manhood, and work with their hands. The passion proves how beautifully right were the Greeks when they explained the connection between brains and body and contentment. Most of these businessmen and professional men like camping because they like to share in the actual work of camp, and most of them like to live in log-cabins because they feel that they are starting

housekeeping again and because log-cabins give them so much opportunity for tinkering. They are prouder of some little contrivance
they have made at the blacksmith or carpenter shop than they are of
all the business honors that have come to them.

I have already spoken of how the doctor with whom I first came
to Wyoming spent his time building rustic furniture; last summer a
retired engineer, a lawyer, who is also a writer, and a banker occupied
many of their hours by putting up a fireplace. They wore overalls
and caps and smoked pipes and got themselves covered with mortar
and were as happy as the day is long. I came back one evening and
saw them on the roof of the cabin to which the fireplace belonged,
outlined against the sunset, inspecting their completed work. It was
a most engaging conference. The appearance of the three was that of
substantial stonemasons; their seriousness would have done credit to
the most conscientious of mechanics . . . of which there are few left.
These were nice fellows; your heart warmed towards them.

Nowadays it is dangerous to speak well of the business man. To
suggest that he has an imagination—which, if he is at all successful,
he is almost bound to have—is very likely to get you into trouble.
Having suggested this, however, I will become reckless and hint at
two more little recognized and perhaps unpalatable truths.

It has been my experience that on the whole women are better
ranchers and campers than men; and it is my belief, having seen
a series of younger generations in a way it seems to me only a
dude-wrangler can see them, that the human race is steadily, if somewhat erratically and slowly, improving.

I do not mean that all women are good campers—by no means;
like the little girl, when they are bad they are very, very horrid; but
women are less complaining than men, more eager, more helpful,
and not half so sure they know all there is to be known. Someone

will say it is because they expect less than men and therefore will put up with more. Not in the least; it is because most of them are more disciplined than men. Up to twenty-five, as far as I can discover, the average woman is more spoiled than the average man; after twenty-five she is less spoiled. God preserve me in the woods—or on a ranch—from the sleek, well-fed, well-dressed, petted man from thirty on who believes that golf—good game as it is—is the apex of all outdoors.

As to the younger generations, or the younger generation, for I will talk only about the one of today, I might as well use a big adjective to begin with; I think it is magnificent; better than we were; better than the young people in between. I have camped with these young people and ridden with them many lonely miles, and I have seen them when they were unselfconscious, and I have seen them in difficult positions, and you must remember that about a dude-wrangler there is none of the sanctity of a parent or a college professor. These young people are franker, wiser, more sophisticated, better sportsmen than we were; more eager and courageous about life. They are seldom foolish, and hardly ever wicked.

Youth has always had too much to live for anyhow to be anything as a rule but fundamentally decent. Besides, it has not seen enough of the world to be really evil. Real evil is the result of weariness. Its heart is an utter unbelief in everything, including yourself.

But then, as I have said, the people who come to a dude-ranch are more or less self-selected, so I lay no claim to being a universal reporter. Furthermore, since we publish a booklet that states implicitly just what we have and what we haven't, we warn away the more egregious. People know exactly what to expect before they arrive. For these reasons we escape the majority of fantastic travelers, although sometimes we get them. But even when we do it is not such a serious matter. Sooner or later all dude-wranglers—all Westerners and outdoor men—acquire an uncanny sixth sense in dealing with those they may happen to have in charge, and the fantastic traveler usually turns out to be a fairly nice person if correctly handled; pathetic, as are most people. We have our odd moments, however.

I remember once finding an eminent etymologist down near the corrals flapping his coat in the face of a terrified horse.

"What in the world are you doing?" I asked.

"Training this horse not to pull back when he is tied."

"Do you think that will train him?"

The etymologist became incensed. "I was brought up with horses," he observed stiffly.

As the horse wasn't any good anyhow, I walked on without further comment.

This same etymologist when leaving assured us that he liked the country and might come back again, but that on the other hand he liked, every summer, to conquer (his very words) something new. Dear me—he had been with us three weeks!

I have lived in that particular part of the Rocky Mountains for sixteen years and I know no more than one-quarter of it. There is a tiny valley sparsely settled and then, on all sides, spreading like a dark sea about an island, the surging forests and mountains. The hills roll back, range answering range, like the antiphonal chorus of a song so vast that it becomes silence again. It would take a man a month of steady exploration to know even one of the minor peaks thoroughly, and he could spend ten summers from June to November with a pack outfit, each summer in a different locality, and at the end of the ten summers he would be just barely on the edge of knowledge.

While the etymologist was saying good-by I was troubled with an uneasy feeling that, like Ajax, he might be struck by lightning.

. . . In the West they constantly use the old phrase 'the fear of God in your heart.' This does not in the least imply that a man is religious; it means that through some experience or the experiences of a life-time he has arrived at a proper humbleness regarding his relationship to other men and his surroundings. Once more the Greeks, wise people, had a word—I cannot remember it now—expressing the same idea. A bad horse may put 'the fear of God' into the heart of a man who thinks too much of his riding, a courageous man may put 'the fear of God' into the heart of a bully. It is a beautiful phrase . . . .

Perhaps the most fantastic tourist we ever had was a lady whom we got on a horse and couldn't get off again. At least, it seemed for a while as if we weren't going to get her off. We had had great difficulty in getting her where she was and it was impossible to persuade or force her to dismount. We had procured for her the quietest horse in our band, a gentle bay creature named 'Just So,' so gentle and dude-broken that when the previous summer he had been ridden by a woman who experienced difficulty getting into the saddle, he had been known to edge over closer each time his rider missed her objective. Yes . . . a fact! (Like all story-tellers, after having told many stories, I would like to put my confirming sentences in capital letters.)

'Just So' stood with his kind eyes fixed on the distance and shook his ears a trifle to keep off the flies. One of my partners and myself were busy fixing the lady's stirrup-leathers. We were arrested by a high thin inhuman voice and looked up to see our charge staring straight ahead of her as if afraid if she moved her head she would fall off. I have seldom seen naked fear; most people try to conceal it.

"So!" the lady was saying. "So! That is just what I have always heard about the West! Exactly! You take a woman who has never ridden and then give her a broken saddle."

"Madam," I objected, "we are adjusting your stirrups—people's legs are not always the same length."

For a moment she was silent and then she found her voice again. "Take me off," she demanded. "This is a much too vigorous horse!" I repeat her exact words.

"He is not a vigorous horse," I said mildly. "This is old 'Just So,' the quietest horse in western Wyoming . . . . If you fall off he will stop and pick you up."

"Take me off!"

"Try a little ride."

"No, take me off."

"Oh, very well." But, when we invited her to dismount, we found ourselves just where we had started.

"It is impossible," she announced.

"Take your right leg," I said slowly, as if talking to a child, "and swing it over the saddle. Take your left foot out of the stirrup and slide. We will catch you. In other words, reverse exactly what you did while getting on."

"Don't argue with me!" she retorted. "There are some things some people can do and there are other things they can't—it's a matter of psychology."

I became hopeless. "But, madam," I asked, "what in God's name do you propose? Either you will have to get off or else we will have to tie your horse to a hitching-rack and leave the two of you there until he dies under you. And it won't be a bit easy to eat your meals where you are."

When we started there was no one in sight but the lady and my partner and myself, but when we finished there must have been at least forty people gathered in a circle, and each time a word was said it was greeted with shrieks of laughter and contortions expressing mirth. A few rolled on the ground, one man took photographs, and I am sure that several ranch-hands who couldn't possibly have known what was going on came in from adjacent fields. The problem was solved by the sudden appearance of our foreman, who rode innocently around the corner of a saddle-shed. "Here, Joe," I said, giving him the lady's hackamore rope—I owed him something, anyhow, for several recent practical jokes—"Mrs. Smith" (Smith will do as well as any other name) "wants a little ride down-country. Lead her." And without being aware of his victim's anguished cries, Joe set off at a gentle trot.

After that 'Mrs. Smith' rode every afternoon on a leadstring—she had a curious way of saying that she was going to ride 'a block or two down the road'—but she never got to like riding; she said 'you got sand in your clothes,' whatever that might mean, and that 'there were not enough places to hang things.'

We had at that time on the ranch a very melancholy mature man with a drooping mustache. He was a queer man, for when he finally left the valley he left with six or seven decrepit milch cows, intending to drive them all the way to Arizona. We appointed this man to catch 'Mrs. Smith' when she dismounted. The ceremony occupied several minutes and was invariably witnessed by numerous uninvited guests. There was much backing and filling on the part of 'Mrs. Smith' and innumerable statuesque poses on the part of the rescuer. Naturally the lower-minded around the corrals twitted the unfortunate man about his job. After a week or so he came to me.

"Look here," he said, "I like you and I like this here outfit fine—I ain't got one single complaint; but if I have to keep on a-catching of that there lady I'll have to ask you for my time."

'Mrs. Smith's' avowed purpose in coming to Wyoming was to find out if it was as 'bad' a country as she had heard, and nothing happened during her stay to disillusion her. It is a dangerous business asking Westerners foolish questions. Joe, the foreman, swore that she slept with all her clothes on and in her shoes, for several mornings he had to awaken her early and he assured me that there was not a moment's interval between his knock and the patter of her heels on the floor. But her leading complex was horses. Horses depressed her; she would sit for hours looking at the mountains, and brooding about horses. Once she called me over and confided this to me in her absent-minded voice.

"A pretty country," she said, "a very pretty country, but filled with horses . . . horses everywhere . . . I look in one direction, and there's a horse; I look in another direction, and there's another horse. There are too many horses."

The day she left, the car that was to take her over The Pass did not arrive on time, so I commandeered a small buggy that was going down-country and asked the driver to set 'Mrs. Smith' off when he met her original conveyance. She climbed drearily into the narrow seat. It was raining. She stared at the misty hills, then her eyes met mine.

"Horses again!" she said.

XVI
DUDE-BROKEN

THERE are four things in the world that all people think they can do without previous training: fishing and riding and camping and writing.

It is easy enough to see why they think this about writing, because writing uses as its material words, and words, of course, are the commonest things there are—almost every one possesses at least a couple of hundred. Besides, the American attitude toward writing is queer. I am collecting a book of quaint remarks. At least six times a year some old friend whom I haven't seen for a long time asks me, 'Are you still writing?' 'Why, yes, of course. Are you still banking?' But why this insouciant attitude should be prevalent about riding and fishing and camping remains somewhat more of a mystery, unless it be that these things have been done by the human race for so long a time that they have become race memories.

I dare say they look easy. All you have to do to ride a horse is to get on him and stay there, and all you have to do to catch a fish is to find some water, put together a fairly complicated bit of rigging, and then, grasping the rigging firmly in both hands, lift it above your head and bring it down like a Russian knout. As to camping, what, after all, is that? Nothing at all but living in the woods . . . . Sarcasm is so generally misunderstood that I hope you understand I am being sarcastic.

As a matter of fact, there are no more delicate and complicated and esoteric sports in the world than fishing and riding. And the ability to take care of yourself in a wilderness or comparative wilderness is not intuitional. You can blunder through by what is known as 'main strength and awkwardness,' but if you do you are lucky. I remember two young men who turned up at the ranch one spring before the snow had gone in the higher country. They wore light serge suits and felt hats and stubby patent-leather shoes, and they had walked over from Idaho, thirty miles away, through one of the passes of The Tetons, skirting hidden precipices and snowslides just on the point of running. They were quite unaware of what they had accomplished. But this is exceptional and not to be recommended. It reminds me of a story of a friend who, resting in a hut in the Alps, after making an ascent with guides and paraphernalia, was suddenly interrupted by a little American with an umbrella and spectacles who opened the door of the hut and asked when the next train left from the Italian side.

The suburbanite who threads his way to the station every morning through the automobiles of his neighbors becomes frequently too fearless.

Not a summer passes during which I do not have trails taken away from me—trails I know as well as I do the foot-path from my house to the corral—by people whom I am guiding. With infinite secret pleasure I allow them to lead me into "jack-pots" where they have finally to admit that it was they, not I, who were lost. Also, every summer, I am told numberless things about my business, although I dare say that is a fate common to everyone. I do not keep track of the occasions when I am informed that there are 'no fish' in streams and lakes I know are teeming with trout, nor do I mark all the new facts that are discovered about horses whose characters I know considerably better than I do the characters of most of my cousins. There are times, however, when I find myself wishing that my informants could see a dry-fly fisherman at work, or could live for a while with horses as a man on a ranch must of necessity do.

A dry-fly fisherman stalks fish as a hunter of big game stalks rhinoceroses. But even apart from dry-fly fishing, I have waded a river time and again between two men, one of whom was getting a strike almost every time he cast, and the other of whom failed to get even a rise. There is a clergyman and university professor—also a poet and short-story writer and essayist and diplomat and naval reserve officer—I might as well tell you his name, Henry van Dyke, who casts one of the most beautiful flies I have ever seen. He is also, incidentally, one of the most charming men to be out in camp with I have met in many years of camping. He is seventy-one, but a hardy, courageous gentleman and a veteran camper. Two years ago 'the doctor' came to my ranch. It was late in August and the fishing in the Snake River—the finest trout-fishing, in my humble opinion, in the world—was just coming in. As usual, several accustomed fishermen had gathered for the occasion, but they had not been having very good luck. 'The river wasn't in condition yet,' 'Possibly something had happened to spoil the fishing for good.' The little doctor—doctor of divinity—arrived at noon, had his lunch, and afterwards disappeared. I saw him crossing a field with his rod and basket. In a few hours he returned with ten fish, the largest weighing five pounds and the average from one pound to three.

And what applies to fishing and camping applies equally, perhaps more so, to horses.

It costs us and every other dude-ranch thousands of dollars annually to maintain our bands of saddle ponies. In our case, we not only have to think of replacing every year the misfits and cripples, the mares who have colts, the horses who die, but we have also to think of winter feeding. To feed a hundred or so horses requires at least two hundred tons of hay. And dude-horses are in a class by themselves. They are not easy to find. They must have a combination of qualities rare in any single animal, and certainly non-existent in the human animal. They must be young and fast, yet gentle and easy-gaited, and infinitely wise. We have combed the country for our 'cavey' and are still combing it. Some of our horses come from Idaho; from Black-foot, or the Bannock Indian Reservation—although Indian ponies are to be avoided. Like their masters they have 'no heart.'

The favorite Indian method of breaking a horse is to tie everything movable to him and then to turn him loose. At the end of a few days the horse is broken, but his spirit is broken as well. Some of our horses come from Wind River—the ranches over there, or the Arapahoe or Sho-shone Reservations; although, if possible, we avoid the latter as much as we do the Bannock Reservation. An Indian is a difficult person to buy a horse from, anyhow; he will not sell unless he is hard up. You have to catch him in just the right mood. Many of our horses are picked up singly here and there as we happen to come across them. We are continually buying and inspecting and trading.

We have strange experiences. Some of our gentlest horses have had bad reputations, but have worked out beautifully when properly handled; others, gentle when bought, have been ruined in one summer by an ignorant or bad-tempered rider. One of my partners seems unable to buy a horse for his own use, no matter what the previous performance and history of the horse has been, without the horse turning into a fence jumper. It is a standing joke on the ranch, but no joke to him. He uses side-hobbles, cross-hobbles, ties the tail to the front hobbles, without effect. Another partner seems always to buy 'bad' horses.

He bought one buckskin horse that I myself saw a young Easterner, clad in a slicker so long that he tripped over it, climb on as if he were going up the ratlines of a ship. My partner turned this gentle creature out on the range for a few days and at the end of that time found his new purchase would do almost anything you wanted, so long as you restrained your desires solely to bucking.

Given a chance we will guarantee to teach any one, old, young, male or female, to be comfortable in a Western saddle within a short time. But we are not always given the chance. Sometimes prospective riders won't even take the trouble to find out what a cow-pony is, let alone believing us when we tell them.

A cow-pony is a work-horse, he is not a park-hack or a hunter. He is trained to work at top speed and strain every muscle on a round-up or when he is pursuing something, but he is not expected to take much more than a gentle jog-trot—a cowboy trot—when on the road. And being exceedingly intelligent—that is, within equine limitations—as most semi-wild animals who have to look out for themselves are, he is not going to do a bit more work than he has to. We have in our band numerous horses who are favorites with our cowpunchers, and yet often these same horses are the ones tourists hate the most because 'they won't go.' And we also have in our band several high-headed fools, without heart or common sense, who do not look where they put their feet, but who are greatly beloved—especially by young ladies—because they haven't the brains to take care of themselves.

'Won't go!' A curious phrase. I am afraid too many modern people are used only to engines. Why can't they learn to say, 'won't walk up,' or, 'trot,' or 'lope' or 'gallop?' 'Won't go!' It is in the same class as the odd habit so many Easterners have of calling all horses 'she' whether 'she' happens to be a she or not. Horses are never battleships.

I am no sentimentalist about a horse, that most sentimentally regarded of animals. George Borrow was right when he said the horse was a good friend of man, but that death resided in the crescent of his hoof. I know that a horse has far less brains than many another less-considered mammal. He is ruled by fear, he is subject to absurd panics, and if one of these heady frights seizes him he will do his best to kill the person upon his back, no matter how well he knows that person, but considering his lack of brains, there are times when I admire him—especially the dude-horse. It is astonishing how well the dude-horse takes care of his charges. Our older horses actually acquire a conscientious look in their eyes, and it seldom takes more than a year or two for almost any horse we buy to become wonderfully tourist-broken. I have seen the ignorant perform about them, and on them, feats that leave the cowpuncher gasping. Twice I have seen people get on backward. Yes, they put the right foot in the left stirrup and with the utmost abandon swung the left leg over the horse's head and landed facing the horse's tail, an exploit difficult for even the trained rider. I will do them the justice, however, of saying that there was a slightly bewildered expression on their faces when their respective horses, being well-trained horses, set off down the road. One of these acrobats was a learned and absent-minded judge who had never ridden before, but the other was a woman who had fox-hunted all her life, though never on anything but a side-saddle.

Such experiments as getting on a horse tied to a hitching-rack and then trying to start off without first untying him, or going off for a picnic with a dozen things dangling from your saddle, each one flapping at every movement, or throwing down your reins on the horn and burying yourself for a blind moment in a slicker or raincoat, are too common to mention. A favorite hazard is to remove your saddle and drag it along back of a row of horses, your latigo and stirrup brushing against their heels as you go. Unsaddling and throwing your saddle to the ground without untying the rope of your hackamore is perhaps a trifle rarer, but it is none the less popular. Many a peaceful moonlit night has been disturbed for me in this fashion. A horse will stampede with the saddle on the end of the fifteen-foot rope, cutting down anything in its way, like the scythe of an Assyrian chariot. And people, for some strange reason, like to stand with their mouths open. I can't tell how many times I have had to dive for them—literally—and shove them out of danger, yelling: "For God's sake, get away!"

A couple of summers ago the doctor discovered a young man getting on his horse from the wrong side. Now only Indian ponies are broken so that you can get on that way. Most white men's ponies will kick you if you try it, for a horse is even more conventional than a Philadelphian. The doctor called the young man's attention to his error. "Oh, that's all right," said the young man cheerfully, "I'm left-handed."

I once saw a boy weighing about a hundred and ninety pounds try to swing on his waiting pony relay-race fashion, that is, by grabbing the horn and vaulting into the saddle without using the stirrups. He missed his jump and, his right heel catching in a pack he had tied on back of the cantle, the whole affair turned with him and left him, securely entangled, swaying gently backward and forward underneath his horse's belly. As a general rule the one thing that sends a horse completely insane is to have the saddle turn. I did not know what to do, for I was twenty feet away and on foot and was afraid that if I made a jump I would only make matters worse. Since the gate was open, there was no particular reason why the horse and what was left of its rider shouldn't have ended up in Yellowstone Park, a day's journey north. But as a matter of fact the horse did nothing. Instead, he trembled in every limb, and after a while, very cautiously, looked down between his fore legs at his squirming burden. I thought then, and I have thought after-wards, that if you only do something sufficiently outrageous to a horse, frequently you 'buffalo' him—'buffalo' being a Western equivalent for 'rattle.' I imagine he says to himself: 'Great Heavens, this must be rather a fellow. I don't believe I had better try anything with him.' But anyone who wants to make such investigations can do so without expecting me to follow.

The Westerner, never eager to give advice, believing that the best man is the man who looks about him and sees how a thing is done and then does it for himself, has a curious way of expressing his feelings when confronted with an absurd happening. He remains immobile, unless his help is needed, but his eyes, without any expression in them, seek and hold the eyes of some other understanding person. They linger there interminably. The next time you are near a corral look about you and you will catch these level glances.

After many years of dude-wrangling, in a moment of passionate reflection—and this is not a contradiction in terms, for moments of passionate reflection are the moments in which all poetry is written—I composed the following epic, and it is now posted in a conspicuous place on the walls of our main cabin. I give it gladly to the world and to other dude-wranglers. It is entitled: 'Something About Western Horses.'

* * *

Please do not ride your horses about the cabins or tie them to trees. The reason for the first request is obvious; the reason for the second is that ropes kill trees.

* * *

Learn how to tie a bowline knot and a tie knot.

* * *

Remember that the most dangerous part of riding is the mounting and dismounting. More people are hurt getting on or off a horse than in any other way. BE CAREFUL.

* * *

Learn how to put on a Western saddle and be particularly careful of your saddle blanket. If the saddle blanket rides back on a horse it is likely to give him a sore shoulder.

* * *

Let your horse drink whenever he wants to. The hardest thing to find in the West is a water-foundered horse.

* * *

But do not let him eat while on the trail. Nothing spoils a horse quicker than this.

* * *

When stopping for lunch give your horse a chance to feed. Do this by keeping bridle on but slipping bit out of mouth.

Be sure, however, that your reins are untied. Better still, take off your bridle and let your tie rope trail. DO NOT LOOSEN SADDLE— although many experienced riders do. In any case, watch your horse from time to time so that he does not leave you a-foot. Learn his disposition in this respect. Western horses are trained to stand when the reins are on the ground but most of them forget to some extent this training.

* * *

Whenever you mount your horse be sure that your cinch is all right. It does not, however, have to be too tight.

* * *

If your horse stumbles look at his feet and his legs. If there is nothing the matter with them, then there's something wrong with the rider. One of the purposes of reins is to keep your horse awake and on his feet. Few sound horses, properly shod, have a habit of stumbling except for two reasons; carelessness on the part of the rider; leg weariness on the part of the horse. The latter is due to continual riding. A HORSE HATES TO FALL JUST AS MUCH AS YOU HATE TO HAVE HIM FALL.

* * *

If your horse fails to keep up with the others, or has tricks you don't like, or is lazy, before you blame him, figure out how much you really know about riding (or, if you are an experienced Eastern rider, how much you know about Western riding). Riding is a lifelong study. If you watch five cowpunchers you will see that each one has a totally different horse but that all ride abreast. Only Indians and tourists ride single file in an open country. REMEMBER THAT A HORSE KNOWS ALL ABOUT YOU THE MINUTE YOU ARE IN THE SADDLE. HE SIZES YOU UP A LOT QUICKER THAN YOU CAN SIZE HIM UP.

* * *

A fast walk is not a natural gait. Use your heels.

* * *

It is, however, the most useful gait for distance riding a horse can have.

* * *

Loping, trotting, or hurrying a horse over rocks or a rough road is like running over mountains with hob-nails. TRY IT!

* * *

Always start your horse off quietly and do not hurry him at the beginning of the day. A good rider brings his horse in fresh at the end of the day and also makes quicker time than the man who has no mercy on his horse. ONLY IN WESTERN NOVELS DO PEOPLE GALLOP 'ENDLESSLY OVER THE PRAIRIES.' A cowpuncher on a round-up has a string of horses like a polo player.

* * *

For most of your riding use a slow trot and a fast walk. Every now and then lope your horse for a change; he likes the fun of it. But save most of this for the end of the day when it is cool.

* * *

Remember that Western saddle horses are grass fed and also that, instead of going out for 'a brisk canter' of an hour or so, or hunting twice a week, you are using your horse continually and making trips of from five to twenty miles each time you ride.

* * *

Almost anyone can learn to stay in a saddle under ordinary circumstances, especially a Western saddle, but out of every hundred riders anywhere there are only a few HORSEMEN and HORSEWOMEN. It's a fine thing to be and makes riding twice as much fun.

* * *

When you ride BE RIDING ALL THE TIME. That is, think of your horse and what you are doing. It's a sport; you might just as well be absent-minded playing tennis or football. If you don't keep your mind on what you are doing, some day your horse will make a fool out of you, or you will make a fool of him.

* * *

If you injure your horse by carelessness or lack of mercy, please be ashamed. Everyone else will be for you.

* * *

Henry Ford has invented the only thing that works without rest and without much need for brains on the part of the person in control.

* * *

In short, treat your horse as you would like to be treated yourself and you can't go far wrong. In any quandary think of this. He is not a machine. He is a living creature and what brains he has are working continually.

To this has recently been added an addendum having more to do with what is known as road manners, or horse etiquette. The addendum was composed by a well-known professor of law who, although he had done no riding until he came to Wyoming, was able within three weeks to get to the heart of things. The result is an example of what trained powers of observation and an analytical turn of mind will do for a man.

HOW TO BE POPULAR ON THE TRAIL

1. When approaching a gate, place yourself in the middle of the party. This will insure your not having to open or close the gate.

A1. (The numbering is not mine but the professor's.) If you succeed in managing so that one of your companions is left to close the gate, it is on the whole better to proceed without him. This prevents delaying the main body, and may result in an accident which will enliven an otherwise uneventful day.

a2. If any of your companions exhibits any defect or peculiarity of horsemanship, do not fail to call it at once to his or her attention. Or better still, imitate him or her to his or her face. This will speedily cure the fault and will restore the external harmony of the party.

II. If the leader of your party seems to wish to slacken his pace, lope past him at full speed. This shows your superior staying power and has the added advantage of starting his horse up when he least expects it.

III. By the same token—the best way of starting your horse is to ejaculate "Clck! Clck!" This acts broadly to start all other horses and contains the element of surprise.

IV. An excellent method of ridding your horse of flies is to let him rub his head against your companion's horse, or better still against your companion's knee.

V. One way to avoid a reputation for being fussy or an old fogey is to lope your horse around a blind corner.

VI. Perhaps the pleasantest place for a lope on returning to the ranch is between the gates of the ranch enclosure. There are not as a rule enough children so that their rights or safety have to be regarded.

a6. On the return from the ride visit the kitchen and bother the cook. Remember that you are welcome there day or night, and that cooks are easy to obtain.

VII. The East was settled before the West, and therefore knows more about riding. Treat, in general, suggestions in regard to horses made by Westerners as so much "Bull."

It is frequently a pleasure to be facetious. Caricature, as all politicians know, sticks in the mind longer than the best of portraits. An absurd or an unpleasant incident is more dramatic, unfortunately, than a pleasant one, save when the latter is heroic, and is always more dramatic than the usual pleasant average of intercourse. There is not much to say about the usual pleasant average of intercourse, or the usual pleasant person. These stir your heart but do not stir your lips. The more you love a woman the less you like to talk about her; the better you like a friend the more the friendship becomes unconscious, like breathing, or fine weather.

I have little to say about all the charming and interesting and kindly people who have come to our ranches—hundreds of them—many of them now life-long friends. If I started to say anything I would have to write a separate book, and what could that book be after all but a repetition of gratitude? A 'Memory Book.' And as for 'Memory Books,' they were treasured but not read, and nowadays they are no longer even written.

I have a thousand and one golden memories as well as a thousand and one tales. Memories of faces and voices and laughter, of rides and camps and loveliness seen in company. Of crisp mornings when snow-clad peaks soared against blue skies with the still whiteness of gigantic pelicans, of nights when the moon, coming up behind the sleeping ranges to the east, picked out for a moment a ragged pine, and made isolation suddenly another companion, and flooded the sage-brush with light so that you saw ambergris floating in a sea of silver. For a week or two in the late autumn when everyone is gone a dude-ranch is a lonely place—haunted.

XVII
The Outfit

A FRIEND of ours, a rancher from many miles away—three mountain ranges, two valleys, and a desert—came to visit us unexpectedly and found us in the midst of a fancy-dress party. I was dressed in some sort of a silly costume and the doctor, my partner, was dressed in something even more silly. We give these parties every now and then, usually on the spur of the moment, and it is extraordinary what can be done with skins and Turkish towels and Indian relics and curtains. The near neighbors drop in, and it is all very colorful and amusing... the big log-cabin lit with candles, the fire smouldering in an open fire-place, the fiddlers over in one corner, and, unlike most fancy-dress parties, the cowboys real cowboys. But the visiting rancher, being a simple man of cattle and arriving after dusk when the party was at its height, was taken aback and for a while imagined himself, I dare say, in a place where the inmates had overpowered their keepers, as in De Maupassant's story—or was it Edgar Allan Poe's?

He regarded the doctor and myself sympathetically. His voice was full of concern.

"So you have to give these things in order to keep the dudes amused, do you?" he asked.

"Not at all," retorted the doctor, "we and the dudes give them in order to keep the outfit amused."

And this statement has not always in the history of the ranch been an exaggeration. There have been summers—as was the one in question—when we had working for us a particularly difficult and restless group of young men and women; a group infinitely harder to satisfy than double the same number of tourists. Nor can you, on a dude-ranch, light-heartedly dismiss your employees once the busy season has started. You are too far away from the nearest centres of population; by the time July has come all the available local youth, male or female—the country does not boast of any great number— are already spoken for. And, once a dude-ranch is in full swing it is like a fairly complicated machine whose parts are hard to replace. If one of the cogs breaks you must work frantically to repair the break and, at the same time, you must try to keep the machine running as if nothing had happened.

There are days in the histories of all ranches when trouble seems to come to a head, and this is especially true on a dude-ranch. I don't know why this is so, but it is. For weeks everything has been going smoothly, and then suddenly, out of a clear sky, disaster piles up like a thunder-storm.

Visualize the circumstances, and, in order to help you visualize them, I will hint to you what the system on a dude-ranch is.

Here then is a supposedly self-contained place, usually miles from any source of supplies, upon which temporarily anywhere from seventy-five to a hundred and fifty people are living—in our case, an average of seventy-five people: fifty dudes, twenty-five or so ranch-hands.

During the busy season we employ two cooks, a dishwasher, two waitresses, two cabin-girls, a house-keeper, two laundresses, a rast-about, a carpenter, a rastabout's helper, two horse-wranglers—day and night, the latter in Western parlance called a 'night-hawk'—a team-ster, a foreman, two young dude-wranglers—usually Eastern college men—a truck-driver and two guides, two camp horse-wranglers and two camp cooks, the latter frequently increased by from one to three other camp outfits. If you add to these three partners and the wives of two of these partners, you will see that our visitors do not lack for attention . . . twenty-nine people in all, or considerably more than one-half the total number of our tourists, this disproportion being partly due to the fact that some of our arrangements are necessarily primitive, so that personal service has to take the place of mechanical contrivances, but mainly due to the diversified interests of a ranch, increased fourfold if the ranch happens to be a dude-ranch.

This is the outfit. Now we can turn to the dudes—fifty of them, and we will take this as an average assortment.

Eight young men around university age, and six or seven young women, somewhere between flapperdom and womanhood. These are easy to account for. They are constantly off on parties of their own, and have the pleasant carelessness concerning details characteristic of the young. Five families, mother, father, and their broods, ranging from elder sons and daughters to the youngest flowers of the flock; the older sons and daughters being lumped with the class first mentioned—the young men and women—and therefore little trouble, but the mothers and fathers and the youngest flowers of the flock demanding infinite thought. About the youngest flowers of the flock one thing especially is to be remembered: they must have milk and plenty of it, and they must have green vegetables; about the fathers and mothers several things are to be remembered: bridge (and now, God save the mark, Mah-Jong!), instruction in horseback-riding, and a reconstruction of a frequently narrow point of view, so that instead of thinking they are there solely for their children's health and pleasure they will realize eventually the benefits and pleasures they themselves are deriving. That takes care of about thirty-eight people, and the remainder of the fifty is made up of a dozen or so bachelors and unmarried women who, if you give the former plenty of shooting and fishing, and the latter plenty of riding and scenery, are as easy to account for as the younger men and women. Indeed, possibly easier, for it is amongst such people that the dude-wrangler frequently finds his most accustomed and sympathetic guests. They know what they are West for and they know how to look for it.

Naturally, amongst all these fifty or so souls, some of them millionaires, some of them hard workers, some of them from New York, some of them from San Francisco, there are bound to be a few dyspeptics—however kindly-intentioned—and formalists, and perfectionists. The first understand no breakdown in the food-supplies and no bad cooking, the second understand no delay of any kind—in meals, horses, or people—and the third frequently understand nothing at all. These must be soothed and made to understand, but on the other hand they must be given as little just cause for complaint as is humanly possible. But this is not always humanly possible. One of the last—a perfectionist—once asked us why we didn't sweep the corrals out every day. We do clean them frequently, but it takes a scraper and two horses to do so, and even Hercules, with his experience of the Augean stables, couldn't sweep them.

Back of these fifty souls, or rather, I should say temperaments—taking care of them, ministering to them—are the twenty-seven or so other temperaments I have mentioned, incalculable as all temperaments are, equally incalculable as are the temperaments of the tourists. The problems and perplexities of a dude-wrangler do not end with his dudes, they only begin there. When he has his dudes all nicely settled and contented, he must see that his outfit is also nicely settled and contented. And his problems are increased because of the material out of which much of his outfit is made.

Some of our outfit—they call themselves 'roughnecks' in contradistinction to dudes—are professionals—the cooks, the waitresses, the housekeeper; and through the years we have built up a nucleus of trained assistants for such crucial positions as that of the rastabout and horse-wrangler. Most of these professionals come back to us season after season, but on the whole the outside hands, the assistant horse-wranglers, the teamsters, even the cabin-girls and laundresses, are for the most part local boys and girls, to begin with raw and untrained, and, with all their virtues, Far Westerners are a restless people with not the slightest sense of personal service. Moreover, you have to handle them differently from the average run of employees, you have to appeal to their common sense and decency and loyalty, and when you ask them to do things it is politely. Exactly, of course, as you should ask them.

Youth, moreover, demands amusement, and there is not much formal amusement on a dude-ranch after dark, the time the young people working for you have at their disposal.

Dancing is a great solution. It always has been to a Westerner. If a Westerner is in a bad humor, all you have to do as a general thing to get him out of it is to let him dance. The same is more or less true of the Easterner, of course, but the dance has never been such an essential in civilization as it has been in frontier countries where—until the radio and phonograph were invented—it was frequently the only form of amusement. The Mormon Church made it practically a part of their ritual, and the ancient Jews, being cattlemen and frontiersmen, glorified it. I have known men to ride forty miles or so through the bitter cold of a winter's night merely for the purpose of 'shaking a foot.' In the old days when women were scarce, some of the men would tie handkerchiefs on their arms and take the places of the missing ladies. 'Bill' Newbold told me that over in Wind River there was a time in his youth when there were only two ladies who attended dances and, since they didn't like each other, they had threatened to shoot at the slightest jostling. I imagine that this made for good dancing.

But the reverse side of the Far Westerner's fine sense of independence is not quite so commendable. When carried to an extreme it means an entire lack of understanding of system. Having been born into a world where there is plenty of space, he—or she—the Far Westerner, sees no reason why an empty tin can, for instance, shouldn't be given to the elements. You open a tin can, you use its contents, and then you throw the can out of the window. What could be simpler? And if it happens to be a tobacco-can you throw it down wherever you are standing.

It has taken us years to impress upon our outfits the need for order and cleanliness; years to impress upon them that a rake and a broom are the greatest labor-savers, if used in time, man has yet invented.

XVIII
System and Lack of It

I HAVE already built up for you the background—the seventy-five or so people, each with a different personality and a different incalculability to be found on a dude-ranch. Now we can see just what is supposed to be taking place when everything is functioning normally.

The static conditions are these: in the ice-house there should be beef and mutton and pork and ham and bacon and butter and eggs and fruit; the fresh vegetables that cannot be grown in the vicinity; and the fish and game-birds caught or shot in season by the guests of the ranch and ourselves. In the milk-house there should be dozens of pans of milk and cream, and in the food storehouse, flour, cereals, canned goods by the scores, preserves, jams, and so on ad infinitum. All these in sufficient quantities to last at least a week and to supply not only the ranch itself but any pack trip that may be going out in the meantime. In the other storehouses are supposed to be duplicates of everything on the ranch, so that any article can be replaced immediately.

Such are the static conditions; the mobile conditions are, a horse for every person and always on hand when desired; a constant supply of wood for the cabins and kitchens, a constant supply of hot and cold water; three meals a day; picnic luncheons prepared when wanted; cleanliness; laundry taken away and delivered back on time and in good condition; and pack trips constantly going out and coming back, and so scheduled that the guides have not more than one idle day between their return from one trip and their departure on another.

The mere outfitting of pack trips with their varying numbers of tourists and their varying lengths, and the fitting in of them so that the guides, with their short season, will be kept busy and the tourists, with their conflicting desires and necessities, will be satisfied, is an enormous undertaking in itself, requiring great experience and forethought. As to the food-supply on a pack trip, you dare not leave anything out that is necessary, not when you are going into an actual wilderness, yet, at the same time, you must avoid sending anything that will be merely extra weight. Various tastes have to be consulted; some people like pickles and some like sweets.

But even with all the system in the world there are certain of these static and mobile conditions that cannot always be predicted. You cannot, for instance, buy butter in too great quantities, or meat, or anything that is likely to spoil, and yet there may come weeks when more butter than usual is used, or some of the butter you have turns rancid. And horses are invariably uncertain. No horse-wrangler or 'night-hawk' is so expert that at times he will not lose part of his 'cavey,' especially in the fly season, when his charges are restless. There are bound to come days when this person or that is riding a horse to which he or she is unused, or not riding any horse at all. Sometimes we have had two or three men, including frequently ourselves, riding for half a week simply in order that one tourist may not be for too long discomforted. And there are other occasions when burly cowpunchers ride for butter as, at times, they ride after stock.

Yet despite all the perversity for which inanimate objects are famous nothing has been found to equal the perversity of the human mind once it is thoroughly aroused.

For years I had a Japanese cook who got drunk regularly once a summer and stayed drunk for three days. During this time his one desire was to be a dude. He said he could easily afford to be a dude because he had a tea-plantation in Japan he could sell by cable. After the Eighteenth Amendment went into effect—that is, at first, until the inevitable efficiency in bootlegging set in—he was in the habit of making a disgusting brew out of raisins which he would hide behind the stove until my foreman and myself would discover it and bury it. After several years of these gaieties, which used to wake me up at two or three o'clock in the morning, and overturn the system of the ranch, my nerves were worn thin, and I told 'Jimmie' that the next time he got drunk I would probably shoot him. He seemed to take this threat to heart, for his annual diversion was delayed longer than usual, but one night late in August he stuck his brown face in through the window of my cabin and interrupted on my part a peaceful slumber. I was really angry. I grabbed my gum, wakened my foreman, and together we went up to tell 'Jimmie' what we thought of him.

He had no opportunity to bother us with his usual formula; we drove all thoughts of being a dude out of his head by our bitter personal comments. Finally I told him that if he left his cabin again that night I would tie him down and leave him tied for two days, and I showed him my gun, and impressed upon him how near he had come to being shot in the leg. Very drearily he got back into bed.

The next day he was ill and sent for me. I had no sooner entered his cabin than he fell upon his knees, took my hand, pressed it three times to his forehead, and asked me if I wished him to kill himself . . . hari-kari. I said no, certainly not, and I said it very coldly—I said that I did not want a dead cook about the place at all. "Well, you see," he explained, in his almost indistinguishable English, "I have had a great sorrow . . . otherwise I would not have done this evil thing."

My all-too-easily-touched heart was wrung. "What has happened, Jimmie?" I asked.

"I have received word from Japan that my mother is dead."

"Your mother!" I was conscience-stricken. "When did she die?"

"Seven years ago, sair."

But because of Jimmie and a great many other people and events connected with a dude-ranch I have learned one thing. By nature I am an impatient and irascible person, but these characteristics do not pay. They pay neither objectively nor subjectively. When things pile up and the end of the world seems near, the most satisfactory defense is to work hard and try to get under the obstacles, not over them. The same principle applies to making yourself heard in a crowd. Misfortunes are like waves; if you try to jump them they will knock you down, but you can easily dive through them, or let them wash over you. A high voice and a worried expression are temptations to universal catastrophe; a soft voice and a smile are likely to turn even the most excitable human being into something less like a horse or a cow and more like a man or a woman.

As much as possible we try to get the dudes and the outfit to mix. It is good for both the Westerner and Easterner to know each other, and once the initial embarrassment is over and the provincialism on both sides dissipated, the Easterner and Westerner as a rule like each other. And, where the Easterner is concerned, much is lost in a visit to a ranch if he fails to learn something about the people who live on ranches.

Summers vary in this respect. It depends whether imaginative people are in the ascendancy or not. Fifty or so townbred people, living together, can capture an atmosphere utterly and make it their own and go blithely about their occupations totally unaware that they are missing the most valuable experience the West can give them. It is not worth while coming to Wyoming merely to get a little slice of Bar Harbor or Southampton . . . . I do not always love bridge as that noble game should be loved, and I have learned to hate continual talk. I do not love either bridge or talk when the whole wide silvery world of Wyoming is sleeping under a great moon or an incredible galaxy of stars . . . cowpunchers out on the range, ranchers in their cabins, bucking horses knee-deep in grass, steers, silent black shapes in the darkness, elk in the leafy shadows of their summer haunts, and, in canyons not four miles from where the bridge-players and gossippers are, bear following trails that in many cases no man has ever followed.

At night, by a Western stream, whether it be a forest stream or a stream that moves slowly through the marshes, there is the sweetest and most pungent of smells—the smell of coldness and mist and damp mud and weeds that grow in water. This has always seemed to me to be the epitome of loneliness; wild and lonely as a single mallard winging through the red dusk of an autumn sky. And people who play bridge or talk all night miss such things . . . .

Perhaps the most fundamental difference between the Far Westerner and the Easterner has to do with time. I once worked on a ranch where the home pasture was a wooded tract of over a hundred acres. We had some Easterners staying with us, fairly ponderous business men—'executives'—and in the morning they would come out with khaki gaiters wrinkling over their ponderous executive legs and demand their horses. I never lost my delight in what would then happen. The horse-wrangler would sit on his heels and roll a cigarette and stare at the sky, while the executives would become angrier and angrier. After a while the horse-wrangler would pick up some hackamore ropes and disappear in this direction or that. He never told the executives what he was doing, and perhaps if he had they wouldn't have understood him, but he was doing that most un-urban of things, thinking. Having a wooded pasture in which to find his horses, he was thinking just where he had seen them last, and just where the feed was best, and just what the conditions of the hour were—heat, files, and so on—and when he had finally made up his mind, he walked in a straight line to where the horses were. The executives would have preferred immediate action, even if it only consisted in running about in circles.

A famous head guide who worked for us was always driven into a frenzy by questions having to do with hours and locations. "How do I know?" he would complain, waving his hands. "How in h— do I know when we'll get there? There might be a washout, or a flood or a blizzard, or one of you fellows might break a leg. Or how can I tell where I'm going to camp? A man can't tell where he's going to camp even if he's been over the same trail only the week before. I'll have to see what the feed's like when I get there."

And, incidentally, this last sentence contains a frequent source of disagreement between Westerners and inexperienced Easterners—no honest guide, except in a water-hole country, can tell you at noon exactly where he is going to camp that night. In making camp the Westerner looks first for grass for his horses, next for water and wood, and last for the aesthetic pleasure of his party. He does his best to balance these considerations, but if any one suffers it must be the human beings. Horses are not as adaptable as men; they have to be more looked after. It takes a horse about eight hours to fill up on a good range and, if he doesn't fill up, then after a while you will be afoot and that will be the greatest inconvenience of all.

In this perennial quarrel about time, I am heartily on the side of the Westerner, and one of the reasons why I like to see Easterners go on a pack trip is because on a pack trip they learn better than anywhere else that efficiency has nothing whatsoever to do with haste; is, as a matter of fact, opposed to haste. We live in an absurdly hurried age, we run where we ought to walk, and we walk where we ought to sit, and we blow our motor-horns if we are held up for a minute— all for the purpose of getting nowhere as quickly as possible. As a result, we spend half our time undoing decisions that we would not have made at all had we taken the time to think them over. But the frontiersman has long ago learned that frequently it is impossible to undo decisions in a country where haste usually leads to disaster and sometimes even to death, and that if you go gaily up a trail without stopping to consider whether it be the right one or the wrong one, you may find yourself at nightfall many miles from where you wanted to be. And you are in a country where there are no convenient inns and where you can't take short cuts.

Thoughtful and slow-moving by necessity, except in moments of danger, the Westerner has preserved many virtues the more modern world is in sore danger of losing. For one thing, he is the repository of the far-famed but nowadays almost non-existent American sense of humor. A few mechanics still have it, a few farmers, practically every Far Westerner. On the whole we are getting to be a grim, hurried, harried people. We have wit but no longer humor. We are becoming gray and crackling. But the cowpuncher and the rancher, having time, are essentially gay-hearted, although by the same token they may also be essentially caustic and outwardly grave. They live close to reality and their talk is pungent and filled with figures and conceits. The Far West is the one place I know where irony is always completely understood. You never experience the horrible sensation of saying something obliquely and having it taken literally. If you say of a man whom you despise, "He's a fine fellow, isn't he?" the Far Westerner knows instantly what you mean, and frequently a charming conversation is started in which not one word spoken is supposed to be accepted at its face value.

And then, above all, there is the Western method of telling a story. Casualness is the most salient characteristic of the Far West; casualness of speech and action. Overlying an extraordinary fundamental directness, a real starkness, there is always this casualness, this—what shall I call it?—this slow blitheness. I don't know why this should be. I suspect that it comes from many causes, from the adventurous character of the people who settle in countries like the Far West, from the fact that they have plenty of room and time, from the fact that nature is so gigantic and ruthless that they have learned patience and stoic laughter. At all events, it makes for authentic wit and drama. A Far Western story is told like one of Browning's longer poems. You are carried along, that is, on a low level of interesting detail, purposely related in a low key, and then, suddenly, you are brought up all-standing—breathless—by a twist of auger-like laughter or beauty or tragedy.

With all due respect to the education, learning, and ability of the city-dweller, one who has known the allusive soft-voiced talk of the frontier cannot but be at times homesick for it. Those long hours when you sit up around a camp-fire! The light spreads out to hang tapestries of faded flame upon the great walls of columned pine, and beyond that you cannot see except for a hole in the night where, directly overhead, the stars shine through. Every now and then you or your companion moves to throw on a log or poke the smouldering sticks together. And all the while your comment is filled with sap and with brooding—real conversation, about horses and steers and dogs, and trails and moose and elk and bear, and men whose isolation has made them individuals marked with comedy or terror.

XIX
On Getting Lost

SOMEWHERE in a short story I have attempted the following philosophic description of 'getting lost,' and I don't know that I can improve upon it.

Now, being lost is a strange thing, largely a matter of psychology, and it is difficult to explain the phenomenon to a person who never has been lost. It is almost impossible to lose a man who refuses to submit his mind to such a surrender. The difference between an old hand and a new one is that neither may have the faintest idea where he is, but the old hand isn't alarmed and the new hand is. Perhaps the distinction is best illustrated by the story of the Indian who was found two days away from where he should have been and when interrogated, replied, "No, me not lost—teepee lost." The Indian was right.

Men have run themselves to death in a ten-acre wood-lot; they have followed water up-hill, thinking they were following it down; they have shrieked themselves into exhaustion; they have been found stark, staring mad; they have built little fires to keep themselves warm at night and have seen eyes that were not there across the flames, and dusky predatory shapes equally non-existent; and they have held long, rigidly logical conversations with ghosts. All this may seem very funny and exaggerated, but it isn't; try getting lost.

Nearness to death is a pleasant interlude compared to it. . . A man is going through a forest; he is happy and contented; the rays of the setting sun are falling in gold through the trees; he is thinking of something else; and then suddenly he looks about him and everything is different and faunal and terrifying; and, unless he uses a great deal of self-control, the thing has happened. Undoubtedly this was part of what the Greeks meant when they spoke of meeting Pan.

I might have added that getting lost also has its parable for the over-busy and the overstimulated. In eighty cases out of a hundred a man gets lost not because he has been careless but because he has been too careful in a hurried way; not because he hasn't been thinking but because he has been thinking too much; because he has mistaken the trees for the forest, and because he has smothered the important in a mass of unimportant details. The unaccustomed traveler following a trail tries to remember every foot of it; the old-timer remembers only the exceptional features; the twisted tree, the strange-looking rock, the sudden turn, the ford. Stewart Edward White has pointed this out, as he has also pointed out why the tenderfoot finds it so difficult to see the game his guide sees at once. The guide, as he sweeps with his eye a country—a valley or a distant side-hill—is looking for the exceptional; the tenderfoot sees everything and therefore sees too much. In trail finding and big-game hunting, as in everything else, quality is to be preferred to quantity; discrimination is the secret of distinguished success.

I might add Kephart's advice in order to make my philosophical dissertation somewhat more practical. When you know you are lost, sit down just where you are and try to forget all about it. If you smoke, light a pipe. After a while, when you are calm, try to recollect your back trail, and then try to work your way back to where you first went astray. But above all things, be unperturbed, and do not try to go forward.

I am not, however, writing a text-book on wood-craft. My object in bringing up the subject of getting lost was because getting lost has a direct bearing upon the life of a dude-wrangler, a practical bearing as well as a spiritual one.

My country is a singularly difficult country in which to get really lost; nothing like the desert or the rolling forests of Maine or Canada. To the west are the gigantic peaks of The Tetons, to the east the high, if less spectacular, peaks of the Continental Divide. If you ascend almost any rise of ground, or, in an extremity, climb a tree, you can see these peaks and get your bearings again. Besides, to the west, every stream runs into the Snake River, and to the east, every stream either runs into the Snake River or into a subsidiary of the Snake River; so all you have to do, even if you cannot see the peaks, is to follow water down-hill. But getting lost, as I have pointed out, is more than this: it is a psychological affair and the direct opposite of common sense, and since my country is also in places one of immense forests, although it is not easy for the experienced person to get seriously lost, it is not hard for the inexperienced person to spend the night out. Only once in sixteen years have we had a serious alarm of this nature, but almost every second summer or so we have to saddle horses at twelve or one o'clock at night and organize impromptu search-parties. This is where getting lost has to do practically with dude-wrangling.

Half the time the missing ones are not lost at all, merely delayed, and even when they are lost, they are easy to find and are speedily comforted. The average tourist knows nothing of the season of the year in the Rockies when even the most experienced are frequently lost permanently. On a winter night you cannot always see the peaks and you cannot follow the courses of the hidden streams, and you cannot lie down casually in the brush and wait until dawn. Not so many winters ago a number of people were sitting by the ranch fireplace, cheerful and warm, and only half a mile away, on the flats above, an old man, the father of one of the girls working for us, was struggling step by step to his death. They found him afterwards under the snow.

And I recollect one winter night when I was carrying fifty pounds of mail—too much—on my back from the post-office, eight miles below, to the ranch. Twice a week one of us skied down for this purpose. It had been a clear day and it had settled into a clear night, sharp and silent and filled with stars—like a frosted bell that has not been struck. The slightest sound, the creaking of a branch, the snapping of a twig, rang with resonance. Just at sundown I dropped one of my gloves, and my hand was nearly frozen before I could put it on again. I skied into growing darkness and came at length to the thick fringe of cottonwood that bordered the stream a mile to the south of the ranch buildings. In the shadow of the trees I could see nothing, and before I had slid twenty feet my right ski struck the soft snow that always surrounds a hidden log and, plunging under the log, threw me my full length and more. I struggled to my feet, and in a moment the same thing happened again. By now my pack was loosened so that every time I was thrown it came over my head and added impetus to my fall. The buckles and straps were frozen stiff and I dared not take off my gloves to tighten them.

I do not know how long I was in that narrow belt of trees, stumbling to my feet and falling again, probably not over twenty minutes, but it seemed an eternity, and a witchcraft sort of thing in which the 'witch-hobbles' of the fallen logs reached out and pulled me down. I had gone into the shadows completely untired and confident, I came out exhausted and bewildered. A mile away, across a level stretch, were the faint lights of the ranch, but it took me two hours to reach them. Sometimes I crawled on my hands and knees. When I came at length to the high bank of snow before the south door, where the prevalent winds had blown a clear space, I slid down on my back and had barely enough strength to turn the knob. Inside there were lamps and people reading and the peaceful smell of supper, but I might very well have been dead out there in the night only a quarter of a mile away, or a hundred yards away, or even fifty.

But these things do not happen as a rule to tourists, and even if they did, interesting as they are, they are not as interesting for my present purpose as what effect the usually harmless straying of the summer months has upon the minds of those who stray. Here is where the spiritual side of getting lost has to do with dude-wrangling.

I have said that I have discovered—or think I have discovered—after many years of dude-wrangling that most people are what they are and that as a rule they only take away from a country what they bring to it. In the main this is true, but every now and then the country, so smiling and apparently gentle in July and August, or even September, does reach out with a mighty hand that grips an unsuspecting shoulder.

A very dear friend—one of the most charming women I know—came to Wyoming first because she thought she was suffering from a nervous breakdown. Her husband had just died and she had had other misfortunes. She thought herself incapable of action or decision. One night she was lost on the slopes of The Tetons. She had been mountain-climbing with a party and, coming down in the dusk, had followed the wrong fork of a stream and found herself eventually in a precipice country where she was forced to stop. Meanwhile, the rest of the party, thinking she had gone on ahead, descended to the horses and, not finding their companion, back-tracked without success. At midnight one of them rode into the ranch and a search-party was dispatched. The 'stray' was found in the grayness of early dawn. But she was not the same woman, and never has been since. She had entirely regained her grip upon herself. She has never again thought herself incapable of action or decision. During that lonely night she had had to make many decisions, and she had spent her time in thought.

I recall a gray, rainy dawn when there came a knock at my door and I was wakened out of a sound sleep by a game warden, who brought word from one of our hunting-camps, thirty miles to the east, that a hunter was lost and had been lost for four days. Shivering with cold, I caught up a horse and followed the warden. On our journey across the valley we issued a general alarm. The later morning found us threading our way into the tangle of hills that led towards the camp.

There was hardly any conclusion to come to except that the hunter was dead. At least, that was the conclusion that all knowledge of the hills and all experience of hunting presented to our minds. This young man was a careless undergraduate and he had had a gun with him. It never occurred to us that, without accident, any one could have disappeared for so long a time in a country such as the one in which the camp was situated. To be sure, it was a trappy country of many confusing small streams and valleys, but it lay to the north of a well-defined little river, and every valley within a radius of ten miles and every stream within the same radius met the little river. Even had the boy wandered ten miles north and crossed the divide, he would have found himself in a country similar to the one he had just left, where all he had to do to reach safety would be to follow a stream.

But the permutations of the human mind are unaccountable. This young man, to begin with, had run away from his guide, under the delusion, apparently, that he could outdistance a bull elk on foot. The two were hunting in the fading light of the afternoon on their way back to camp and had just climbed to within a few feet of the top of a hill.

"Sit down and rest," said the guide, "and then we'll look over the other side."

For a few minutes the guide had turned away his head and when he looked again the boy was gone. But at first, of course, the guide was not alarmed; he merely thought his charge had crept over the edge of the ridge. When he came to the edge, however, and looked down the bare slope beyond, there was no one in sight. Nor was there any one in sight in the open meadow, surrounded with heavy timber, far below. The guide called; finally he shot off his rifle. There was not a sound in answer. He plunged down in pursuit, calling and at intervals firing. Up until midnight he continued to search; a rather hopeless search, since it was too dark to follow tracks. Then he went back to camp and signal-fires were lit, and for four days an organized search was made.

What had really happened was this. While the guide had his back turned, the boy had crept to the summit of the ridge, and, looking over, had seen, down in the open meadow, several elk, a magnificent bull among them. He had been too excited to notify his guide; instead, he had jumped to his feet and had run down the slope and, incredible as it may seem, had continued to run blindly after his quarry—now, of course, miles away—running on until he found himself completely lost. Without trying to remember his bearings, he had kept on going. Morning found him miles away. He had a general idea of his direction and he knew that any time he wanted he could follow any stream down to the valley of the little river. Several times he saw the valley of the little river from the tops of the hills. But he was obstinate, and he insisted to himself that he would find his way back as he had come. He had some matches and some chocolate, and fortunately there were plenty of berries, but he was pretty nearly exhausted when, at the end of four nights and three days, he stumbled into another hunting-camp and stayed there until our men found him. And he had reached that state of panic where he saw things at night.

He told me that when he built his fires he could not sleep because he imagined that across the flames coyotes and wolves were sitting gravely on their haunches waiting for him to die. That was pretty bad. This young man matured considerably. And with all my genuine respect and admiration for the present day generation of university undergraduates, the generation would not be a human one if it did not contain many members similar experiences would not hurt.

Hunters who run away from their guides are not always so fortunate. Several years ago I sat in the grand stand during the annual Frontier Show, given every autumn in the valley, and looked, through the haze of a September day, to where, miles to the west, the densely timbered slopes of some mountains arose. Word had been brought that a hunter, camped there with a single guide, had been lost two days, and the search-parties were out. They found the hunter a week or so later, crumpled up over a log, his rifle, which he had tried to drag after him by the barrel, and in which there was an empty shell, pointing at his chest. His guide had left him alone for a few hours to hunt for some horses, and the hunter, although he was an experienced man and knew that he was breaking the law, had gone out by himself.

This story has a curious sequel. Not long ago I was down in the same country hunting bear in the late fall. There were two women in our party, one a particularly sensitive, high-strung, clever, imaginative person. For a week or so we camped in a narrow little open space with a stream on one side and on the other a precipitous wooded slope. It was a gloomy country, shut in and damp, with a sun that only reached us for a few hours in the middle of the day. Historically it was a gloomy country as well, for two or three summers before a feud had broken out down there that had resulted in the killing of a couple of men. The sensitive woman had heard of this feud, but whether it affected her or not I do not know; I only know that after a few days she told us, in an amused fashion, a dream she had had. She had dreamed that a man had crept down from the wooded slope to one side of the camp and, lifting the flap of her tent, had, apparently without noticing her, crawled anxiously about on his hands and knees searching for something.

"He seemed to be hurt, and I think he was looking for a gun," she said. "Did any of the men who were mixed up in that feud ever camp here, Frank?" She turned to the only member of the party who knew that particular country well.

A negative shake of the head and a slow "No—never," was the only answer.

But in the light of what subsequently happened, I believe—or, at least, imagine—that there was a curious narrow-eyed intentness in the stare of the man she interrogated.

A few days later the same woman, still in the amused fashion characteristic of her, told me that the night before she was so sure she had seen a figure standing just outside the circle of the camp-fire that, thinking it was I, she had been on the point of speaking until, counting heads, she had discovered every one who should be in the party lying around the blaze.

The following morning 'Frank' had to ride into town—twenty miles away—and did not get back until the second day of his departure. He rejoined us while we were eating supper.

"Smith," he announced, "wanted to come up here and camp, but I told him we were already here. He was put out; this old camp of Lankenau's is a favorite place of his . . ." And then the words faltered as if the speaker had suddenly remembered something.

"Lankenau! Why, this is the camp, then, from which that dude who shot himself accidentally was lost, isn't it?" I asked.

"Yes." The answer was reluctant.

After a pause the sensitive woman asked: "Where did they find him?"

There was a sweep of the arm to the north. "Up there in that timbered slope."

I am not trying to prove anything; I am simply stating facts as they happened.

It isn't always necessary for people to be lost, however, for them to realize the full weight of the country and their own smallness in the scheme of things.

There are other adventures equally clarifying. There was the episode of the lady and the bears, for instance.

She was a very young lady and a very charming one—the serio-comedy might have as its title, instead of 'The Lady and the Bears,' 'Beauty and the Bears.' A tall and slim and blond and blue-eyed young woman, beautiful to look at, and sufficiently civilized to be an excellent sportswoman and to fall immediately in love with the West. But most of her life had been spent in Paris, and even in New York she wasn't accustomed to going about very much without her maid, so you can see that for all her gaiety and courage and good sense, she didn't know much about bears.

Eight of us—men and women—had gone on a mountain-climbing expedition. We had left the ranch in the morning, and, crossing the sage-brush flats, had come about ten o'clock to the forest that runs along the base of The Tetons. Here we had tied our horses and had proceeded on foot. Our objective was a narrow saw-tooth ridge that fell away to the north from one of the minor peaks, and the best way to reach this ridge was up a contracted draw that carried a turbulent stream down from the snow-fields. For a while we fought buck-brush and giant wild carrot in the warm quiet of the August morning, until finally we found the course of the stream and the farther slopes of rock and moss. By noon we had climbed to a little valley, with immense wooded slopes on two sides of it, and, on the third side, where the mountains were, rock walls and cramped canyons so precipitous that the latter could almost be called chimneys.

Here we rested and ate our lunch. Afterwards the heroine-to-be complained of a headache, so we left her and continued our climb. I presented her with a can of tobacco to keep for me and a sweater I did not need.

One of the younger men asked me if I thought 'it was quite safe,' and, imitating the skipper of the *Hesperus*, I laughed a scornful laugh, and replied that 'it was the safest place in the world, infinitely safer than New York or Paris.'

And so it was—actually.

We were soon out of sight of the little valley and, the party splitting into two, I found myself, with only one other man and a solitary woman as my companions, scrambling and plodding up a draw that gradually grew narrower. Somewhere around five o'clock we reached our goal. It was sufficiently dramatic, sufficiently worth while, as all high mountain places are. Curious that flying, apparently, gives you so little the impression of flying—skiing seems to give more— while of all things a man can do, mountain-climbing gives most the exultation that would be yours were the wings of an eagle suddenly granted you.

The canyon we had climbed had by now so narrowed that there was barely room for three people to lie down abreast and look over the edge. The other side dropped away to a nothingness— sheer snow-slopes that seemed to roar into silence down to the dark, pine-hidden bed of a valley beginning to be powdered with the gold of dusk. We lay along that knife edge and drank our fill of space and silence, and we must have been there a minute at least before we became aware of a faint halloaing far down the slopes up which we had come. We thought it was the rest of the party pleading with us to hurry back before dusk overtook them and we were indignant. "They've seen all they want to see, and now they want to hurry us. We'll take our time."

And so we did. We peered and chatted and smoked and did not turn back until half an hour had passed. The faint halloaing that had kept up incessantly for five minutes had died away into silence.

But on the way down we were puzzled. We saw the rest of the party on some rocks just above us and they denied any halloaing whatsoever. We hurried on, by no means so well satisfied. After all, it was a lonely country and it was growing dark.

When the little valley came into sight once more we saw, greatly to our relief, crouched on a conical rock perhaps ten or twelve feet high, a human figure and, as we drew nearer, we confirmed our first impression that it was the girl we had left. But she did not wave to us or respond to our cheery greetings; instead, she waited until we were right under the rock and then climbed down and stared at us with eyes twice their natural size. There were dark circles under them, and her face, beneath her jaunty small hat, was pinched and white.

"What's wrong?" I asked harshly, and the next moment burst into roars of laughter, for the girl waved an arm in the direction of one of the wooded slopes and whispered "Bears!"

And sure enough there they were—four of them; two of the biggest black bears I have ever seen and two yearlings. By this time the quartet was almost at the top of the slope, virtuously engaged in searching for the harmless food that black and brown bears live on. They were distant and dusky shapes, more than half hidden in the pines, but they were unable to escape the eyes of the girl. For the moment she had become one of the most accurate observers of game in the West. As long as those bears were anywhere in sight she would see them.

My laughter was ill-timed. It took me three days to apologize, and I am not at all sure that I have apologized sufficiently yet. The girl, you understand, had gone through two or three hours of mortal agony, and I must say she was exceptionally brave about it. We had left her a gay, frivolous young person and we found her on the way to being a woman. She dreamed about bears for nights afterwards and she was ill in bed for a week. She was an example of how ignorance can make one suffer.

By and large, black bears are, of course, amongst the most innocent creatures in the woods. They would not think of harming you, except upon just provocation, and if they catch your scent they run like hares. But the girl didn't know this; she had been brought up to think that the favorite food of bears is human flesh, the younger the better, as in the Old Testament.

After we had left her, she had dozed for a while and then had sat up and looked about her. The horror of that awakening I can well imagine. Coming down the slope towards her, slowly but undeviatingly, were the four bears. They were coming to the stream to drink, but again the girl did not know this, and the dilatory habits of bears only made her agony more difficult to sustain. She was afraid to run, afraid to call. Very slowly—it seemed to her hours, and probably it was—she wriggled on her face towards the rock where we finally found her, and climbed up its reverse side, and lay down again. But even then she was within fifty feet of her enemies. She had carefully thought out what she was going to do in case they followed her—she was going to throw the tobacco I had left with her into their eyes and, while they were blinded, strangle them with the small patent-leather belt she wore around her waist.

(Oh, charming! Better than any fairy-tale ever written! I cannot even now think of that grave-faced declaration without the delight that comes to one in the presence of something exceedingly quaint.)

Once in my life I have been thoroughly lost and several times I have come near to being lost. The man who says he never has been lost, or can't be lost, handles the truth irreverently. The time I was

thoroughly lost I was in camp in British Columbia and had strolled
out late in the afternoon to look for deer. I made a big circle and
finally came back to the stream upon which the camp was located. I
had been paying no particular attention to my steps and suddenly I
realized that I did not know whether camp was upstream or down.
From that time on I was lost. I sat on the banks of the little river for
fully half an hour trying to figure out, by the way the water flowed,
which direction to take, before I realized the utter folly of my inquiry.
When I realized my folly, horror left me as quickly as it had come. All
I had to do was to walk down the stream a mile or so, and if I didn't
find the camp, turn around and walk up a couple of miles. I marked
a tree with my eye so that I would know it again and, to make sure,
cut a notch in the bark with my knife. Then I set off down-stream.
The camp was in that direction.

It is very easy to lose yourself when tracking game. You are intent
upon your quarry and not upon your trail. Once in Wyoming I came
extremely near to spending the night in a patch of timber not over a
mile from the ranch. I had as company, however, a newly arrived missionary of the Episcopal Church—a 'sin-buster' or 'sin-twister'—which
made matters better, although it might very well have made them worse.

The missionary had ridden up from the little town to pay his first
official call, and he and I were having lunch together, when one of
'the boys,' who had been cutting fire-logs up in the timber, returned
to the ranch with the news that he had seen a band of elk enter the
trees only a short while before. It was a gray November day and
there was about a foot of snow on the ground. Excellent hunting
weather, and, besides, we needed meat. The opportunity seemed too
good to be lost, so I asked the missionary if he wanted to go along
and, although he had only been off the train four days, he eagerly
assented. We climbed on the log-cutter's wagon and dropped off

when we came to the tracks the elk had left in the snow—the tracks of seven animals; four cows and three calves.

Now, the timber the elk had entered lies on a curious formation, an island that rises to perhaps fifty feet at its crest directly out of a sage-brush flat, and which is distant a quarter of a mile or so from the main body of the forest. This island is about five miles long by not over half a mile wide, and, although there is a great deal of down timber and the firs are thick, it would seem a difficult place for any one to get lost in, especially any one who knew it as well as I did. But no place is difficult for that purpose if the hand of the dial has reached the appointed hour.

The missionary and I took up the tracks about two o'clock in the afternoon and followed them without stopping until dusk, although at times the going was hard where the snow had collected in hollows. Just at the edge of dusk we overtook the elk, but it was too dark to shoot. I sighted along the barrel of my gun but couldn't see the ivory front sight, and if there is one thing I would rather not do than another it is to take a chance of wounding game. So I let the elk go unharmed. By now it was quite dark, and, being a gray, snowy night, there was not the slightest chance of telling your direction from the sky. That, however, did not bother me. The parson and I were in a draw and it stood to reason that any draw, on a piece of land as narrow as the island, would lead us down to one side or the other.

I set out resolutely. I could no longer see my way at all, but I knew, of course, that I was still in the draw. I walked for perhaps half an hour and then, to my astonishment, felt tracks under my feet. Somehow or other we had crossed the tracks of the elk, although they hadn't been in the draw at all. I lit a match. The tracks were not those of the elk but of two men, one set smaller than the others—the parson was a giant of a man—and the smaller set fitted my galoshes perfectly. We were circling, there was no doubt about it. I said nothing to the parson, but set off again, trying to bear off to the right. In ten minutes or so I felt the tracks again and a further match disclosed that there were now—as far as we had gone—four sets of tracks.

For a second there was just a trembling inclination on my part to become really lost; there was a surge of the feeling that always accompanies really getting lost; the feeling that somehow you have lost your willpower, that you are the plaything of dark and necromantic forces. I imagine that half the tales of mediaeval sorceresses came about in this way. Some knight, going astray in a forest, and, being a knight, refusing to admit that it was his own fault, accused the next nice woman whom he met dwelling alone in a solitary tower. If he subsequently tried to misbehave with her, as very often, being a knight, he would, all the more reason for an absolving tale. Had he not—to begin with—felt the spidery, intangible threads of magic? Yes, but then a modern man can feel exactly the same threads.

"Do you know what we are doing?" I asked the parson.

"Oh, yes," he replied coolly, "circling."

"Do you mind if we spend the night out? I have plenty of matches."

"Not in the least."

I loved that man immediately, and I have loved him ever since. I knew he was going to be a good 'sin-twister.' Unlike most of his clan the Church sends West, he was neither a valetudinarian, nor a fool, nor a failure. I loved him because he was so unperturbed, but I loved him especially because, knowing that we were circling, he had said nothing about it until I spoke to him. Later on I will come back to him.

"This island," I said, "is five miles long—we may have to walk that far. I don't seem to be able to keep straight, but I'll try to keep you from bearing off to one side. You go ahead. We'll abandon this draw for good. I don't understand it."

We stumbled on, falling over down logs and wallowing waist-deep in snow, but I did manage to keep the parson straight, and finally I saw the tips of the trees getting sparser. We came out of the island two miles above where we wanted to come out and on the opposite side from where we had entered.

Later on I went up to investigate that draw. It was the one draw on the whole island, so far as I could make out, that instead of falling away to one side or the other, followed in a complete circle the circumference of a knobby hill.

XX
Faunal Democracy

MY friend John Dodge, a Harvard man and the nephew of General Dodge, who built the Union Pacific Railway, has a passion for mules. There was a time when he had four of them, Hobo, Bobo—and I forget the names of the other two, but they ended in -bo, also. Once upon a time Dodge was crossing the Rocky Mountains with a pack outfit when he came upon an old prospector, and joined forces with him, and fell to arguing concerning the respective merits of his favorite quadruped as compared to those of a horse. The argument waxed, diminished, and waxed in the manner of a Western argument, until finally, in a fit of exasperation, the ancient prospector said this:

"Dodge," he said solemnly, "when you have a horse you have a horse; no matter how ornery he may be, a horse is always a horse. But when you have a mule, why—the first thing you know—the dang thing may turn into a congressman."

A ranch, to be thoroughly understood, must not be visualized as a place where Mr. Smith lives with his family and ranch-hands; it must be visualized as a place where Mr. Smith and his family and his ranch-hands live as citizens of a republic which also includes horses, riding and draft, dogs, milk cows and range stock, pigs and chickens and cats, geese and ducks, and probably a number of unregistered wild animals as well; skunks in the willow patches, ground squirrels out in the open, beaver and fisher and otter along the river, martin in the timber, and, every now and then, in the tarnished silver of the sleeping night, a moose or an elk or a coyote slipping past from one range to another. And each species—with the exception of the unregistered wild ones—is going about its business in an outwardly casual but inwardly enthralled manner, and is quite sure, to judge from the expressions of its members, that without it the ranch could not exist.

The men and women are sure of their own importance, but the horses and dogs and cows and pigs and geese and chickens are even surer. You can see them reassuring themselves whenever anything has happened to depress them temporarily. The cow says to herself: "Oh, yes, it is all very well, you may chase me about, and swear at me, but what would happen to you if I didn't permit you to use my milk?" And the horse says: "You can spur me and quirt me, and climb on me with your big flapping chaps, but if I took it into my head to run away and leave you afoot, you'd have a fine time walking with your bow legs, wouldn't you?" And as for the dogs, well, all you have to do to see how seriously they take their duties, is to get up early any morning. They make a house-to-house and place-to-place inspection, and then—if everything is all right—turn the outfit over to the men.

Sometimes you stop and say to yourself: "Why, great guns, here are dozens and dozens of living creatures all of whom look upon this place as home!" Then you feel your responsibilities ever more deeply than ever.

Into the making of the Westerner's character go the many things I have already mentioned—loneliness, self-reliance, patience due to the fact of being always at the mercy of a gigantic environment, but there is nothing that more moulds his personality than his intimacy with animals. Loneliness, self-reliance, patience give him humor and philosophy, but his intimacy with animals increases this humor and patience and, incidentally, doubles his profanity. For no one can remain totally humorless and have much to do with the grave absurdity of animals, their profound self-importance, and nobody, even the man of best intentions, can remain totally blameless of speech and pit his will against the perverse will of the cow or the horse or the mule.

I love to hear horse-wranglers bringing in their 'caveys' from the range to a ranch at sunup, especially if there are benches or draws that give out reverberating echoes. Horse-wranglers have a way of whistling to their charges very high and sweet, cool and clear as the dewy freshness of the early morning, and being young men and healthy, you feel that the whistle is a part of their cheerfulness and their quick blood at this most inspiring hour of the day. You can hear them coming from a long distance, the rattle of stones, the thud of hoofs, and then, suddenly, the flute-like whistle, the Grieg-like Spring Song whistle, will be interrupted by a most unearthly flow of profanity as this horse or that lags behind or indulges in some of the tricks a horse thinks funny. The whole proceeding is like a Wagner opera in its passionate change from wood-wind to roaring brass.

A witty lady staying on my ranch, having been awakened one morning by a horse-wrangler at his duties, remarked that 'although she could understand a horse accepting in good part one of the terms she had heard applied to him'—a term having to do with his ancestry—'she could not understand him not resenting the other term'—also having to do with his ancestry—'because, obviously, he wasn't that sort of an animal.'

Other men besides the Westerner, however, are brought up with animals and live with them and think about them eighty per cent of their time. In this respect the Westerner is no different from the farmer, or the master of hounds, or the breeder of stock; the difference lies in the fact that the Western animal—all frontier animals—are herd animals. Even the master of hounds' knowledge of animals as herd animals is confined as a rule to one species, the hound, but the Westerner's knowledge of animals as herd animals embraces every species and extends not only to domestic animals but to wild animals as well. He knows his animal not only as an individual, but as a member of a band; he not only knows personal psychology, he knows also the psychology of the mob. And knowing this he is frequently able to perform feats of deduction that seem to the uninitiated black magic. He will be able to predict, for instance, in which direction a startled band of elk or mountain-sheep will run, and will cut directly across country and place himself in their way; and he will know in just what direction, even if he can't follow the tracks, a strayed horse has gone; and he knows how to outwit horses so that in most cases they have trouble in getting away to begin with.

Remember that the Westerner has few fences, and uses them as little as he can, having to preserve his pasture for the late autumn. At the end of the day he turns all except his work-horses loose upon the world, and there is nothing that so astonishes the newly arrived Easterner as the Westerners calmness under these conditions. I could fill a volume with the strange questions that have been asked me upon this subject alone. A great many people, coming to a ranch for the first time, and seeing horses only in corrals, imagine that that is where they are kept continually except when being ridden, and they cannot understand the apparent lack of provision for feeding. Their humanitarian impulses sometimes lead them into absorbing a great deal of misinformation.

But if the processes of a ranch are mysterious, those of a camp are even more so, for at the end of the day the Westerner takes off his riding-saddles and packsaddles and slaps his horses on their flanks, and off they go into miles of open range or thick forest. To be sure, he bells one or two and puts hobbles on most of the rest, but even the inexperienced can see that hobbles are not especially effective once a horse is used to them. I have seen plenty of horses, and so has everyone else, who can travel faster with hobbles than without them. Hobbles seem to encourage certain horses as the cheers of a grand stand encourage certain runners.

The Westerner, however, knows very well what he is doing, and he expects to see, the following morning, unless something out of the ordinary happens, all the horses he has turned loose the previous evening, for, before he turned them loose, he has sized them up carefully as individuals and as units of society. He has put bells, for instance, on the most popular and trusty members of his band, frequently old mares; if he has two bands, or three—horses not as yet used to running together (horses are proverbial snobs)—he has belled the leader of each band; the ordinary horses he has hobbled; a 'renegade' or two—a horse who pulls away by himself and is an anarchist—if he or they are bad enough 'renegades,' he has staked out with lash-ropes or lariats. But he doesn't like 'renegades'; it is not always easy to find good staking-grounds when making camp, and a 'renegade' may tempt other horses, so, if possible, 'renegades' will have been avoided in the first place. Some of the best camp-horses, horses that seldom try to go home, will have been rewarded for their faithfulness by having been turned loose without hobbles.

The first night out from home is the dangerous night; after that the average horse is too well aware of the distance to be travelled, too tired to be anything but content if the feed is good, although there are some horses that never can be trusted. When you buy horses in a distant country and bring them into your own, the geldings as a rule will settle down in a year or so to the new range and after that will not have to be watched, but a mare will never be content until she has foaled. At every opportunity she will try to go back to the range where she had her last colt. Once she becomes a mother again, however, she is safe. Yet even the least restless of horses are strange animals. Until they become used to a new range they will leave the finest grass in the world to get back to a desert where they almost starved to death the winter before.

(I don't know that they are so strange, after all—at least, when compared with human animals. There are a great many men and women who feel the same way, or else why would cities and summer resorts be crowded?)

Two autumns ago I went into the hills with another man, riding a horse I had just purchased for my wife—I wanted to try the horse out. It ended, as you will see, in his trying me out. My companion and myself had three horses in all, two riding-horses and a pack-horse, and the first two nights, not knowing the horse I was riding, I was extremely wary about him, but on the third day I thought I could relax my vigilance. We were miles away from home and we had crossed a particularly rough country, and this was such a good horse, so meek and easy to catch, such an honest and faithful horse! The hypocrite! I'd have liked to have shot him in the head!

The afternoon of the third day we ascended a huge mountain and dropped down on the other side. The going had been so steep, both in ascending and descending, that part of the way we had had to get off and lead, and, during the descent into the little valley where we intended to camp, over a stretch of shale rock and then mud, my horse, the timid, kindly fellow, had trembled violently and had with difficulty been persuaded to continue. We made camp at four o'clock and for a while I even contemplated not hobbling my horse at all. To add to my sense of security there was beautiful shoulder-deep grass in which the other two horses promptly buried themselves. But finally I decided to be on the safe side, especially as we were going out for an hour or two to prospect this new country on foot, and so I put the hobbles on. I could take them off when we returned.

We were gone only an hour—an interesting hour, for we were within a few yards of a wolf trotting through the timber—but when we got back my horse was not in sight. The other two, my companion's horse and the pack-horse, had hardly moved ten feet from where we had left them.

Now, it is the rarest thing in the world for a horse to leave the others; besides, the day's trip had been a hard one, the feed was excellent, my horse had been hobbled, and, finally, witness his terror when, unhampered, he had had to descend the mountain to the south. At all events, he couldn't have been gone very long. I left my companion cooking supper and set off blithely up the trail we had made coming down. After a while my blitheness departed. The hobbled tracks led straight back to the mountain and up that slippery slope and down the other side. From the top I could see in the waning light the valley beyond and the slopes of the hills through which we had passed that morning. On the whole, an open country, in which any moving object would be visible. But there was not a sign of the renegade; not a sign of life except, along a neighboring ridge, black against the glare of the sunset, the wolf. I am afraid I forgot my horse for a moment. Afterwards I remembered him, and searched some more, and finally went back to camp in the darkness a soberer man. . . . I had eight days of walking ahead of me over some of the roughest country in the Rocky Mountains.

I did not love that horse when, almost two weeks later, I saw his gentle, honest face again. I was sorry that his expertness with hobbles had prevented him from getting any noticeable hobble sores.

None the less, although it is humiliating to admit it, and is a fact usually concealed, the 'renegade' or the 'outlaw' is usually a horse with more sense and character than his brothers. A Toussaint l'Ouverture among horses. A horse who, if he were a man, would be leader of an insurgent political party, or, at least, in 'Who's Who.' A 'renegade' is merely a horse who is courageous enough to think for himself and not be afraid of the dark or a lack of companionship, and an 'outlaw' is a horse who knows that if he makes up his mind it is going to be hard to ride him, it will be.

It is lucky for mankind that both kinds of knowledge are rare in horse circles.

XXI
HORSES, MULES, AND OTHER ANIMALS

SOME of the happiest hours I have ever spent and some of the most profitable, philosophically speaking, have been spent on the top rail of a corral fence, the favorite sitting-place of all Westerners if they have nothing else to do—and, sometimes, even when they have something else to do. I don't know which makes you the more homesick for the West when you are away from it, the thought of shadowy forests and cool water, or the recollection of warm dust and the top rail of a corral fence and, on Sunday afternoons, the shady side of a cabin or saddle-shed, where you sit with some chosen companions and roll cigarettes and converse at intervals. Not long ago my small daughter, without any prompting, remarked that she 'loved the smell of dust.' If she has been born with this final love of the confirmed Westerner in her heart, I doubt if she ever gets the West out of her mind.

The most unpopular horse in a corral I have ever seen was a horse named 'Luthy.' I should like to get to the bottom of this—the reason for a horse's unpopularity with other horses. I wonder if it is a question of smell? At all events, 'Luthy' was unpopular with his own race and he was almost equally unpopular with human beings. He was the first horse the doctor and I bought when we started our establishment, and we named him after the cunning man who disposed of him by selling him to us. Subsequently, we spent six years trying to get rid of him. He wasn't exactly the sort of horse you could kill for bear bait, for he was strong, despite his years, and not bad to ride, and a good pack-horse, and he worked well in light harness, but he was the sort of horse you long passionately to sell at a fair profit to a neighbor. He was the most hideous horse imaginable, a pinto horse with great irregular brown-and-white splotches all over him and china-blue eyes that had no more expression in them than you see in the eyes of the modern young woman. A coarse black bang fell down between these eyes. When you were riding through timber and looked back at 'Luthy,' he resembled exactly one of the palfreys damsels were supposed to ride in fairy-tales, and at night his china-blue eyes shone with a phosphorescent gleam. I have never known a horse to be so bitten at and kicked at and struck at by other horses.

He wasn't always popular with me either, although I derived much secret amusement from him. He had two of the meanest tricks a horse can have: when you were driving him with other horses he would hang back until he got you within range of two extremely scientific heels, and, when you were leading him, he would wait until you came to a stream or arroya, and then, just when you were in the worst possible position ascending the opposite bank, he would sit down on his tail and refuse to budge an inch farther. Several times he nearly cut my hand in half, and once or twice he nearly pulled my own horse over backward. Otherwise he was gentle and willing and, in the words of the horseman, 'a child could ride him.'

Years after we had purchased him, the doctor, going over to the Arapahoe Reservation to buy some horses, took 'Luthy' along because he had heard—and correctly—that Indians loved pinto horses. One day the doctor passed an Indian policeman sitting on a fence and stopped to chat with him.

"Want to buy a horse?" said the doctor.

"What horse?" asked the Indian.

"This horse. Fine horse, but too lively for the dude-business—bucks."

The Indian looked at the sky and then he looked at 'Luthy.' "That horse?" he said dreamily. "I raised that horse myself nineteen years ago and sold him over into your country. . . . We used to call him 'Big Paint.'"

In my own string there is a little buckskin named Joe, with a black stripe down his back, whom I ride more than any other. I bought him when he was four—he came originally from Nevada and has some 'desert blood in him,' I think; that is, the blood of the wild horses that still roam some parts of the Southwest—and I have had him twelve years, so he is now sixteen years old. But he is as good as ever and has a trick of keeping himself marvellously fat and sleek. There is a tradition in the West, how true I don't know, that a buckskin horse is stronger than his fellows, but, at any rate, it is true that the grass-fed Western horse does not 'burn out' as quickly as his more pampered grain-fed cousin of the East. He develops more slowly and lives longer. If the East would feed its horses a little bit less and work them more, and if the West would feed its horses a little bit more and work them less, a happy medium would be reached. And if a horse would be broken not to buck, as the Easterner breaks him, and not to run away, as the Westerner breaks him, you would have a thoroughly competent animal.

If the Westerner exercised as much care about his horse's back as he does about his mouth, and the Easterner exercised as much care about his horse's mouth as he does about his back, you would have fewer bucking horses and fewer stampeders. The Western horse never has a bit in his mouth until he is three or four years old; he is broken on a hackamore, and consequently has a mouth like velvet; the slightest touch of the bit stops him. Nothing more annoys a man used to Western horses than to get hold of the average hard-mouthed, lunging Eastern horse; although I dare say nothing annoys an Easterner more than to get hold of a Western horse with a constant tendency to pitch.

Joe has always had a tendency to pitch if anything went wrong, and for twelve years we have fought out our differences along this line, he bucking me off every now and then and I sticking him about an equal number of times. But we love each other like brothers and he has never, I am sure, had the slightest intention of hurting me. When he does manage to throw me, he instantly stops and waits quietly until I get on again.

When I bought him, I found him so clever that I could not imagine why the man who had raised him had ever sold him; then I threw a rope at something one day and made an evil throw, and found out. Joe has an objection to bad technic and does not hesitate to show it. He isn't steady enough for a top cowpony.

You will have gathered from this that I don't like to ride bucking horses. I don't, and thank goodness I have now reached the age where I am not ashamed to say so. I think it a most unpleasant experience, a cross between being hit over the head with a crowbar and being beaten in a lower part of your body with a poker, although, of course, the better you ride the less you feel these blows. But there is no romance in it for me. However, since you can't always keep off a bucking horse, I'll admit that, like a great many other things, the anticipation is far worse than the reality. Indeed, once the performance starts, there is a fierce sort of joy in trying to get the better of the mad thing between your legs. And it is not nearly as dangerous as it looks. As a matter of fact, you can wager fairly safely that no sport is in which men commonly partake. Neither war nor diving from heights to a greased board occupy many men's holidays. And riding bucking horses is even less risky than several other sports that could be mentioned. It is the rarest thing in the world to see a man hurt by a pitching horse unless he happens to get caught in the saddle or the horse falls on him. All horsemen know the principle involved. The faster a horse is going the farther you are thrown from the source of danger and the more you hit the ground at an angle. Indeed, if you are anywhere around a bad horse, the safest place to be is on his back.

A man once told me that a long while ago he came upon a lonely white-bearded old rancher down in Nevada sitting on a horse in the middle of a corral. The old man had an obstinate look on his face and so had the horse.

"I'm right glad you've come," said the old man wearily; "I've been on this here cayuse near to two hours, and I'm tuckered out. I can't get near th'fence so as to make a run for it, and if I git off otherwise he'll tromple me under . . . . Would you mind snubbin' him?"

But to return to Joe. However careful he may have been of me physically during the past twelve years, he has at times been by no means as careful of my feelings. There have been occasions when he has wounded my dignity mortally. I remember one warm afternoon when he threw me off in the presence of about twenty-five of my dudes, mostly ladies, and when he threw me it was good and hard. About four times I reached for the saddle-horn—'choking Susie' it is called in some parts of the West—and each time it got farther away from me. Once I saw it when it looked like an eagle in the dimness of Yellowstone Canyon. After that I decided I might as well go, so the next time Joe was anywhere near the ground, I rolled off and rolled right under a lot of other horses, where I lay watching the flickering heels until such time as I felt I could with safety emerge. It hadn't really been Joe's fault; he thought I wanted him to buck, and he had a puzzled expression on his face when I climbed on him again. The twenty-five dudes—mostly ladies—were lined up in a double row about ten feet apart, waiting to go somewhere on their horses, and a young cowpuncher was trying to catch a loose calf with a rope. He missed his throw and the rope hit Joe on the flank. I never did have a chance; I was half asleep in my saddle, leaning over to one side, and I never got straightened up, and, to add to Joe's mistaken idea that I wanted him to buck, one of the twenty-five ladies got in my way—I mean our way—and jammed my right leg into Joe's side so that my spur raked him.

I shall never forget that girl; she was sitting on a small black horse directly in my path, her back to me, and as I thundered down on her she never even moved. "For God's sake get out of the way!" I yelled, and she slowly looked around with two dark, expressionless eyes. The next moment we hit her. Whereupon she promptly reined in her horse. My right leg was brushed from the stirrup and caught under the skirt of her saddle, and, as Joe went by, I had a distinct impression that my tibia was being pulled out like a rubber band. When we finally did jar loose I had a torn ligament that lasted me several months . . . . I wouldn't like to be with that girl in a shipwreck. She is too calm.

I am not, as I have said, sentimental about horses; I have never seen a man yet a horse liked half as well as a nice bundle of hay; but, on the other hand, if you have ridden one horse a great deal and know all his little ways and he knows all yours, and if you have ridden many lonely and, sometimes, dark miles with him, after a while you begin to cherish an affection for him against your better sense. There's a sweet warm companionable feeling to the rippling muscles of his neck when you put your bare hand against them on a black, deserted trail. And as for Joe, if you miss the trail in the dark and try to turn off it he will do his best to buck with you.

But there are some features about being with such short-lived things as horses and dogs that aren't pleasant. You understand too soon what age is. You get too much an impression of the flight of time. A wise man should keep an elephant and always feel young.

Here is Joe getting old—and he's only sixteen, and last summer I helped bury my setter, 'Shot.' Good old 'Shot'! Poor old pup! It seems only yesterday that he came to the ranch, a scrawny thin thing, quivering with excitement. Wyoming is a heavenly place for a scenting dog—filled with the richest and sweetest and most uninterrupted of smells. The cool smell of early morning, the warm smell of noon, the heavy, cold smell of night. And then, every now and then, the thrilling wild smell of a coyote or a rabbit or a fox.

About mules I am non-committal. I don't know much about them except that those who, like Dodge, admire them seem to do so with a fiery sort of devotion. I notice, however, that even these devotees are exceedingly respectful around the heels of their favorites and that they always have to blindfold them whenever they pack or saddle them. Personally I don't think I could love permanently anything quite so calculating; I prefer more impulsiveness. I don't mind so much being kicked in a moment of fear or sudden anger, but to be kicked on Friday for something I did the previous Monday seems to me unpleasantly revengeful. The average mule is a good deal like the average Socialist; he knows too much but doesn't know enough. If you could teach him a bit more and make a man out of him, all well and good, but since you can't, I think he should be kept in his place. A mule carries a pack beautifully and lightly, however, and he is tireless.

Down in New Mexico years ago I knew a lop-eared mule named 'Lily.' She was a very famous mule. In the near-by mountains there were some wild horses, and the method of catching them was to build a corral with a gate that opened inward but wouldn't open out, and in the centre of the corral to place some salt. About once or twice a week a wild horse would be found snared in this fashion. The method of bringing him, or her, down to the ranch, five miles off the mountainside, was to neck-yoke the unfortunate to 'Lily' and turn 'Lily' loose. 'Lily' would deliver her captive in the most scientific manner! Once a wild stallion tried to commit suicide by jumping off a cliff and 'Lily' snubbed him around a tree as handily as a man could have done. And I have seen her snub horses in front of the corral to which she was supposed to bring them in a way that could only elicit admiration. There was a large piñon about twenty feet out from the corral that was scarred with 'Lily's' endeavors.

When she struck the flat about five hundred yards above the ranch, she would give her companions their heads and lope beside them, until, just when they were going at full speed, and hence were easy to unbalance, she would come to the tree and run to one side of it and let them run on the other, and, sitting back on her heels and nearly breaking their necks, would whirl them about and shoot them into the corral, where she would fall placidly to eating grass. If, in their astonishment and admiration, her victims tried to make friends with her, she would kick them.

'Lily' was also famous as a dude-mule. If any Easterner with a bad sense of direction came to the ranch and no cowpuncher could be spared to guide him, the owner would give the visitor 'Lily' and tell him, when he had ridden as far as he wanted, to drop the reins on 'Lily's' neck and allow her to bring him home. She always did, but as she invariably came in a straight line, sometimes she forced her riders to lie down on her back and stay there. One unfortunate chose a direction that placed a section of cactus and thick chaparral between him and the ranch-house. They say that when he finally reached the ranch he had practically nothing on but his scratches.

Concerning burros, the little ancestors of the mule, I have more to say, but I am not going to say it, because, even more than in the case of the mule, the Western world is divided between those who adore the burro and those who do not; and since those who adore the burro are frequently fierce old men who live much alone, I have no desire to antagonize them. I will say, however, that the burro is bad in mud or snow, for he bogs down at once, and will make no effort of his own, and if you try in a friendly manner to help him out without using a pole he is likely, having the jaws of an alligator, to bite your arm or leg off. And I will further say that one summer I thought it would be a good idea to have a burro train at the ranch for short pack trips, but that I speedily abandoned the idea. I abandoned it because burros will eat anything that isn't locked up and padlocked. They have the most extraordinary appetites and stomachs of any animals I know.

As to their stomachs, you learn about them when you cinch up their owners. First, you pull up your latigo-straps until you think you've cut the unfortunate little gray beast almost in half; and then half an hour later you do the same thing again; and then, half an hour after that, you find the latigo-straps looser than ever. Nor are the stories about their omnivo-rousness fables. I have held a bunch of succulent grass up in one hand to a burro and a bundle of cigarette-papers up in the other, and had the cigarette-papers chosen. And I remember Dodge complaining bitterly because some neighboring burros ate up half of a waltz called 'Love's Dream,' while his back was turned.

Dodge plays the flute and was in the habit of cooking his breakfast on a camp-fire outside his ranch-house on warm mornings and practicing flute at the same time. The neighboring burros would gather at the feast and he would feed them flapjacks. But once he went into the house, leaving a pile of music by the frying-pan, and when he came back a few minutes later half the music was gone. I agreed with him that this showed a lack of honor.

One afternoon I took my burro train up to a lake about five miles away from the ranch and made camp and tied the burros to some trees. One of the advantages of a burro train—you think it is an advantage until you know better—is that, if it isn't convenient, you don't have to feed it regularly. How those particular burros got loose I don't know; they must have unraveled the knots with their teeth; at all events they returned to the ranch in the early morning and ate fifty pounds of newly arrived butter that the cook, knowing them to be at what he thought was a safe distance, had innocently left on the curbing of a well. Another time the train was taken on an expedition into the mountains to the east and the guide and his party foolishly left the camp unguarded to climb a near-by hill. To be sure, they covered their supplies with all the tarpaulins and pack-covers and tents they had, and weighted these with rocks, but when they reached the summit of the hill, they looked down and saw all the burros holding a conclave around the canvas-covered heap, and when they hastened back to camp the burros came out to meet them, with their jaws white with flour and sticky with syrup. The camp was two days from the nearest source of supplies and there wasn't a thing left—not even coffee—except canned goods.

Dodge had two mules who could do more than untie knots with their teeth. They were fence-jumpers, so he used to neck-yoke them together to keep them in his pasture. In the morning he would find them outside the fence. Perhaps you can figure that out. The only possible explanation is that they counted three and then jumped at the same time.

But then you never know what a mule can do and what he can't. I am sure that this summer I saw one I was trying to head, change his pace and footing, like a football half-back, as he dodged past me. A horse will hardly ever do that; a horse usually runs in a straight line, and if, when he tries to leave you, you can make a half-circle and cut in ahead of him, he will usually give up in despair. The motto of a mule, to the contrary, seems to be never to abandon hope.

Nor, coming to the cow and the bull and the steer—the most important animals in ranching—have I much more to say than I have to say about the mule and the burro. I can finish with them speedily, although I am ashamed, after living so many years in the West, to find what my fundamental attitude toward them is. I admire their financial value, but I have no real affection for them. And I was astonished at my indifference at the first—and only-bull—fight I ever saw. I expected, like the proverbial American, to be out-raged; I wasn't; I was merely bored. (There were no horses hurt.) Recollecting all the misery that bulls and cows and steers had dealt me in the past, I didn't much care who won. I will admit, however, that in all the world there is no finer sight than cattle grazing upon a thousand hills, nor one more thrilling, nor one that can more cause a man to sing:

"My soul shall be satisfied as with marrow and fatness, and my mouth shall praise thee with joyful lips."

I shall quote from another part of the Old Testament. These are lovely lines:

"Surely the mountains bring him forth food, where all the beasts of the field play.

He lieth under the shady trees in the covert of the reed, and fens.

The shady trees cover him with their shadow; the willows of the brook compass him about."

Strange that the Psalmists and the prophets should have loved so much all the scents and sounds and green freshness of the world and that there are no people so little interested in these things as their present-day descendants.

XXII
The Question of Game

IN the heart of the most civilized man there is a wildness thousands of years old that smoulders and leaps into a little flame at the sight, far or near, of the tawny shapes his ancestors hunted. This is a fundamental thing, as inherent as the desire for survival, and it is a sign that we have advanced somewhat, that we have bound this thing with definite laws and that there is an increasing number of hunters who please themselves more with the pursuit than with the actual slaughter, many even who avoid the actual slaughter except when it is necessary. Real blood lust is a rare thing—at least among Americans—and it is not pleasant to behold. Oddly enough, I have seen it most in small and somewhat deformed men. Possibly it furnishes them compensation and a sense of power they cannot otherwise possess.

I know the answer to fanatical humaneness, and, unfortunately, as the world now is it is a true enough answer. Men must eat meat and unless the game population of a country is held down by hunting it will eventually overrun the country and be its own worst enemy. You cannot teach the moose or the elk or the deer the principles of intelligent race-control, and if you wish to see the practical working out of Malthus's theory all you have to do is to fish an over-stocked lake. Once, in the Canadian Northwest, an Indian and myself came upon such a lake. The water boiled with the rising of the starved inhabitants to our flies—dreadful fish, with huge heads and staring eyes and bodies as thin as snakes. We caught them three at a time as fast as we could cast, and as a matter of charity we fished all day, and built a pyre, and burned our victims. Dynamite would have been better. And near my present ranch there is a lake where the same conditions obtain. It makes you shudder a little for the future of democracy, inclined to listen with tolerance at least to those who would restrict birth.

Besides, even if they did not propagate so rapidly, manufactured death to a wild animal is usually pleasanter than natural death. A bullet is more merciful than nature. The herd animal is always driven out to die, or, if he be a carnivorum, is eaten by his companions, while the solitary animal takes a long while at his agony. But even at that, nowadays I would prefer to leave the merciful bullet to some one else and, in the album of my memories, the pleasantest hunting pictures are not those when I have made a good shot, but those when, along some lodge or in the grass, I have watched an unsuspecting creature and, having had my fill of watching, have gone about my business and let him go about his.

Man is by far so much the most dreaded animal in the forests and by far so much the most deadly that I for one feel always a trifle cowardly when I take advantage of these facts.

The man who has lived in the Far West has in the background of his mind a series of game pictures upon which he can draw at will. Just three months ago I had to spend a night in Yellowstone Park after the season was over, and I could not sleep because of the bull elk who bugled all night about the huge deserted hotel—so close you could hear their snuffling and breathing and the tramping of their feet.

I remember once making camp after dusk in a little half-moon valley with great bare ridges, flanked with timber, rising from it. The dusk was of October and a heavy snow-storm had brought the elk down in thousands from their summer range. But the weather had turned warm again and had confused them, and they had stopped in the forest to the north of the little valley. By night they went south along the ridges to a salt-lick, and just before dawn they migrated back. Two or three stumbled over our tent-ropes and woke us up, and all through the hours of blackness we heard them near at hand. At dawn, high above us, with the rising sun back of them touching with misty light their antlers into gold, so that they looked like stags of St. Hubertus, three great bulls took the air and watched us.

A shining and most transcendental vision. After a while the bulls moved off into the timber and the procession of the returning elk began—hundreds of moving shapes in single file, the head of each one almost touching the white rump of the one preceding.

Later on in the morning, going north, I came upon a small band feeding in an open valley and stalked against the wind into their midst. I had no cover, but when they lifted their heads I 'froze,' and when they put their heads down again I crept forward. Finally I was within ten feet of the nearest cow. All the deer family have poor eyes—in fact, outside of the cat family and the hunting-birds, there is no animal who has the sight man has. A sudden movement will alarm elk, but if you stand still and the wind is right, they do not know what you are. And, as is the case with all wild animals, it is the females who do the watching and give the alarm. There is cynical amusement to be found in the attitude of the males, especially if you happen to be a male yourself. Bull elk, bull moose, stags, buck antelope are so thoroughly pre-occupied with their own beauty and importance. Death steals upon them while vanity is making of them easy victims.

I crossed a ridge on my way back to camp, which was at the head of a lake lying at the base of The Tetons. It was about four o'clock in the afternoon and already the great square mass of rock, twelve thousand feet high and over, to the south and the right hand of me, was throwing its purple shadow out over the forests. Away off to the northeast was another lake, shimmering and molten. Below the ridge a moraine came down, and amongst the heaped-up boulders a stream trickled, and here and there were clumps of willows and alders. And then I caught sight of a movement in the underbrush and fell flat upon the face of a granite ledge and peered below me. Three moose, two cows and a young bull, were feeding in the alders.

If the elk is the most stately and beautiful of Western animals, the moose is the most symbolic. There is something about its darkness, its gigantic uncouthness, that seems to sum up all the histories of forests since the world began. The elk, warm and golden, is a creature of sunlight and open spaces fringed with aspens, but the moose reminds you of hidden moss and the damp boles of gigantic trees.

My young bull left his companions and came down the moraine until he was directly beneath me. He had, I think, to begin with, the thought of a little food and a little sleep and a little rolling in nice hot dust. A pleasant interlude for a young bachelor recently caught in the chains of wedlock. But the leading characteristic of most wild animals, of all possibly, except the grave and wise mountain-sheep, is a lack of consecutiveness. Even the beaver works half the time without using his head, and it is a poor compliment to say to a man that he works like a beaver, although a great many do. This young moose could decide upon nothing. He would start to dig his bed and then a tender willow shoot would attract his attention and he would reach out his great overhanging lip to grasp it. Perhaps it was just beyond his reach, but it never seemed to occur to him to move. He would strain the muscles of his neck until his eyes bulged. More often than not he would forget the first morsel in the sight of another. Finally he decided—it could not have been I, for I was hidden and the wind was not blowing from me—that mysterious enemies were near. Perhaps he was merely practicing the role of a male. At all events, he obliterated with care all his tracks and, arching his neck, challenged the world. There being no response, he dug his bed again and prepared once more for the long-delayed nap. I barked like a coyote.

Now that he had a real enemy the young bull was no longer suspicious, but alert and angry. He struggled to his feet and looked about him. He hadn't the faintest idea where I was and I don't think he even knew to what species of enemy I belonged. I barked again, and he pleaded with me to show myself and do battle, pawing up the earth and throwing it back of him, and lowering his horns threateningly to all points of the compass. He could not understand my reluctance. I barked a third time, and very much against his will, but overcome with the mystery of the situation, he turned about and walked slowly off, stopping from time to time to look back of him. At length he broke into a trot, the boulders of the moraine bothering him not in the least.

I have seen moose trotting in the winter—they take a long, swinging trot, so fast that it outdistances the gallop of a horse—through snow that no other animal could even walk through. They are, indeed, fitted for survival. They have no competitors in that direction except the bear. Their only serious enemy is man.

A moose will live close to settlement—he is not afraid of man; in fact, although harmless, as all American wild animals are if not molested, he will fight a man quicker than most. It is not safe to dispute trails with him. Leave him alone and he will multiply and take care of himself. In the winter he 'yards up' with several companions and lives contentedly upon willows and bark and the grass he can dig down to with his sharp hoofs. But man can destroy him in no time, for he is even easier to shoot than an elk.

When I first came into my country there were not many moose about, although the country to the west in Idaho had been, until it was cleaned out, a great moose country. In the past ten years the moose, entirely protected from hunting, have increased mightily, but now they stand an excellent chance of annihilation. For the past two years the State has sold a limited number of licenses, and there are not yet enough moose to warrant any shooting whatsoever. They should have been given at least five years more. This summer I rode from the headwaters of the Yellow-stone to the headwaters of the Lamar, down the Yellowstone and back, through the greatest moose country in my part of the world, and in all those eight days I saw only thirty moose, and of these only four were bulls, and I could see only five cows with calves. Such observations are not scientific, they are by no means accurate; a cow of any species seen at a distance may very well have a hidden calf with her, but I for one was convinced none the less that the penny-wise were at work again, and that the females of the moose family were being too rapidly widowed.

Wild swans are the most mysterious and beautiful of birds. Like the rattlesnake, their marital faithfulness is touching and a lesson to humanity. It is more than ordinary brutality to shoot one of a pair, for you leave a survivor who will never remate. Last summer a rumor reached us that two of these stately and dazzling birds—a fairy prince and princess spellbound—had settled in a lake to the northeast. I did not believe this rumor until I saw with my own eyes, for wild swans are rare in our country, and a lack of knowledge may confuse them with pelican, but one dusk I came to the lake through a gap in the hills and saw the bride and bridegroom floating in the still, many-colored waters—translucent spots of whiteness in waters the color of the flamingo's breast and the color of the wings of the oriole. I think they must have chosen the lake deliberately, for it is a lake that resembles a primitive Italian background, with round hills where saints could have set up chapels, and clumps of spruce and fir that resemble cypresses.

When we turned our horses loose, the swans, hearing the bells, stopped in their occult, imperceptible swimming and craned their necks and floated near to the shore. The bells, tinkling and huddled, seemed to enchant them. Until darkness blotted them out we could see them swimming to and fro, and at sunrise they were still there.

In the saffron twilight of a gathering thunder-storm, my wife and myself, the following afternoon, poled an ancient raft we had found across the lake. I was whistling and singing, and the swans, hearing a new sound, consulted together and followed us. They make no move without first turning their heads and staring questioningly at each other, and in the end it is the woman, I think, as always, who decides. When we came near to the other shore we stopped poling and began to fish. The swans lost interest, so I had to sing to them again. Then they came closer and circled about us. I sang 'Lohengrin' and they apparently appreciated the compliment. The storm was drawing nearer. The afternoon grew impeccably quiet. There came a great splash to the right and left of us and we saw the heads of two beavers swimming. I cannot make understandable how panic—pantheistic and essential—the hour was. It was like the Wind in the Willows. We seemed caught up in a spell of the forests, and of water and of hills, and of the emptiness before storm, when instead of creatures dreaded and fled from, we spoke a universal language and our intrinsic innocence was understood.

A passion for bears is an idiosyncrasy. I confess to it. The brown and black members of the family are the most amusing denizens of the forests, and their gray kinsmen, the grizzlies, the most thrilling. When you are in the presence of a grizzly you know that at last you are in the breathless presence of the wilderness.

Last summer we came upon four of these silver-coated monsters—a mother and three yearlings—high up in a mountain meadow on a divide between two creeks called Gravel and Wolverine. I am told that probably two of the yearlings had been kidnapped, as grizzly mothers have a way of fighting off other grizzly mothers and stealing their cubs. I do not know how true this is, but I do know that triplets are rare in grizzly circles, for grizzlies propagate sparsely and are so unsocial that they even mate with difficulty.

As we came out of the timber—we had a pack-train of twelve horses with us and had been riding all afternoon through the fog and shadows of a rain—the old mother rose to her hind legs and lifted her great arms above her head. It was a warning and we stopped where we were. Satisfied that we meant no harm, she dropped to her feet, and, her children after her, disappeared with grotesque incredible speed.

Motherhood is exclusive in its tenderness. Not for nothing have the warlike nations symbolized themselves in the maternal figures of Germania, and Britannia, and Columbia.

Three weeks before I had heard from a park ranger the most amusing bear story I have ever heard—and there are countless amusing ones. Early in his career the ranger was stationed, after Yellowstone Park was closed for the season, at the Lake Hotel. A small black bear began to make himself particularly objectionable; he stole food and entered the kitchen when nobody was about and left it in confusion. The ranger, fairly new at the time to bears, decided to drive the marauder out of the country, so early one morning he started in pursuit, firing his revolver over the bear's head, and throwing rocks at him. All that day and the next he chased his unwilling quarry, and the bear, as all bears do, kept himself just out of range, and when his tormentor rested, rested also, and looked back mournfully and scratched himself in the sun. At the end of two days the ranger and the bear had travelled about thirty miles and the ranger was tired. The next morning he went home. The bear was nowhere in sight, but, as the hotel was reached, the ranger heard a noise and looked around, and there was the bear just behind him.

Back of Old Faithful Hotel they have a tank that holds the water-supply. This has had to be protected by a heavy grating, because the bears come from all over the park to use the sloping sides as sliding boards and the water as a swimming-pool. They never grow tired of the sport.

Dodge, my friend who admires mules, once figured in a dramatic bear incident. His mules had a habit of running away, but they did no harm. They would run for a while and then stop and eat grass as though nothing had happened. Dodge had started in the direction of Cody, driving his mules attached to a covered wagon with the top down, but on the road he fell in with another Harvard graduate named Jones, and both had been so delighted by the encounter that Dodge had changed his original purpose and had persuaded Jones to return and view the beauties of The Tetons. Jones was one of the most hairless men I have ever seen; a round-faced, bald young man, with huge spectacles. He never spoke, but about his lips hovered a perpetual vague smile, as if he was amused by the echoes of a joke he had heard years before. On the return journey Dodge and Jones met a man with a bear cub, and they bought the cub for ten dollars.

This is the prologue; the drama in one act and the epilogue occurred a week later.

Leading down to the ranch where I was then staying was a dug-way, and at the foot of this dug-way were several log buildings. One warm August afternoon a terrific hubbub broke out on the other side of the hill into which the dug-way was cut, and over the hill, in a cloud of dust, with a creaking of chains and a rattle of wheels, came Dodge and Jones and the bear, Dodge's mules running away. Jones, sitting in the back of the wagon, seemed utterly unperturbed; he was viewing the country with his usual absent-minded smile. But the bear was more temperamental. Half-way down the dug-way, being restrained only by a log chain which was fastened to nothing, he leaped upon Dodge's back, and, reaching around, began to claw at that frantic driver's eyes. Jones never even turned his head.

Since it looked as if the whole entanglement was going straight through the log buildings, the few spectators withdrew to a discreet distance. But as usual the mules stopped long before danger was reached and, breathing heavily, looked about them with a proud and amused expression. Dodge, red with anger, dropped his reins, and without a word threw the bear over his head and made a flying dive on top of the squirming mass of fur. Locked in each other's arms, the two rolled down the slope. It was a question whether the bear was scratching Dodge more than Dodge was bruising the bear, or the other way around.

The epilogue occurred that night.

Dodge and Jones had made a little camp and I went down to see them. They were drinking soup out of tomato-cans, and the bear, tied to a tree, was winding and unwinding himself on his chain. Whenever he had unwound himself as far as he could, Dodge would put down his tomato-can and arise solemnly and go over and smack his pet in the face. All the time the bear whined mournfully.

It is not a very sensible citizen of a Far Western State, nor a very imaginative one, who refuses to give thought to his game. Pennsylvania and New York, Europe for centuries, have proven conclusively that game is merely an added asset to a country, an additional source of meat-supply and revenue, manna dropped from heaven. It is an old-fashioned idea, thoroughly unbusinesslike, that game cannot exist in the neighborhood of settlement. And it is more than an old-fashioned idea, it is sheer ignorance, to believe that there is something shameful about game because its presence presupposes that a country is still uncivilized. Nothing could be further from the truth, and it is the older States, who, simply because they are more civilized, have realized first the depths of such nonsense.

XXIII
An Unnecessary Tragedy

A COMMUNITY that allows its game to be destroyed is like a man who has ten dollars in one pocket and so forgets that he has five in another. This condition of mind is a sign of unaccustomed wealth and is nothing of which to be proud.

And make no mistake. The whole question of conservation in America is again standing at a crisis. Two decades ago it stood at another crisis when it was first introduced as a national policy. Then the conservationists won, but once more the forces of destruction are gathering and the conservationist is finding himself with his back to the wall, preparing to fight a further knock-down and drag-out battle. Furthermore, in the curious way the radicals of one generation have of becoming the reactionaries of another, some of the very forces and governmental agencies who led the original fight for conservation are now, unwittingly, times having changed and the idea of conservation being amplified, leading the forces of destruction.

I have come near to saying that the problem of game is a fairly simple one. Intrinsically it is, but actually it is complicated, as are all problems in which a number of men are involved. It is not the game that makes the problem, nor the increasing settlement—in most game countries an extremely sparse settlement after all—but the way the human mind reacts. If tomorrow the politician would become intelligent and disinterested, the game conservationist open minded, and the government expert practically informed, the question of game in the Far West would be settled forever. Intrinsically the problem is so simple that it can be written as a syllogism.

Profitable things are worth preserving; game is profitable (that game has been proven profitable, and, incidentally, spiritually necessary as well for the health of the nation, only the ignorant will deny); therefore it is worthwhile to preserve game.

Or again:

It has been found that all investments require, to be made successful, some expenditure of time and money; game is an investment; therefore it requires some expenditure of time and money.

A few Far Western States have already managed to get rid of their game but not the majority, and my own State of Wyoming is singularly fortunate because it was settled last and had by far the greatest supply of wild life to begin with. It is even possible, therefore, in view of the increasing intelligence on such matters that Wyoming may awaken in time to prevent itself from being in the position of some of its neighbors who, having lost their game twenty years or so ago, are now buying back at great expense, realizing its value, what they originally had for nothing.

In order to preserve game perpetually two things are necessary: an adequate game-warden service and, where certain animals are concerned, an adequate winter range. For most game-animals only the former is needed. On the whole the majority of States have fairly good game-laws, so it is not so much a question of passing new laws as it is a question of enforcing those already in the code. Nor is summer range a factor, certainly not in the Far West. There will be sufficient summer range for centuries to come, perhaps forever. The first thing to do, however, is to see what animals can be preserved and what animals cannot, and what those who can be preserved require.

Elk, moose, deer, mountain sheep and goat, bear, fish, and all manner of birds can be preserved; buffalo and antelope, mountain-lions and coyotes and wolves cannot. The first two of the second category can only be preserved in national parks, while the last three, romantic as they are in certain aspects, are rightly classed as vermin. Buffalo and settlement, however scattered the settlement may be, do not get along well together. A buffalo-herd will go through any fence except one especially constructed at great cost, while as to antelope, charming creatures that they are, they are none the less fools and need especial guardians, also a warm country in winter. The latter fact is particularly fatal to them. They will not learn to take care of themselves in countries—mountain countries and timbered countries—where there is natural protection. They court destruction. Mountain-lions, wolves, and coyotes are beasts of prey, and even if the cattle and sheep men were not to be considered, a choice would have to be made between these three species and other game. They are the worst enemies, for instance, the deer have. Possibly the same charges can be made against the grizzly bear, but they must be made with care. There is a great deal of nonsense extant about the grizzly. At the worst he is an extremely rare animal, and it is only the killers of the race, easily identified, who do much harm.

The species that can be preserved give absurdly little trouble and an immense return on the investment made. Grant to elk, moose, deer, sheep, goat, bear, the smaller game and fish, only half a chance and they will increase and grow fat.

Sheep need only this; an adequate game-warden service and freedom from their tame brethren, from whom they contract diseases.

Goats need even less; they demand merely an adequate game-warden service.

Bear need an adequate game-warden service and a campaign of education which will show them to be not vermin, but one of the finest and most profitable game-animals a country can possess.

Deer will take care of themselves if their enemies, the wolves, coyotes, and mountain-lions, are kept down.

As I have pointed out, you cannot annihilate moose unless you do so yourself.

The elk present a more difficult problem, but not such a difficult one if handled, as it never has been handled, with knowledge and common sense. Elk are the only one of the animals mentioned who need to any extent a winter range, and this at once presents a dilemma because winter ranges, being for the most part in valleys, are as a rule taken up by ranches. Elk are like cattle; during the summer months they range the high country, but with the approach of cold weather they drift in huge bands to the winter feed-ground to which they are accustomed. They are not by tradition natives of the mountains; in fact, very little game is. Elk are plains animals and in adaptability stand between the moose and the antelope.

The history of the elk in my country epitomizes nicely the whole situation. When my valley was first explored in the early years of the nineteenth century there were no elk; ten years ago there was a herd estimated at twenty thousand individuals, the greatest herd in the world. To-day, due to winter losses and one terrific slaughter in Montana when the great herds summering in Yellowstone Park broke and stampeded before an early storm, there are probably not more than eight thousand, if that many, of the magnificent herd left, although it is still the greatest herd in existence. The herd is slowly building up again, but it is a question, after such catastrophes, whether it can maintain its own unless great wisdom is exercised speedily.

When the elk come down before the snow some of them winter on bare side-hills and do well, but the only range sufficiently large to accommodate them in any great numbers consists of the meadows of natural hay and the swamp-lands surrounding the local town, where, owing to the conformation of the hills and the warm water, the snow never lies heavily. This has been their winter range ever since they entered the country. Unfortunately for them, however, it was also the first land settled by the entering pioneers, so there came a time when the elk, seeking their accustomed feed- grounds, found nothing but fences. This, of course, was an impossible situation and the federal and State governments have bought back some of the land and raise hay upon it to feed the elk. And, curiously enough, this winter feeding does not make of the elk tame creatures, as was at first predicted. The same elk that during the winter will let men come close to them, a day after the winter breaks are as wild as they ever were. They seem to understand the situation perfectly. But neither the State nor federal governments have done enough. With the expenditure of a sum of money which would be to them nothing at all, and which the elk would rapidly repay, the elk situation could be put immediately upon a permanent and satisfactory basis.

All the land that was originally the winter feed-grounds of the elk—only a few thousand acres after all—should be bought back and an adequate game-warden service should be instituted—I don't mean as to individuals, the present individuals are first-class, but there are not enough of them—and the whole valley should be turned into a game preserve. There should be no shooting there at all.

Possibly later on Mr. Roosevelt's suggestion that the elk-herd should be handled as cattle are handled, that is, that annually the weak members should be culled out and a certain number of others culled out as well, the latter to be used as a profitable source of revenue and meat-supply, might also be put into effect.

If such a course was adopted everyone, including the hunter of big game, would be well served. The State and federal governments would make money, the inhabitants of the country would make money, the constant expense and worry of game trials would be eliminated, the conservationist would be satisfied, and the hunter of big game and the local hunter for meat would find that the preserve suggested would supply them with more game than they ever thought possible, for of course a great deal of hunting country would be left on all sides of the valley and the valley would act as a perpetual reservoir. Perhaps even antelope could be induced to roam there again. The question of range for the cattlemen, frequently injected into the discussion by the ignorant or the malicious, is beside the point. The elk occupy no summer range the cattleman uses or ever will be allowed to use.

It seems strange, considering what the history of the valley is, and what it actually is to-day, that the State and federal governments refuse to do what is simple and intelligent. If the valley were the ordinary mountain valley there would be less to be said, but it is not the ordinary mountain valley—it is a unique country, using that abused word advisedly; unique scenically, as I have already pointed out, and unique where game is concerned. It is the last refuge of the big game of America; the last stronghold. Here the game has gathered. Here is an opportunity, if taken in time, to construct the greatest natural-history museum on the hoof in the world, as well as the greatest source of big-game hunting; a museum that would attract thousands of visitors. And, bringing the subject down to one of financial returns, and this must be done if we are to remain sensible, a museum that would pour immense revenues into the country where it was situated.

But there is nothing more disheartening than to try to talk straightforwardness to a politician, or toleration to a fanatic, or common sense to a doctrinaire. Sometimes one wonders if the mistaken enthusiasm of friends is not more fatal than the cynical indifference of enemies.

Reform is a strange thing. It does something to a man's mind, or rather, to be more correct, the man's mind does something to reform. Most people want the world to improve, but after a while the majority of sensible men are so appalled by the personality of the reformer that they decide that if the world can't be reformed in any other way it had best not be reformed at all. You can, at least, argue with the devil, even if you can't convince him; he will at least listen to what you have to say;he possesses some knowledge of humanity; but the reformer will do neither of the first two, nor will he acquire the last. Good fools are infinitely more dangerous to progress than clever knaves.

And the earnest fools of conservation have hurt and are hurting perceptibly that vital cause. They will not, for one thing, admit that you have to approach every man with decency, and consideration, and tolerance. They refuse to argue with the average man along the only lines the average man considers worthwhile, and there is no use in burying your head in the clouds if you don't know where your feet are going.

In order to convince the average man you must show him that the plan you propose will bring him actual dollars or cents, or their equivalents. He has his living to make, he is not a millionaire theorist, nor a supposed expert who sits behind a desk.

The reformer loses his temper. It is the essence of reform to make a gesture and desire the fruits of the gesture to be accomplished immediately. Heaven to a reformer is a place where he can touch a moral call-bell, and the rest of the world, disguised as a sleek-haired bellboy, is instantly at his elbow, eager to carry out his commands. But since humanity is not made that way, the reformer becomes enraged and calls people names. Then he wonders why he makes enemies and why his cause invariably in the end fades into nothingness.

There is not a Western game country the inhabitants of which have not repeatedly been called 'game-hogs,' 'poachers,' 'tush-hunters,' 'horse thieves,' and 'cattle thieves.' My own country, being a famous game country, has suffered more than most. Do you wonder that its citizens are slightly resentful? Even if they were what they have been called, it would be foolish to approach them with such epithets on your lips. But they are, as a matter of fact, most emphatically not. There is no community in America that has a higher level of intelligence. The people are a picked lot and on the whole the best friends the local game has. Again and again, without hope of recompense, at great personal loss and inconvenience, they have fed the elk when the government and State have bungled their jobs. They have driven notorious 'tush-hunters' out of the country. Any serious killing of elk for their teeth is nowadays impossible.

And these statements are easily proven. Paradoxical as it may seem, but not in the least paradoxical when the reformer's mind is taken into consideration, many men who should know the most about game know the least practically. And here is a simple truth they frequently overlook, but a truth which no man who has ever been a game-warden thinks for a moment of contradicting: game cannot survive a decade in a country whose inhabitants are hostile to it. Not all the laws in the world or the best of game-warden services can save it. The fact that game still survives in great quantities in western Wyoming is the only proof needed that my neighbors and myself are not, except in rare instances, 'game-hogs,' 'poachers,' or 'tush-hunters.' This is an ipso-facto argument. It is only a wonder to me that citizens of Far Western States, confused by inept jurisdiction, puzzled by indifference, insulted continually, actually injured at times by the mishandled game, continue to think as clearly as they do on the subject.

Not long ago I picked up the magazine of a humane society and saw a long article dwelling upon the horrors of roping; the number of cattle killed and maimed by the rope. And, coming across the same magazine another time, I saw an earnest editorial denouncing the brutality of the rodeos that have been recently held in New

York—"the poor horses [I am quoting almost exactly] were made to run and jump against their will." Now, what, in the name of common sense, are you to do with such people? Cattle-handling is one of the oldest professions in the world; they handled cattle in Judea; and is it for one instant credible, even if the cattleman was a brute, that he would have been for thousands of years an idiot? Steers and cows are worth money. Have you ever seen anybody but an idiot deliberately throw money away?

As to the poor horses made to run and buck, it would be an infinite pleasure to see the writer of such sentiments climb to the 'hurricane-deck' of a bronco. Old Steamboat, one of the most famous horses in the West, was a lady's saddle-horse most of the year, but when you took him into the arena and blindfolded him he knew just what was expected of him. But these are examples of how the reformer's mind works.

Scattered throughout the West in lonely cabins, on spreading ranches, are any number of men who possess more knowledge of game and what should be done with it than is contained in most game societies and government bureaus. It is a pity that all those whose fundamental desires are the same cannot come together and meet upon a ground of mutual advice and toleration.

And meanwhile the game continues to die.

XXIV
Some Neighbors

MY country, since I have been there, has not changed greatly in the character of its inhabitants. There has been, to be sure, an inroad of rather alien folk in the shape of Middle Western farmers, but the original background was so thoroughly etched in that the new-comers have been pretty well absorbed—hardy, adventuring men, the first settlers, many of them coming into the valley because they wanted to end their days, after years of aridity and water-holes, in a country of greenness and perpetual water. One of them told me that he was 'tired of living in a place where you saw a visitor coming at sunup, and watched him all day long, and then, in the end, he didn't get to your place until half an hour late for supper.'

There are, of course, numerous men who love deserts—'Desert Rats,' they call them—and many more who love the treeless plains, or the burnt umbers and ochres of the Southwest; but the men who come into the mountains and stay there have a vision of trees and waterfalls.

I cannot pick out and describe, even in a line or two, all those first neighbors of mine, fairly distant neighbors most of them, living anywhere from five to forty miles away. I cannot even give a satisfactory composite picture of the curiously cosmopolitan society, surfaced by common desires and common traditions, that distinguishes most cattle countries. In the case of my country, not so cosmopolitan as some others I have known, since my country is a rougher country and a country of small holdings. Not as cosmopolitan, for instance, as that of the little town in New Mexico where English aristocrats and American millionaires rubbed shoulders with cowpunchers and Mexicans, and the 'four pluses' of golf suits were as common as spurs and chaps. And not as cosmopolitan as that of another little town in the State of Washington on whose outskirts for a while lived four gorgeous British ex-cavalry officers who arrived with some capital and the intention of going into ranching, but who spent most of their capital giving champagne luncheons every Sunday in a striped marquee set out on the bare sage-brush flats of their holdings. The neighbors who were not invited fell into the habit of taking up positions of advantage on the near-by hills and watching the proceedings through field-glasses, and the town council finally passed a special ordinance against the ex-officers because one of their guests stumbled in the main street on a Monday morning, and lay there, and blocked traffic.

My own country has always been a grimmer country, but it was, and is, sufficiently cosmopolitan.

When I first arrived there, among the inhabitants was the handsome son of a great New York family, who had been sent West because he was thought to be a drunkard, but who developed (unlike most of his fellow remittance men) into the shrewdest and most sober of cattlemen; and there was the son of an American admiral, the rest of whose family lived in Florence; and there was an ex-policeman from Pennsylvania, who had shot a man justifiably but had decided to emigrate; and there was the illegitimate offspring of a race famous in New England; and Dodge, the Harvard man; and another man whose talk was of the roughest but who occasionally let drop a phrase astonishing in its delicacy and sureness of education; and there was the mysterious heir of a South African official, who carried in his pocket the photograph of two beautiful sisters.

These, and more like them, and then a score of men whose real names and stories were never known.

The heir of the South African official is still in the country, and will be there forever. He was shot a few years ago by a boy who had worked for us, and the shooting was so necessary that the boy was never even arrested. The Boer, between whom and the boy there had been bad blood for a long while, rode over to the boy's ranch, announcing his intention of murdering him, and arriving at the door, placed his horse between him and the cabin and attempted to shoot the boy and his wife through the window. A strange fellow this Boer, a charming, blue-eyed, curly-headed young man with a slight foreign lisp. He had been a mounted policeman in the Canadian Northwest and a top cowpuncher everywhere, but he told me that he had once fallen and injured his head, and I don't think he had ever got over the injury, for he was undoubtedly at moments insane. He could never spend a night at a ranch, for instance, without taking something away the next morning, and then, half an hour later, you would find the thing he had taken, lying in the road where he had thrown it.

Once I was riding with him through the fringe of cottonwood that bounds the ranch on the south. He sniffed the scented air. "This always reminds me," he said, in his soft voice, "of ballrooms."

The illegitimate son of New England was even more dramatic. There is no reason why I shouldn't mention his name, although I shall not do so, for it is not the name of his kin, and he is dead now—blew his brains out a few Augusts ago when he was alone in his isolated ranch-house. They found him two weeks later, the shotgun, the trigger of which he had pulled with his bare toe, between his knees. A tortured, hampered, damned sort of a poet. Dodge, the last person who saw him alive, said he raved all one moonlit night of the loveliness of his lakes and mountains and whispering forests.

Smith—that is what I shall call him—was the son of a Maine seamstress and a member of the famous clan to which I have referred. Some way or other he had obtained a good education and in the late eighties appeared in our country from another part of the West, with a young wife, a couple of children, and a herd of pure-bred cattle. He took up a ranch on the shores of the great lake north of us, twelve miles above the nearest settlement and sixteen miles below the most southern outlying soldier-post of Yellowstone Park. Between him and the rest of the world, on all sides but one, was unbroken forest, through which ran the dusty ribbon of the road from our valley to the high plateau of Yellowstone.

But on the fourth side—to the West—his ranch sloped down to the lake, and across the lake, green where the pines and fir were, gray where the granite arose, white with snow above, floated the gigantic vision of The Tetons.

A beautiful place, the finest for its view I have ever seen, but no kind of a ranch. Smith built himself a handsome log-cabin, long and rambling, and settled down to raising his pure-bred cattle. He was soon discovered to be an odd man, but for two or three years nothing sinister was attached to his name. Then a partner, a man we will call Wheelwright, appeared from the East.

Wheelwright was a good-looking, polished man, the son of a general in the United States Army, who had got himself into some sort of scandal in New York and whose wife had divorced him. He and Smith seemed to be the best of friends, but when there is a pretty woman in a triangle, people will talk, even distant neighbors, and so after a while it was said that Smith was jealous.

The truth of what happened I don't know; nobody knows; at all events, after Wheelwright had been in the country about a year, he and Smith, hunting cattle, went into a ford on the Snake River, a ford Smith knew and Wheelwright didn't, and Wheelwright was drowned. The gossips claimed that Smith had deliberately sent Wheelwright below the ford, but Smith, in a posthumous letter, denied this angrily and said that he had not been within a half a mile of Wheelwright at the time.

This is tragedy number one. Tragedy number two is harder to explain away.

Smith lived on with his wife at the ranch. Two or three more children were born, and then, five or six years later, I am not quite sure how many years intervened, the still young Mrs. Smith was found one bitter winter's night, moonlight and frozen snow, with both her hips broken. Smith said that she had injured herself while skiing, but hips are hard to break, and even those who liked Smith— only two or three—admitted that he had a maniacal temper that came near to, or actually was, insanity. Besides, surrounding this particular incident were curious circumstances.

A soldier from Yellowstone Park discovered Mrs. Smith's condition. In those days, during the winter, a snow-shoe patrol of one man came down from the station to the north once a week to the little settlement to the south, and this scout was accustomed to break his journey at Smith's. But when, on this particular frozen night, he came to the log-cabin, he was refused admittance, although every window was blazing with light and he heard someone playing furiously upon the piano. The soldier, being a wiser man than most soldiers, pushed the protesting Smith aside and entered. In an inner room he found Mrs. Smith. Without wasting time he hurried on to the settlement and returned with a party of men and a sled. I have talked to some of these men and also to one of the women who attended Mrs. Smith, and they swear that she told them that if she got well they would hear the truth, but if she died, no one would know. She died, of course; the nearest doctor was then over two hundred miles away, and The Pass had to be crossed. The little expedition had not gone very far before the young wife with the broken hips succumbed.

Smith, meanwhile, making some excuse to go back to his ranch, never rejoined the tragic little expedition, but snow-shoed straight north, and so out of the country, and out of the country's knowledge for seven years. At the end of seven years he returned, but by that time all his stock had disappeared, and his children, all but the youngest girl, who had been adopted by some wealthy people in Chicago, had been parceled out among the neighbors.

I don't know how accurate any of this is; even the most honest are not to be trusted completely when their prejudices are aroused. Smith claimed that the whole thing had been framed up to run him out of the valley and steal his stock; but I am positive that this is not so, if for no other reason than the personalities of some of the men he accused. At all events, Smith was a broken man and behaved as such. He hardly left his ranch except to come down to the little settlement for supplies, and his attitude toward the world became even queerer than it had been before. After a while he brought back another wife to the lonely cabin beside the lake; a woman as strange as himself, whom he had found playing the fiddle on an excursion steamer in southern California. She was the daughter of some well-to-do people in the East, and they sent her a small monthly allowance. Smith told me that once he had married her he could never again get her to play for him.

"When I ask her to play," he said, "she plays only discords, but once or twice a year—usually late on a moonlight night—she will begin to play and will play like an angel for hours."

I am not likely to forget the first time I saw Smith. I was riding up to Yellowstone Park and a man who knew him told me to be sure to drop in upon him. I came, about ten o'clock of a morning, to the forested road that led off from the main highway in the direction of the lake. It was a very still and warm and sunny morning, the sunlight falling in round patches of gold through the sleeping evergreens. Along the forested road, tacked to a tree here and there, were the bottoms of boxes on which had been written scrawlingly in pencil: "If you love God's creatures and intend them no harm, you are welcome; signed; John and Mary Smith." Presently I came to the cabin and the view of the lake. Around the front door boards had been erected to the height of about two and a half feet, and on the front door was a sign, "Private, No Admittance." I climbed over the boards and knocked. A voice said: "Come in."

A man was sitting by an empty fireplace reading a three-weeks-old copy of the New York *Sun*. On one of the bare walls was a lithograph of John L. Sullivan, and on another was a picture of Bishop Potter. The man did not look up when I came in, nor did he speak for several minutes. After a while he put down his paper and asked me who I was and where I came from—most un-Western questions. He was a tall, slim man of about forty, with straight black hair, worn rather long, and a dark mustache; not unlike Robert Louis Stevenson in appearance; a thin-faced, sensitive-looking man. Down to the waist he was clad in a cowboy's flannel shirt and around his neck he had a red handkerchief, but below the waist were faded Eastern riding-trousers and stained puttees. His conversation was equally bifocal; most of the time he used the slang and solecisms of the cattle-range, but every now and then he would speak with the clipped accents of the educated New Englander. The latter was especially true when he spoke of music. He was passionately fond of music and had a huge Victrola and a library of records. "Did you by any chance hear Tetrazzini sing last winter?" he asked suddenly. This was Smith.

In the midst of our desultory talk a door opened and a woman clad in a straight gingham gown—I don't think she had anything on underneath—her feet bare, and her black hair parted in the middle and drawn down over her ears, came in. Under her arms was a yellow-backed French novel. She stared at me for a moment and then said:

"There aren't many huckleberries this year, are there?"

I admitted that there weren't, and she went out as quietly and as vacantly as she had come in.

After half an hour or so I announced that I must be going, and Smith volunteered to ride a mile or two up the road with me. We went out back of the house to where my horse was grazing with loose reins, and Smith, disappearing for a moment into his kitchen, returned immediately with a black filly on the end of a forty-foot rope. I don't know whether he kept the filly in the kitchen or not, but it certainly looked as if he did.

He and I jogged slowly through the warm, deserted noon, and in all my life I have never seen anyone kinder to a nervous, untrained animal than this man, twice accused of murder, was to his black filly. When we parted he asked if I would inquire after a fog-horn he had ordered for a launch he had just put on the lake.

"It ought to be up in the park somewhere," he said. "Perhaps you could bring it down back of your saddle."

Imagine bringing a fog-horn down back of your saddle! And what in the world did he want a fog-horn for anyway? At that time there were only two other boats on the whole eighteen miles of the lake, and they were twelve miles away.

I only saw Mrs. Smith once again after that first visit. I was coming back from Yellowstone a couple of weeks later and a man came into my camp on the Snake River about five o'clock in the morning and asked where the nearest dentist was—he had been suffering for days with a raging toothache. I told him that there was no dentist in the country, but that if he would ride twenty-eight miles south he would find a blacksmith who pulled teeth. He thanked me and departed, and he must have ridden hard, for, following him, I came upon a silver-mounted spur that he had dropped without stopping to pick it up. I gave it back to him when I found him asleep that night in the cabin of the blacksmith. But in the meantime I had passed Mrs. Smith.

She was lying in the grass where the road to her ranch entered the timber, reading a newspaper, her bare legs crossed. It was merely by chance that she had anything on at all, for she was in the habit of taking sun-baths, and once, when she and her husband were wintering in a small neighboring town, she had tried to take her sun-baths on the roof of the hotel porch which stood at the intersection of the two main streets. On this occasion, however, she was doing nothing more sensational than eating peanuts. There was a paper bag on the ground beside her, and as she read she would reach down, take a peanut, put the nut in her mouth, and flip the shell up into the air, all without taking her eyes off the print. As I passed her she laid down her paper and asked: "How's your tooth?"

Now there was only one road, and I had come from the north and so had the man with the toothache, but nevertheless I answered her gently.

"It was not I who had the toothache, Mrs. Smith."

She stood up, threw the paper down indignantly, stared at me a moment, and then stalked off through the trees.

I had already noticed to one side of the road a newly erected shack to which were attached signs announcing that lemonade and candy and tobacco could be bought, and as I was preparing to continue my journey a red-haired young girl, very charming, came out and spoke to me. This was Smith's youngest daughter, who, that summer, had left the wealthy family which had brought her up and had returned to her own kin. She had arrived, I understand, with a boarding-school education and two trunk-loads of expensive finery.

. . . A boarding-school education and two trunk-loads of finery in this wilderness, where her only companions were a couple of half-insane creatures, so afraid of each other that at nightfall they stole out in opposite directions into the timber and hid themselves. Smith told me he had put up the little store to keep the girl amused.

"It's a lonely life for her," he said.

What I could learn of this girl's subsequent history makes a story in itself. But it is vague; I do not know how true the reports are I have heard. I was told that she went out into Idaho and became a waitress—'a biscuit-shooter'—in a cheap hotel, and that later on she drifted to a big city, where she was arrested for theft but acquitted. After that I lost track of her. A charming girl, her red head shining against the dark green of the pines . . . . I could tell a score more stories about Smith and his second wife. The countryside still echoes with them; they have became traditional. But I have only room for one or two more.

Smith was known to a great many people. One of his especial friends was a university professor who is probably the foremost anthropologist in America. Whenever this anthropologist came into the valley he camped at Smith's ranch. The summer I first saw Smith, the professor arrived with a party. Smith got up a dance in honor of the party and, the afternoon before the dance, suggested a ride in the motor-launch—the one for which I was to trace down the fog-horn. Everybody went except the youthful member of the party who told me the story. He was left sitting on the edge of the lake with Mrs. Smith. After a long pause, during which she stared dreamily at the diminishing launch, Mrs. Smith turned to him and said: "Got the makings?"

"My husband," she added thoughtfully, "is an insanely jealous man . . . . He is reported to have killed two people already." She looked at the youthful member of the party with narrowed eyelids.

The youthful member of the party, devoting a moment to reflection, made some excuse and went away into the woods, where he stayed

until the launch returned. That night, at the dance, Mrs. Smith dancing with someone else, Smith in a fit of anger went to bed in the next
room and refused to get up again.

But the launch-party had not been without its own excitements.
Half-way to the other shore the engine had stopped, and Smith,
looking puzzled, had remarked 'that he didn't know much about
launches, as this was the first time he had ever run one, and he had
left his book of instructions at home.' He had then proceeded to
pour gasoline into every likely-looking aperture, and the launch had
given a tremendous hiccough and had backed for a hundred yards.
"I hope it doesn't explode," said Smith, mildly. "A swimmer wouldn't
have a chance in this ice-cold water."

Smith and his second wife were constantly running out of supplies, forgetting to order them, or sometimes, I am afraid, not having
enough money to pay for them. Every now and then they lived on
berries. A friend of mine once met Smith driving a covered wagon to
the nearest store in Yellowstone Park—two days distant.

"We're entirely out of grub," he announced, "and have been for
three days. We haven't even flour."

The following day the same man came across Smith headed in the
opposite direction.

"Did you get your supplies?" he asked in astonishment.

"No. No—but I got something else. Get off your horse and look,"
and Smith lifted up the back-flap of the covered wagon, and there
was the wagon-bed heaped a foot and a half high with wild roses.
"Mrs. Smith is mad about wild roses," sighed Smith.

Towards the end of Smith's life a man staying at my ranch stopped
in upon my recommendation to see him. He had been there only a
few minutes when Smith drew him aside.

"You have probably," he whispered, "noticed something peculiar
about Mrs. Smith. Well, it is true. I am very much worried about

her. I think it must be the altitude. I would like to get her down to California."

Ten minutes passed and then Mrs. Smith took the visitor aside.

"You have probably," she said, "noticed something peculiar about Mr. Smith. Well, it is true. I am very much worried about him. I think it must be the altitude," and so on.

Poor, haunted creatures. The end of it was a lonely cabin buzzing with flies and a discovering party that had to use sulphur to get in.

XXV
OTHER NEIGHBORS

PERHAPS it may seem that I am going fairly far afield for my next three stories, but the first is so curious and the second and third so typical, that they appeal to me as being worth repeating. Besides, in Wyoming every one is a neighbor no matter in what part of the State he lives.

The Bishop of Wyoming gets about all over his immense diocese, and by nature he is a storehouse of unusual tales. Several years ago he was down in a country to the south, an isolated country, thinly settled, and while he was in the hotel of the little town a tall, sandy-haired man in faded, well-cut riding-clothes came up to him.

"Are you the bishop?" he asked, with an English accent.

The bishop admitted his calling.

"Well," said the sandy-haired man, "my name's Macfarland"—I'm not giving his right name—"and I own the Horseshoe Ranch, about twenty miles south of here. I haven't been to church for years, but I used to be a churchman, so any time you get a chance, drop in to see us."

The bishop promised and Macfarland departed, but it was two years before the bishop had a chance to pay his call, and when he asked for Macfarland he was met with smiles. Finally he elicited this story.

It seems that shortly after he had seen Macfarland, Macfarland's foreman—a man we shall call John—came up to the ranch-house one day and said: "Mac, I want to speak to you."

"All right," said Macfarland, "come in."

When the two were seated in the living-room, John, without any further preliminaries, stated his case.

"Mac," he said, "you've been running this here outfit for ten years and it's steadily getting worse. I've been doing some figuring lately and I've calculated that between what you've borrowed from me and what you owe me for wages, you just about owe me this ranch, and considerable more. However, I'll call it square if you turn the place over to me. I'll come up here and live in the ranch-house and you can take your things down to the bunk-house. You ain't a bit of good, but for old times' sake I'll keep you on and pay you forty a month."

"All right," said Macfarland, "that suits me. But what am I to do with Mrs. Macfarland? She can't live in the bunk-house."

"I've took care of that, Mac," said John. "I've had a little talk with Mrs. Macfarland and she don't think no more of you than I do. She don't think you're any kind of a man. So, if it's satisfactory to you, she'll stay right up here in the ranch-house with me."

"All right," said Macfarland for the third time, and packed his things, and went down to the bunk-house, where he lived very happily for a year and a half. At the end of that time he appeared one night in the sitting-room of the ranch-house with a long envelope in his hand.

"John," he said to his ex-foreman but present employer, "the governor's dead, so I guess I'll be getting back to Scotland."

His wife, or former wife, or whatever she was, looked up from her reading. "You've come into the title, Mac?" she asked.

"Yes."

"Well, I think I'd like that even better than this do you mind if I come along?"

"No. Not in the least . . . . "

In the same country the bishop once met the local doctor driving rapidly in a buggy towards the hills with a rifle between his knees and his medicine-case on the seat beside him.

"Where are you going?" asked the bishop.

"Well, you see," explained the doctor, "they've caught a couple of horse thieves up the canyon on a ranch, and they're besieging them, so I thought I'd better be prepared for anything."

That night the bishop noticed a number of young men in town celebrating earnestly. One of them had his arm in a sling and another had a big piece of sticking-plaster on his cheek. Upon inquiry the bishop discovered that these celebrants were the supposed horse thieves and their besiegers.

Apparently there had been a good deal of 'rustling' going on and the country was uneasy. A description of two of the 'rustlers' had been broadcasted, and a week or so after the broadcasting two young men had ridden up to a ranch in the hills and inquired from the owner whether his father, who owned a horse-ranch farther up the canyon, was at home.

"No," the young rancher had replied, "but he'll be back to-morrow."

"Can we go up and wait for him?" the strangers suggested. "We have important business."

"Sure," said the young rancher, "help yourselves."

But afterwards, thinking it over, it had suddenly occurred to him that the two young men looked exceedingly like the 'rustlers,' and he also remembered that his father's ranch was, at the moment, deserted. He at once aroused the neighborhood and a posse started in pursuit.

The posse arrived at the little ranch up the canyon after dark and, disposing itself so no one could escape, waited for the dawn. Shortly after sunup one of the young men came out of the cabin with a bucket in his hand, on his way to the well, and a nervous member of the posse fired from ambush and narrowly missed getting his mark in the leg. The mark, being a wise young man, asked no questions, but ducked back into the cabin, shut the door, and began to reply to the hail of bullets that was now striking the logs. His companion joined him and the battle continued for several hours. Finally the sheriff suggested a truce and went forward, waving a white handkerchief. The two young men came to the door.

"Surrender," said the sheriff.

"What in h— for?" asked the young men.

"What've we done?"

"You know what you've done," said the sheriff.

"No, we don't," they retorted angrily. And they didn't, for they were entirely innocent young men who had legitimate business with the father of the man who had given the alarm.

"You see," said the bishop's informant, "the boys sorter felt they ought to do something for 'em."

Two hundred and fifty miles and more east from us there is a colony of Englishmen which has been in Wyoming many years. Two of these Englishmen are the thirteenth and fourteenth sons of a Scottish baronet and the uncles of a Scottish duke, and another is the next heir to an English earldom. The thirteenth and fourteenth sons of the Scotch baronet and the next heir to the English earldom have been everything from cowpunchers and sheep-herders and camp cooks to members of the State legislature. Now they have prospered, and although they are American citizens they have built themselves—in the way the British have—ranch-houses that resemble as much as possible English country homes. It is strange to come out of the sagebrush and into the shadow of great shaggy hills and find copper jugs filled with hot water, and port after dinner, and, in the case of the thirteenth son who graduated there, an Oxford accent.

Seven years ago I went over to see these Englishmen—really Americans. I could have reached their country in a few days by motor, but I preferred a pack-train—eight days across two mountain ranges; and I did not resort to a motor until I came to the flat country beyond.

Part of the last two days we ran through the Crow Reservation, a splendid rolling up-land with the blue Absorakas off to the southwest and the blue Big Horns off to the southeast. The Crows are a stalwart race; huge, the squaws as big as the men. The men wear immense black pointed sombreros and their hair in plaits. In one of the agency stores we came upon a list of Dead Indian Lands—lands, that is, for sale to white men under what seems to me to be a by no means wise government ruling. On one side of the list were printed the Crow, or Absoraka, names, and on the other the quaint English translations.

Mint or Peppermint.
McKinley Backbone.
Many Wives.
Mary Wears Nothing.
Takes His Enemies in a Fog.
John Slides Down Well.
Don't Care.

And then, lingering and lovely, Sits with the Stars.

In the Crow country I saw an ancient squaw and a thunder-storm. We had missed the road and late in the afternoon we turned into a little Crow ranch—the only one in sight—to ask our way. Dusk was approaching, and over to the west the Absorakas were caught up in clouds, and to the east the Big Horns were a wall of darkness. But in front of us, from zenith to horizon, above the rolling country where the grass trembled in the wind, the sky was blood-red—red as in any painting of Remington, whose colors artists deny. Standing before a great white teepee that had been erected to one side of the log ranch-house was the old squaw wrapped in a blanket. She did not move as we stopped our car, she continued to lean upon her cane, and her face had no expression in it. Her little eyes were like burnt-out coals and she was so old that the skin of her face was hardly visible for the wrinkles. She would not answer us, but presently a young girl came out of the cabin and directed us with the beautiful straight-handed, fingers together, gestures of the Indian. We turned about and climbed a hill, and as we did so I looked back.

Outlined against the approaching storm and the blood-red sky was the old squaw, her shawl flapping like the coat of a scarecrow, her stick raised in the air, cursing us. She looked like some dark fragment of cloud blown out before the thunder . . . . Two hours later we were in a modern Montana town and in the bedroom of a hotel, the furniture of which was covered with cretonne.

The following day we came back to the Crow country again and the company of its big-hatted residents, and that night we found another contrast even more dramatic than the hotel with its chintz. Our lamps picked up in the darkness clipped hedges and white fences, and pretty soon we turned in through a gate and found a lighted house and a lawn as smooth as velvet and shaded by trees exotic to Wyoming. Beside the car trotted a man in white flannels, who carried a lantern and greeted us in the accents of the Thames valley. Across eleven years and thousands of miles, at the foot of great mountains only known well for half a century, and at not such a distance from where, but four decades earlier, Custer and his men had been massacred, I came once more into the presence of the Char and the Isis. They are a great people, the English—quietly unconquerable.

At the moment the brother of the English earl was away, helping as best he could the England whose citizenship he had given up, but to whose aid he returned when she was in trouble, but his youngest son was there, a completely American boy of eleven, who, so far as I could make out, had never been out of the United States, and who resented the slightest implication that he wasn't an American—which, of course, he was. And where this boy was concerned something interesting was going on. This boy—they were afraid to tell him because he was such a thoroughgoing American—had at the time every chance of becoming the next Earl of So-and-So, whether he wanted or not, for his oldest brother, who had been brought up at Eton in order that he might be prepared to accept the title his father would never claim, was at the front in a Guard regiment. As things turned out, the elder brother came out of the war unscathed, but all that summer and the next the small boy in the heart of Wyoming stood upon the brink of a hazard that would have changed his life forever.

They tell a story about his father—a very absent-minded man. Whenever, in the old days, he went down to the station riding a pony, to see any one off, the station agent would take out his jack-knife and stand by to cut the reins of the pony as the train departed, for the brother of an earl was in the habit of tying his mount to the railing of the rear car and forgetting him until it was too late.

I have left the young missionary—the young 'sin-twister' whom I took out and lost on his first visit to me, and who for a while was a near and dear neighbor—to the last, on the principle, now abandoned, that everything ought to start or end with a grace. He was a good missionary; a blue-eyed, rosy-cheeked, light-haired young missionary, who bought a horse and put on a flannel shirt and chaps, and rode up and down the country doing an immense amount of good and talking about everything but holiness. He had not a trace of the sanctified attitude which seems to be given away nowadays with the diplomas of most divinity schools. In his presence you felt somehow that with all your faults you still had a fair chance of heaven. Even old Bill Holliday, after observing him in silence for two years, remarked: "That fellow's pretty near as good a man as if he wasn't a parson, isn't he? "

The young parson came into the valley first in answer to an advertisement inserted in a church paper by the bishop, who was in despair of getting anybody to fill the job, but who, none the less, being an honest man, painted the situation in the blackest of colors. The young parson accepted the call in a letter in which he said he had a large and wealthy parish on the Hudson, but that he was 'tired of trying to save the souls of people who were already sure they were saved.' He had only been in the valley a short time before he built two small log churches—beautiful little log churches—and a log hospital, that has saved many lives, and a parish house of logs, where he had his own quarters and a man's club-room with a library and billiard-tables.

I recall snowy winter evenings when I had skied down from the ranch and the young parson would greet me with a fire and supper, and a long talk afterwards, and, finally, a white and cool bed. Also, at times, a glass of sherry—yes, Heaven be praised, a glass of sherry! For, although a most abstemious man, in this respect he agreed with St. Chrysostom and all the other fathers of the church. One moonlit night in summer the young parson christened my youngest child on the front porch of the ranch. The congregation sat about on Navajo rugs on the grass. To the west rose the black rampart of The Tetons, like the last hills of life before the wide and vacant plains of death are reached, and to the east and north and south the silver valley spread away soft and obscure with the obscurity of life. Picked out by the moonlight, and in the halo of the lamp on the table beside him, was the big missionary with the little child in his arms.

He has left the valley now, alas, the young missionary, and is over doing what he can with the Arapahoes. He has a log chapel there, too, with a huge plate-glass window back of the altar that is the most beautiful church window I have ever seen. I heard service there once in the early morning, and the rolling valley beyond the chapel and the snow-capped mountains that bounded the valley made a stained-glass panorama far finer than any man could contrive.

I like ministers—if they will only permit me to like them. When I was a little boy I once pinched out of pure affection the legs of a bishop who was staying with my grandfather.—My grandfather's house was always filled with bishops and clergymen. I admire the clergyman's calling and his supposed single-mindedness. Besides, being an outdoor man, I am inclined to be religious. The out of-doors is mysterious and brooding. But I do not like indoor men to tell me about it, and I do not like them to tell me of a God who knows nothing of forests and quiet places; a small and spiteful God occupied solely with what his neighbors eat and wear and drink.

XXVI
BAD MEN

ON an unfortunate day, and a good many years ago, someone confused the extreme western edge of Wyoming, due to a similarity in names, with the 'Hole in the Wall' country many miles to the north and east, and ever since then the extreme western edge of Wyoming has enjoyed a reputation not at all deserved. Not long ago my partner, the doctor, while on a train, was asked his destination by an elderly gentleman, and when he replied the valley, the elderly gentleman pursed his lips and inquired whether he was 'after someone or making a getaway.' Furthermore, when alert and temporarily unoccupied citizens—every now and then a girl—held up the stages in Yellowstone Park in the days, not such a great while back, when the stages were held up, even the newspapers of eastern Wyoming, who should have known better, spoke of the ease with which the hero of the 'stick-up' could escape to the 'notorious' south, and his immunity from arrest while there.

Nothing, of course, could be further from the truth. To begin with, the valley is a small and open country surrounded by immense forests, and anyone entering it, unless he were able to live indefinitely upon berries and bark, would eventually have to show himself and would be immediately recognized, and, in the second place, there are only five roads from the outside. And finally, the valley isn't that sort of a country and never has been.

The 'Hole in the Wall' was a real Lorna Doone community to which most of the road-agents and train-robbers of that part of the Northwest fled and where they lived, some of them with their families, very contentedly. The one entrance was through a narrow, precipitous canyon, guarded day and night by men with Winchesters. The 'Hole in the Wall' no longer exists, although I was interested to read in a book written by two men who a few years ago made the trip from the headwaters of the Green River to the outlet of the Colorado that they had discovered a similar 'bad man's' village in southern Utah. But at no period of its history, even in the beginning, could there have been anything less like the 'Hole in the Wall' than our valley.

It never had for any length of time more than one famous bad citizen, and he moved out—or, rather, was moved out. This gentleman rejoiced in the name of 'Teton' Jackson, and he used to run stolen horses in from the East and sell them in the West, and then run stolen horses in from the West and sell them in the East. He is now, from what I have heard, unless he is dead, a respected and substantial man somewhere to the south—a bank director, unless my informant was mistaken or jocose. Black Horse, the Arapahoe policeman I have mentioned, was the man who finally captured him, but Black Horse himself admits that he followed 'Teton' and his wife several days before he dared come up with them, and then only arrested them when both were sleeping peacefully one hot noon under their wagon.

The chances for arrest or non-arrest seem to be largely a matter of fortune. The last man who held up the stage in Yellowstone Park was finally caught only because he made the mistake of thinking a cow-puncher was a sheep-herder, and Hugh Whitney, a young ranch-hand who went 'bad' over in Idaho and killed a bartender, and afterwards a sheriff and a conductor on the railway, disappeared completely after living for several years in the mountains south of us. The supposition is that he went to South America.

Concerning Whitney's diagonal flight across country to his hiding-place, the story is told of a man of boastful proclivities, one of the pursuing posse, who came too close to the fugitive. He is supposed to have ridden up to a ranch and inquired from the owner if 'a red-haired freckle-faced young fellow had gone by.'

"Yes," said the rancher—"about five minutes ago."

"Oh!" replied the subpoenaed limb of the law thoughtfully. "Well, I must be getting back to the other fellows and tell them about it—they're five miles back."

The last man who held up Yellowstone Park—un-aided he held up eighteen stages—was a rancher out in Idaho. Before embarking on his adventure he stole two horses from the outfit I was then with, and it was these two horses that led to his eventual downfall. Several years later, long after pursuit had been abandoned, he rode into a sheep-camp with these two horses and asked the solitary herder if he could have supper. The herder answered "Yes, of course," and while he was preparing the meal—Stafford—that will do for his name—held his host up, tied him to his wagon, and stole everything he had. But un-fortunately for Stafford the sheep-herder had been a cowpuncher, and he remembered Stafford's outfit in detail and also that the brands on Stafford's horses looked as if a wet blanket and straight iron had been used on them. Stafford was arrested for horse-stealing and his latest robbery, and, through this, his exploit in Yellowstone Park was traced.

It is claimed that at the time of his arrest he was working on an armored car, which he intended to use to kidnap the president of the Mormon Church and hold him for ransom.

Rapid and easy communication is the destroyer of marked local traits and since, even now, rapid and easy communication is difficult in a big mountain country, mountain valleys retain their characteristics long after the plains have been ground down to a dull similarity. The inhabitants of mountain valleys talk differently, think differently, have different customs, and even dress differently from their neighbors. My country, far from being the haunt of bad men, has always, if anything, been more peaceable and less dramatic than the three valleys immediately adjacent. The contrasts between these four countries are interesting.

To the northeast is a country that has for years been a tourist country, root and branch; all other industries are subservient to this main industry, and perhaps for this reason, and for others as well, such as the original temper of the inhabitants, it is a country known for the ornamental dressing of its citizens and the fact that they wear guns. Gaudy handkerchiefs, flaring silver-studded chaps, buckskin shirts are common, and the last time I was there I camped near a schoolhouse where a dance was going on, and I have never heard so much unnecessary shooting in my life.

Directly to the east and the southeast are two other valleys, different from the first in the common facts that both are essentially cattle and sheep countries, and yet different in details from each other. The upper valley is smaller, farther from centers of population, and more feudal, having been held for years by a number of long-settled families. It is, therefore, conservative, peaceable, and self-contained. Moreover, being close to a couple of Indian reservations, its whole essence has been altered by this fact.

The valley below it, cut off from the valley to the north by huge mountain ranges, is in closer touch with the railway and is more subject to the vagaries of a floating and uncertain population. How it is now I do not know, but a few years ago it was fairly turbulent, and many of its inhabitants did not think themselves properly dressed unless they had a piece of steel hanging to their hips. And it was out of this country there came one of the grimmest stories I ever remember hearing, of a girl who was branded by her father because of some trouble she had with a young man, and of how her father was shot from ambush the next day, and his murderer never discovered.

My own country has never been given to wearing guns. It is considered the height of bad manners, and—what is more effective—

ridiculous into the bargain, to carry a gun unless you are going into the hills. By the same token, it has always been a country of conservative dress. The universal uniform is a pair of overalls, or ordinary wool trousers, a denim shirt, an unobtrusive sombrero, and a pair of worn chaps. Even neck-handkerchiefs and cow-boots are confined as a rule to those actually engaged in the stock business, or to the dude-men and the younger generation. Incidentally, the female portion of the younger generation has recently taken to wearing overalls, also; a curious sign of progress if you recall the time, only a short while ago, when even riding-breeches were looked upon with disfavor by Western maidens.

This lack of flamboyancy on the part of my country has been due largely, I imagine, to the type of settler who first located there, but also, to some extent, to the situation of the country itself. The valley is entered from the west, so it is in closer touch with countries farther away than it is with its neighbors immediately to the east, and, owing to its great forests, it has never been a big stock country, but a country of small holdings—an essentially neighborly, law-abiding, and peaceful community, attracting in the beginning not so much the cattleman and his swaggering buckaroos as the quieter and more solitary frontiersman—the miner and small rancher, and trapper and hunter.

These reflective and lonely men established a civilization after their own liking, and even to-day, when the cattle business has expanded greatly and the cow-puncher has drifted in, and the sons of the original settlers are cowpunchers themselves, the color and disposition of the valley are the same. Furthermore, and most important of all, you must remember that big game has always been the predominant feature and most pressing question. It is at the back of everyone's mind and conditions thinking.

A ban upon guns and extravagance in general is an aid towards keeping the community which wishes to be peaceful all the more peaceful, but naturally no sparsely settled country, settled by individualistic thinkers, and where the hand of the law is light, gets along altogether without adding an occasional chapter to its history, and I will say that when the valley does add a chapter to its history it seems always to add a more than usually exciting one.

On the road between the local town and the great lake to the north, forty miles away, are two graves that have been there a long time. No one knows who occupies them or ever will know. Two young men—well-spoken, pleasant-appearing young men—rode into town one summer afternoon and let it be known that they were looking for a ranch. A few days later, hearing of a ranch, they went up-country to investigate. They had no sooner left than a third stranger, claiming to be a sheriff, arrived on horseback, followed by several men. He said that he had a warrant for the young men's arrest on the charge of horse-stealing, and demanded that he be shown where they were. For this purpose he took along with him several of the settlers.

So far everything had been entirely normal, but from then on events were out of the ordinary, for the supposed sheriff and his men, arriving at the ranch where the two young men were, sent in one of the local ranchers to call them out, and when the two young men appeared, shot them down without a word of explanation. He then held off the local men at the point of a pistol and rode out of the country as mysteriously as he had come. Afterwards the resident end of the posse remembered that at no time had it seen the supposed sheriff's papers.

But the most curious and dramatic chapter in the valley's history was written only a short while ago in connection with the feud—the range war—I have already mentioned. It took eleven years in the telling and it is not finished yet.

Fifteen years ago in the spring, after the snows had gone, up a mountain draw directly opposite our ranch and only a couple of miles away, the blackened remains of a wagon were found. Evidently the previous autumn someone had camped there and before leaving had built a huge fire and had destroyed all traces of occupancy except the charred ring the flames had left and the steel parts of a wagon—wheel rims and bolts and chains and so on—that would not burn. I saw these twisted relics in the yard of the local justice of the peace where they had been taken. The discovery was made by a game-warden and a young cowpuncher who had gone up to estimate the depredations amongst the moose five brothers, recently come from Colorado, had committed during the winter. The five brothers are not essential to the story; they are all by now worthy citizens in various parts of the West; but they had come into the country absolutely without money and practically starving and, taking up an abandoned trapper's cabin on the shores of a lake, had lived on the game and defied the game-wardens to come and get them. They had left by the time the game-wardens arrived, and subsequently, when questioned, proved that they knew nothing whatsoever about the main incident of this tale.

Here were the strange features of what came to be known locally as 'the wagon mystery.'

In the first place, camp had been made in a draw over a quarter of a mile from water—a spot no sensible camper would choose; in the second place, the wagon had been a new one and therefore somewhat valuable as a foundation for a bonfire; in the third place, no one remembered, in a country where every horse and wagon is instantly marked, having seen the wagon or its occupants the previous autumn; and, in the fourth place, even if a murder had been committed, and that was the obvious explanation, what had been the purpose of burning the wagon? The horses had not been burned, and if a man could take the horses out of the valley, he could have taken the wagon too; indeed, the burning of the wagon was a bit of flagrant stupidity, since it left unmistakable traces and aroused a hue and cry. Whoever burned the wagon could have driven it out quietly and no questions would have been asked.

Casting around in a circle for other clews, the game-warden and the young cowpuncher came upon perhaps the strangest relic of all. Cached under a rock fifty yards or so away from where the wagon had been burned was a rifle of special make wrapped in oilskin. This presented a bit of psychological evidence if nothing else. Evidently the man who had placed it there so carefully had been unwilling, however he might have felt about another man or a wagon, to destroy this fine firearm, and had intended some day to return and recover it. And, as time went on, the rifle proved to be not only a piece of psychological evidence but the only evidence that proved of any value at all.

The firm that had made the rifle was written to and replied that, although in most cases they would have no idea to whom their special makes were sold, in this case the buyer had written directly to the factory and that his name—let us say—was Greene, and that he had lived in a small town in Montana. Upon further inquiry it was found that Greene had only lived in the small town a short while and had left the previous spring in a new Studebaker wagon with a man named—let us say—Thompson.

In other words, either Greene had killed Thompson and then had burned the wagon, or Thompson had killed Greene and had burned the wagon, or no one had killed anyone, and between them Thompson and Greene had burned the wagon for some reason much more unaccountable than the desire to hide a murder. But the last was not very reasonable, because of the finding of Greene's gun, and the first was not probable for the same reason. Undoubtedly Thompson had killed Greene, and undoubtedly somewhere in the maze of forest and lake and canyon was Greene's body . . . .It is there to-day. It has never been found. The clew presented by the rifle petered out. Greene and Thompson had been swallowed up in thin air.

All this took place fifteen years ago and for eleven years nothing more happened. As we take up the story again you must listen for a while to something that apparently has nothing to do with the original plot.

Far to the south, at the end of the valley, a small range war that had been smoldering for a couple of years burst into flame, and two men were killed and two others were arrested.

The principal figure in this range war was a man of evil reputation, although how much he deserves this reputation I do not know. He is a handsome fellow, white-haired and fine-featured, and the very day the killings he is supposed to have instigated were taking place I saw him in the local hotel—establishing an alibi, some say—playing most charmingly with his little daughter. But years before he had killed a man under suspicious circumstances and had served a term in the penitentiary, and it was known that he had warned all newcomers to keep away from the part of the valley in which he lived, and to leave his range alone. The majority obeyed him, but a few didn't, and among the latter were two mature bachelor brothers—fine men and pleasant—who homesteaded and began to run a small bunch of cattle directly in the middle of the forbidden territory. One day they were reported missing and a posse went down to investigate.

A burned ranch-house was found—the fire had taken place a week or so earlier—but no traces of the brothers save this, a charred torso with two bullet holes in it under a fallen ridge log. Save for the ridge log there would have been, as in 'the wagon mystery,' another case of a missing body. But the torso was identified and proved sufficient evidence and, because of what had been going on for the past two years, the exclusive cattleman and his eldest son, just discharged from the army, were arrested. The cattleman was able to prove an alibi, but the eldest son wasn't, and then, to the astonishment of every one, the sheriff arrested a man named—let us say—'Bearcat' Roberts, who lived on a little place next door to the cattleman and who had worked for him. A man so harmless—so the country thought—that the name 'Bearcat' had been given him in derision; a shuffling, quiet, peaceable man. Bit by bit the evidence was pieced together, and it was found that 'Bearcat' and the eldest son had shot one of the brothers, a man crippled with rheumatism, through a window of the cabin, and afterwards had ridden out on to the range and had shot the other brother and had packed his dead body back on a saddle-horn to where the holocaust was to take place.

Fairly cold-blooded—to shoot a man and throw him over your saddle and ride with the dripping body in front of you for a couple of miles or more. 'Bearcat' and the eldest son were sent to the penitentiary.

But here is where the strange grim story draws together. Up in Montana, a ranchman reading in a paper a description of these murders and of 'Bearcat,' and something stirring in his mind, wrote to the penitentiary and asked if 'Bearcat' had certain marks upon his body. The warden wrote back that he had. 'Very well,' said the ranchman in his second letter, 'then he is the man who formerly called himself Thompson, and who eleven years ago left this country with a man named Greene and was subsequently never heard from. If you can find Greene's body you've got the man who killed him.'

Greene's body, however, as I have said, hasn't been found and never will be found; in fact, no one really knows that he is dead; so 'Bearcat' is just where he was before. But imagine the mental background.

Facts in themselves are never as interesting as what makes the facts, and here is a man—that is, if any of the story is true—who killed another man under peculiarly haunting circumstances, yet who calmly came back in five years or so to the country where he had done the killing, and settled down, and, after a while, killed two other men. Probably the only thing he regretted was that the beloved gun he had so carefully cached had been found.

In connection with this tale there are two vivid complementary incidents. The night the murder was discovered the cattleman, a gun on his hip, strode through the hall of the little hotel of the nearest town to a room where a preliminary hearing was being held. The narrow hall was lined on either side with men, also armed, who hated the cattleman, and their nerves were on edge. Had he at any time touched them with his elbow or pushed one of them aside, another murder would have been added to the already long list. A man who was there told me that you could feel the tenseness. And five miles or so from the cattleman's home, up a lonely valley, lives a Swiss who was the first man to suspect that anything was wrong and who was the man who rode into town to give the alarm. But he had difficulty getting away the night of his discovery. He crept out of his cabin and as he did so he saw, high up on a ridge above him, some one strike a match and light a cigarette, and he realized that he was being watched.

There is no doubt in my mind that the real 'killer' is a homicidal maniac, a man with a kink in his brain to whom the object of a crime is as nothing compared to the interest taken in the perpetration of it. 'Billy the Kid,' in the Southwest, who murdered twenty-four people before he was twenty-one was undoubtedly insane, and so was 'Shorty Smith' up in our country, who added to his list by shooting, several years ago, for the seventy-five dollars he had in his pockets, a boy with whom he had spent four snowy solitary months winter-keeping a government road-house. You don't shoot the only living thing in sight, especially for seventy-five dollars, unless you are mad.

But if real 'killers' are homicidal maniacs and therefore likely to kill any one at any time, they are, fortunately, extremely rare, and the average man who has been called 'bad' is either not bad at all or, at the worst, merely a coward. Not that cowardly 'bad men' are to be encouraged; they are almost as dangerous as the real 'killer,' and, their numbers being greater, have probably done far more damage. The old Western saying that 'the fellow you want to watch is the fellow whose finger trembles on the trigger' has much sense to it. But if the weakness of the cowardly 'bad man' is appreciated he is not difficult to handle. The majority of 'bad men' anywhere in the world are men who have killed some one accidentally and are too cowardly to stop—they are haunted by ghosts and see a potential enemy in every one who comes over the nearest hill.

My former partner told me that he knew in Nevada a little sheriff, crippled with rheumatism, who never packed a gun and who never failed to bring in his man. When he overtook the fugitive he would sit calmly down under the other's leveled revolver and argue the matter out. "There's no use your killing me," he would say. "I'm old and all worn out and haven't a gun. They'll catch you in the end, and if you've killed me you'll sure hang; otherwise you've got a chance." The brave men needed no second invitation to surrender themselves, and the cowards were paralyzed by bravery, as they always are.

The 'good bad man,' the man who does not know what fear is, but who, for some reason, has turned his killing abilities in the direction of law and order, is, in my private opinion, just as insane as his homicidal brother and just as mysterious in his impulses. I do not understand the pleasure of tracking down or killing another man, even if he is an outlaw. I should imagine at the best these to be grim and unpleasant duties. The average detective is no engaging figure in my eyes; his job has to be done, but I believe that in most cases it is done by men who through no virtues of their own but by mere good fortune find themselves using their unstable mentalities in the prevention instead of the accomplishment of crime. Down in New Mexico I came across a sheriff who had a record of twelve Mexicans with crippled right arms. He never killed a man; he always shot his victim's biceps out as he tried to draw his gun.

A great many men who have achieved a reputation for badness have achieved it undeservedly. In the West to steal horses in your youth used to be—and still is to some extent—an exploit of wildness somewhat similar to getting drunk, although it was, and is, rarer and more dangerous. Some of the finest men I have ever met had a faint aroma of this juvenile un-sanctity about them. One man who subsequently worked for us was a famous bad man when I first came into the valley. The third or fourth week I was in the country I passed a number of horsemen riding in the other direction, and when I asked one whom I knew what they were doing, he replied that they were after Tom, who was travelling due north with a band of horses.

Tom established a name for himself for casual bravery and carefulness in certain respects. He never tried to shoot anyone, and he never stole horses from a friend or from his own country. As to the former quality, on one occasion, when followed by a sheriff's posse, he pushed his stolen horses into a river raging in flood and, swimming after them, from the other bank kissed his hand and waved his hat to his baffled pursuers; and on another occasion, being warned that a man was in town who had sworn to kill him on sight, he went over to the saloon where the man was, walked twenty feet or so from the door to the rear of the room in the face of a drawn revolver, took the revolver from the hands of its owner and slapped the owner's face.

But Tom was not a bad man; he was merely an unstable man with a childish love of action and adventure, as we unfortunately discovered when we hired him. He was anything but a bad man; he was the most genial and the kindliest soul alive, gentle and generous to a fault. Nor was he always brave. At the height of his career—my first summer in the valley—he was brought up by night in order that he might consult the doctor, who made furniture, about a painful swelling that appears sometimes on the neck and sometimes where you ride horses, but which is never dangerous. Tom, however, thought he was going to die.

Nate, the lanky ex-cowpuncher who went on the original antelope hunting-party, and who, when the other doctor and myself started our ranch, worked as our head man for a while, also had a reputation for badness when I first met him. I was warned that he would steal the rope off my saddle—and while I was looking too. As a matter of fact, I have never known in all my life a more honest man, or one more sensitive to obligation. He has almost too sensitive a sense of obligation; he refuses to be under obligation to any one, and he is not happy until he has paid a favor back.

His history is a curious one. His first recollections are of an Arizona cow-camp where he was a child of four with long golden curls—he has no knowledge of his father or mother—and it must have been a poor sort of a cow-camp, for the outfit was in the habit of drying its hands on Nate's curls after the evening wash-up.

"If I ever see one of those sons of so on," Nate once informed me grimly, "I'll kill him even if he is a grandfather."

After Arizona, Nate drifted to California, to Nevada, to Oregon and Alberta and Montana; finally to Wyoming. He chose his own name and taught himself to read and write when he was about thirty-five years old. Starting with nothing at all, he has by now acquired two profitable ranches, and during the winter indulges a taste for travelling. Not long ago a famous motion-picture actress patronized him in the following manner, and received the following answer.

The blond-haired screen star was doing a Western and was on location in the valley, and was being very kind and gracious, indeed, to all "the dear simple people."

Having heard that the proper way to address a native when first meeting him was to ask him how he had wintered, she asked Nate.

"Fine," he replied. "I wintered in Paris, Berlin, and Rome."

Several years ago, just before the war, Nate made a triumphal tour of the East, starting in Chicago, where he speedily became a civic institution, and ending up in Philadelphia and New York. In Chicago he fell in with what he called the "Alley" Bazaar, not inappropriately—each city at the time vying with the others in the expensiveness and labor of these bazaars—and met any number of opera singers and actors and 'Follies' girls and millionaires. Two months later, when I went through Chicago on my way West, I found that all I had to do to introduce myself was to mention Nate's name.

Nate was so popular in Chicago that, as he himself expressed it, he had to make his getaway from that city between sundown and sunup. His next stop was Philadelphia, where he went hunting with the fox-hunting crowd, and after an initial hunt, in which he lost his seat several times, never having ridden an English saddle before, became one of the first flight. In New York he stayed with the portrait-painter who had been our first dude. The portrait-painter gave a dinner in Nate's honor and put him next to a newly arrived French countess—a French countess who was the very last word in worldliness and who was famous for her somewhat decadent tastes. Nate, I may add, has a way with women. After dinner the portrait-painter asked him what he thought of the countess, and he replied that he had found her one of the nicest, simplest, commonest—used in the correct sense—little women he had ever become acquainted with . . . .

The very worst man I ever met was a white-haired, kindly-looking man—until you scrutinized his eyes—who wore a conservative sombrero without any dents in it, and a black suit, and who looked exactly like a New England deacon. He was the worst because he had all the coldness of the New England deacon turned bad. I only heard him laugh once, and that was when we were nooning one day in the shade of some cottonwood trees out on a partial desert. The "deacon" was lying on his back, his hands crossed behind his head, staring up at the cloudless sky, when suddenly he began to chuckle.

"What are you laughing at?" I asked.

"You remember I told you I once ran a gambling place in Juarez?" he replied. "Well, when the revolution broke out I and a nigger cowpuncher manned a machine-gun, and I was just a-thinking of the didos them Mexicans cut up when we turned loose on them. Laugh? I near died!"

XXVII
'THE OLD WEST'

IT is very difficult in writing of your memories not to bewail the past. The only thing that prevents you from doing so is your knowledge that in twenty years you will be weeping over what is now the present. Once upon a time I started a private investigation of my own.

I had heard that the cowboy 'was dead' and although in the twenty-odd years of my Western life I had seen a great many young men and mature men and even elderly men who thought themselves cowboys, I wanted to be assured of the facts. I asked the oldest man I knew when the last cowboy had hung up his saddle and put away his spurs and chaps.

"About eighteen eighty," he said. "There haven't been any real cowboys since then."

This was a trifle startling, for, if true, the cowboy had died almost before he was born. Up until the Civil War there weren't many cowboys outside of Texas.

Unperturbed, I continued my research. The next man I asked was a middle-aged man who had abandoned the range and settled down to ranching in the late nineties.

"Max," I asked, "when in your opinion was the real cattle life over?"

"Well," he replied thoughtfully, "I should say about nineteen hundred."

My last informant was a young rancher who, beside a red-hot stove one winter night, had been telling me of a cattle drift in a Montana blizzard five years earlier. "We followed 'em," he said, "three days with not a thing to eat, froze to our saddles. And then we come to a deserted cabin. Whoever had been there had left some soup in an iron pot and it had turned to ice, but, before turning, two mice had drowned in it. We heated it up and swallowed it down." . . . He sighed. "It ain't what it used to be. They're all Montgomery Ward buckaroos now."

And this, mind you—this cattle drift, the most epic and dramatic of all possible incidents in a cowpuncher's life—had taken place thirty years after my first witness claimed that all cowpunchers were dead, and ten years after the date set by my second witness.

"Dick," I said to the young rancher—his nickname was 'Dismal Dick '—"what year do you set as the year the old West vanished?"

"About nineteen thirteen," he decided finally.

"And when, Dick," I continued, "did you quit riding and take up a ranch?"

"About nineteen fourteen."

So you see my theory was vindicated and a perfect chain of evidence was formed. The psychology underlying it is common enough. Having been a university man, I have met with the same phenomenon before. Most universities end—that is, all the heroism and hardihood and good times end—as each class graduates.

Now that I myself am in my middle years I find that, like everyone else, I have to catch myself constantly lest I fall into this intellectual error. "Neither the West nor life in general is as adventurous and authentic as they were in my youth." Aren't they? They really are. It is I who have changed, not the West nor the world.

It is a very difficult thing to keep young, but it is very necessary.

In the eyes of the Westerner the cowpuncher dies whenever that particular Westerner, if he has been a cowpuncher, gives up punching cows and settles down to ranching. In other words, the cowpuncher has ceased to exist every day of every year since he first became a distinct national figure. Meanwhile, scattered all over the Rocky Mountain States, and in Texas and Oregon and Washington and

Nevada and even California, are thousands of young men who regard themselves as cowpunchers and who are earning their forty dollars a month, much as their fathers and grandfathers did before them. If you asked one of them if he was a cowboy he would be as much astonished as a broker's clerk in Wall Street would be if you asked him if he was a broker's clerk.

The cowboy cannot die for the simple reason that there are millions of acres of land that can be used only for grazing purposes, and while such acres exist the cowboy will exist along with them. Nor has his life changed as greatly as many imagine. To be sure, there are no longer the drives of hundreds of miles from ranches to shipping-points, or from the arid Southwest to the summer grass ranges of the Northwest, but there are still drives of respectable length, length sufficient at least to invoke the qualities and atmosphere of the longer drives, and there is loneliness, and there are bucking horses, and stampeding cattle, and the use of a rope, and cold and heat and dust and wide horizons.

Moreover, as my good friend, Philip Ashton Rollins, who has written that excellent book, 'The Cowboy,' has said, the West is a state of mind, and a state of mind lasts longer than any material circumstance. It is the most intangible and at the same time the most immutable of things. Even in the present-day Western towns—Far Western towns, I mean, of course; towns somewhere near the sweep of mountains and deserts—there lingers an aroma that strikes the nostrils of your imagination with the sharp, acrid scent of wood smoke curling up from a log-cabin chimney on an October morning. The Far Western town outwardly is utterly changed from the collection of log or adobe houses that marked its beginning, but it is not changed spiritually. There is the same largeness and warmth and casualness; the same exotic exhilaration. All the latest secrets of plumbing cannot wash away the fact that here is a community set down in a country whose boundaries fade into the level infinity of plains or the perpendicular infinity of hills and skies.

And in scores of places the old West not only has not changed spiritually, it has not changed actually. The truth of the matter is this. In such localities where soil or climate or altitude permit, the West in its more obvious phases has become a broader sort of East, but in localities where the soil or climate or altitude do not permit, the West is much as it has always been. In short, 'the old West' is spotted; but the spots are large and many of them bid fair to be permanent.

I find that people are astonished when I tell them what should be common knowledge; that there are places in America that have never been adequately explored; that there are still a few countries into which no white man has ever set foot; that there are still huge cattle outfits; that you can duplicate in all respects the adventures and ardors of the pioneer.

In Oregon, in Nevada, in other States, there are towns scores of miles from the railway; in Idaho there are forests where you can travel two hundred miles without seeing a habitation; in Wyoming there are deserts where you can do the same thing. The human horizon is too often limited by the immediate foreground. In the huge dining-room of the Canyon Hotel in Yellowstone Park you can look through the plate-glass windows to a country across the Yellowstone River that practically does not know what a man is. And anywhere in our national parks, off the highways, crowded with motors, are unbroken solitudes. I wonder how many of the tourists in Yellowstone Park, or the other parks, realize this? I wonder if they have ever stopped to think what Yellowstone Park, let us say, is like after it closes—in September, or October, or in the winter? A lonely, majestic place.

In central Idaho there is a huge country so rough that what few ranches there are perch themselves in the little deltas of the rivers twenty-five miles and more apart. And you are not able to leave the trails that lead to these ranches, because they twist along such precipitous cliffs. This is an old country. It was known at the time of the Civil War and has been the scene of several unsuccessful gold rushes. But now its population has almost disappeared. There are a few deserted mines where old mine-keepers live with their Chinese wives, or by themselves, and some of these mine-keepers have not been outside for twenty or thirty years.

In Montana there is a broad valley where every fence is down and the cabins of the homesteaders are falling to pieces, for all the land has been bought back again by the great cattle company that once owned it. And even in my own valley something of this same process has been going on and would have been accelerated had not the cattle business fallen recently upon evil days. Originally, all the land being government land, no man, no matter how rich, could obtain more than a homestead and a desert claim. But of late years, until the years of bankruptcy, the inevitable evolution was taking place and the men who had done well were buying out their shiftless neighbors.

The valley, however, had never been sufficiently overrun by miners or homesteaders or settlers of any kind to make the process obvious. Even to-day most of it is still untouched. Two years ago I took a pack-horse and made an eight-day trip in the mountains back of the principal town. My route lay in a circle and at no time was I more than twenty-five miles away from a motor road, and yet in all that time I came across only one horse track, and that was over a month old, and I took horses into a country where no horses had ever been before.

Last summer I spent a week in a country not forty miles from our upper ranch, that was only explored and plotted and, to all intents and purposes discovered four years ago, and later on, with another pack-train, I wandered for three weeks through the mountains to the east and saw—save once—not a soul outside of our party except on the day before we made the ranch again. On that day I came across an old friend leading a pack-horse across the Continental Divide. But then, curiously enough, the Continental Divide is always an excellent place to meet friends you have not seen for a long time. They appear out of the distance, exchange a few words with you, and disappear into the distance. I suppose this phenomenon is due to the fact that on a height of land as gigantic as this trails converge— Nor are these adventures of mine with loneliness exceptional. Far from it. Unfortunately I am too busy and my travels too circumscribed by my work for me to hunt out the countries I really want to see.

If it is easy enough to understand why the 'old-timer' thinks the cowboy is dead and tells you so solemnly, it is not quite so easy to understand why the Easterner, having just discovered the West, discovered at the same time that not only the cowboy but the entire West as well was 'dead.' For you must remember that the West has only interested the East for the last fifteen or twenty years. The cowboy, especially, as a dramatic and lyric figure, is a recent find; the motion-pictures are not very old; the Western novel has been written by those still in the prime of life; and the magazines devoted exclusively to the West are as yet mere children. Here is a puzzle and a paradox. No sooner do we introduce the cowboy and the miner and the cattleman and the homesteader to ourselves and the Chinaman and the South American and the Hindoo and the Parsee, than we discover that we must proclaim all such types corpses, buried a long while ago . . . . But that we have introduced them sufficiently, even if they are corpses, there is not the slightest doubt.

A few years ago I was back in Oxford for a prolonged visit and a young peer hunted me out because I was a ranchman in Wyoming. He entertained me and followed me about. He was a handsome boy and the possessor of a title famous in English naval history, and he seemed a nice boy, but his family was worried about him because he did nothing but read about the West and dream about the West and practice throwing a rope down on his Sussex estate. I was informed that he had become an excellent rope-thrower.

"I am afraid," he sighed, "I can never ranch myself, but I have a younger brother who can, and I can go out and see him . . . . Do they still shoot many people out there?"

He was bitterly disappointed when I told him they did not and, in reality, never had.

The young peer thought the old West was still alive, but the East knows better. Especially do all literary critics, and motion-picture critics, and dramatic critics, and publishers; in fact, for some odd reason, particularly all those connected with publicity. Not one of these classes mentions the cowboy without referring to his demise and no publisher of Western stories but has a sentence on the jacket of his product stating that this is an authentic description of 'the vanished' or 'fast vanishing wilderness.' Even the motion-pictures, in their wild, moronotic way, know better than this. I saw one such jacket on a recently published book and was amused to find in the magazine of this publishing house, appearing at the same time the book was published, the best articles about the cowpuncher I have read for a long while, and they are written by a man whose profession until recently was that of a cowpuncher.

Even the English papers are joining in the cry. The other day I picked one up and came across this jewel of knowledge: "In the Canadian Northwest in the days when it was real wilderness and a real frontier—" I wonder if the man who wrote that has ever seen the Canadian Northwest, or has heard of the Mackenzie River, or the Peace River, or Great Slave Lake, or knows any of the recent exploits of the Northwest Mounted Police?

Perhaps it is satiation. If this is the cause the East is justified, for during the past decade it has been flooded with lies and truth about the West, and the worm will turn, although, as somebody has said, 'it does him little good, since he is the same on all sides.' I should not like to think, as, indeed, I have pointed out I do not think, that all this interest in things Western is the flowering of the double rose— the final refulgence before dissolution.

I do not believe it is the final refulgence, and I do not even think it is satiation. I think the present point of view of the East towards the 'old West' is due to a much simpler mental reaction, a reaction as simple as that which produces the point of view of the old-time Westerner; something having to do with the aphorism that familiarity breeds contempt. Although, of course, this aphorism—if you will consider it—applies only to dull people. Familiarity breeds no contempt with the wise or the far-seeing.

Anything which you know well loses, unless you are a singularly intelligent person, a fraction of its glamour. If you are a stupid person it loses all of its glamour. A stupid man marries the most beautiful and charming of women and immediately she becomes in his eyes less beautiful and less charming than almost any other woman whom he has not married. The strange is magical, but the magic of your own fireside is merely that dull thing, home. The East has discovered the West and has gone out to it by the thousands and, therefore, although the West may still be a lovely place in which to spend the summer, and although the mountains sleeping in the sun may still be there, and the quiet lakes, and the wide valleys, and the young men who dress like cowpunchers and talk like cowpunchers and think and work and play like cowpunchers, and although prospectors still prospect the hills, the West, having been discovered by the East, is no longer the material out of which conjuration is made. Your uncle, perhaps, or your father, or your grandfather could weave enchantment out of the West, but not you.

Can't you? There are a lot of young men—and young women—who still seem to know the necessary necromantic signs.

I should hate to think what old 'Pap' Nichol once said in his high-pitched voice was true, and that is, that 'the West was a nice place and a real honest place until them damn dudes come.'

Like everything else, it all depends upon the width of your vision. Within the circle of your mind lies the whole world, but the world is no wider than the circle of your mind.

Last summer a newspaperman came into the valley, and spent two days there, and rode from one end of it to the other in a motor-car. He was a nice fellow and a clever one, although his cleverness, as is the case with many newspapermen, was blurred by the percussion of too many events. After leaving the valley he wrote an article in which he described the valley as the 'last frontier' and then went on to say that 'the last frontier' had disappeared. He had found merely a modern and growing community, potentially a great tourist country; he had not 'even been able to discover a bad man.' Bad men are not important; I for one would be happy if the valley were entirely without them; but if I had known that they were one of the objects of the newspaperman's search I could have shown him a 'bad man' not over ten yards away—an excessively bad man. Possibly, however, he wouldn't have believed me. Perhaps he cherished an unobtainable ideal of a 'bad man'—something that roared and stuck a feather in his cap like Macaroni.

As to the rest of it, although the valley never was 'the last frontier,' there being plenty of other countries just as much if not more of a frontier than it is, and although it hasn't been a frontier of any sort for a number of years, it is still sufficiently wild and beautiful and unspoiled.

XXVIII
IN THE HIGH HILLS

AND this brings me to the motor-car and its effect upon the West and outdoor life generally. My friend of the newspapers overlooked the fact that you cannot see much wilderness from the seat of a motor-car. But he could have used his imagination. I wonder what he thought was going on in the great, shaggy, lonely forests and hills that hemmed him in to the north and the south and the east and the west?

No, you cannot see much from the seat of a motor-car, and motor-cars in the West are a mixed curse and blessing—just as they are everywhere else. They are a blessing because they take out of themselves and make travelers of thousands who otherwise would never leave their villages or shops or factories, and because eventually they will build up a nation that knows fairly well even its own vast territory, a nation of fairly good outdoorsmen and campers; but they are a curse because they prevent other thousands who might have seen things intimately from ever doing so, and because, even at their best, like most American institutions, they engender a philosophy that is broad but never deep. They stand for half-way knowledge. You know the highways, but you never know the lanes. You see the mountains, but you never really get into them. You camp out, but you never know the real heart of camping. The one hope is that possibly in the future the ranks of the real campers will be recruited more and more from the ranks of the motor campers, who realize that there are, after all, limits to the motor camp.

A National Park ranger told me that an indignant woman burst in upon him and demanded why, when the park had built its own roads, it had been so stupid as not to build one near a certain famous canyon and waterfall.

"But, madam," the ranger asked, "from what direction did you come?"

"From the south."

"Then for over a quarter of a mile you rode within a few feet of that canyon. There was nothing between you and it but a low retaining wall. Will you go back? It is only a couple of minutes away."

She would not go back, she was in a hurry. But her complaint suggested an investigation. For over a month the rangers at that particular station asked as many tourists as they could if they had seen the canyon. About twenty per cent of these tourists said they hadn't, and of this twenty per cent, five per cent refused to turn their cars about and go back. They, also, were in too great a hurry.

I dreaded the automobile when it first came into the valley; I thought that then surely the 'old West' would go. But the automobile has not been half so destructive as I imagined. Its inherent limitations, at least in countries such as mine, prevent it from becoming too ruinous. It must stay upon certain definite roads and its owners have only certain places where it is possible for them to camp. If you avoid these roads and camps you are not much troubled. Nor at any time, even on these roads and at these camps, are you troubled for long. The main travel only lasts for a month, from the middle of July to the middle of August. Moreover, the country is too large for the motor-car to conquer it. I stopped my horse in the middle of a sage-brush flat and watched a car go by. In a few minutes—moments, rather—it became a dwindling speck upon the horizon, for all actual purposes as far from me and I from it as if we were miles apart. I could have called and the people in the car would not have heard me, and they could have called and I would not have heard them. Even when the car had been close to me it was merely a straddling bug dwarfed by immensity. I realized something more; I realized that nearness is a question solely of the communication of minds and per-sonalities; mechanical appliances in themselves mean nothing. Had I been talking to a man in Chicago over the telephone I would have been nearer to him than I was to that car.

Wherever motors go, of course, there are no fish left, or birds, or cleanliness, but motors can go only a few places. And sometimes even motors promote enchantment. There is an exhilarating annihilation of space about them, if you do not use them too much. It is exciting to see three mountain ranges in a day when it would take you a week to climb the side of one of them with a pack outfit, and it is good for you if afterwards you go back and really look at the mountains.

Indeed, far from the West having lost its romance, think, on the whole, it has achieved more romance; has kept a large part of the old romance and added to it. The advent of the Easterner—of the dude-ranch—has not destroyed romance but increased it. Only those who have never lived on an actual cow-ranch, especially a bachelor ranch, could think otherwise. There is nothing more interesting, as I have pointed out, than the reactions of the Easterner upon the Westerner and vice versa; nothing more interesting, as I have also pointed out, than the effect of a wild country upon a cultivated, or supposedly cultivated, mind. And recently a new element has been added in the shape of motion-picture companies who occasionally wander into the valley and stay for a while in strange gypsy-like encampments.

They are a curious sight, these encampments; the sleek-haired men, the almost beautiful, unnatural, neurasthenic women; the wide-eyed local cowpunchers and teamsters who have been hired to supply atmosphere or do the manual labor. Between the trunks of forest trees swinging signs are put up, that blow down the next winter, upon which with a hot iron is inscribed the earth-shaking news that on such and such a date 'The Greatart Players, Claude Duval directing,

Maria Montesierre and Charles Lovelace acting,' have camped there for two weeks, or three weeks, or a month. Plump young women, dressed in the bathing-suits permitted only in southern California, that curiously unmoral, fiercely Puritanical land, plunge into mountain lakes and eat their meals at long tables unconcernedly without changing into more conventional attire, and languid leading ladies patronize God and the country and any casual visitor.

One famous director took me out into the twilight and stood with his arm through mine, and as we looked at an apocalyptic sunset flaring behind a mountain peak fourteen thousand feet high, said suddenly and dreamily:

"My Tetons!"

I have spoken of 'my country' because that could not be helped and because it is a common phrase that implies no lack of proportion, but it had never occurred to me before that a man could make such an objective thing as a mountain fourteen thousand feet high so subjective as to call it 'his own.'

A blond leading lady whom both my wife and myself had met in California—at Hollywood, which Karl Kitchen so aptly calls 'Moronia'—swam up to us—not literally, but with the swaying lack of interest and large dull beautiful eyes that most motion-picture people affect . . . as if they were living in an aquarium—and said she was glad to see us again.

"And these dear kind people!" she added. "They ask me to lunch and then I discover that they live five and ten miles away."

"I'm so sorry," murmured my wife, "because we wanted to ask you, too, but we live twenty miles away.

Who wrote the picture you are playing in, Miss Thingamabob? "

Miss Thingamabob became even more patiently weary. "I do not know. I never know the names of the people who write the things I act in." Untactful, to say the least, since numerous stories and novels of my wife have been turned into pictures. And amusing in this particular instance, since the play from which the scenario in question had been taken had been written by a man who at one time was the most famous playwright in America. There was only one obvious retort for my wife to make.

"That is exactly the case with me," she laughed. "I never can remember the names of the people who act in the things I write."

The large dull beautiful eyes exhibited no emotion, but afterwards we learned that we had "insulted the profession." An illuminating point of view, because I had always thought until then that writing was a profession, also . . . .

With the going of the brief summer, however, the country comes back absolutely, completely into its own. It is an odd alteration, sudden as the lowering or raising of a curtain; a divestment of one sort of romance and the sight once more of the naked, beautiful romance underneath. The country is like a woman who, bathing in a green forest pool, her summer clothes dropped from her, stands for a moment speculative before she dons the thick, disguising garments of winter. The last motor has gone, all but the hunters of big game and the hardier dudes; the motion-picture people and the quaint, annoying campers have departed, and a sense of loneliness drops across the world like the gold mist of St. Martin. And presently the gold mist is copied by the gold of the aspens. The mountain ash turns red. The hills are a green fire with smouldering edges and smouldering circles where the choked flames have burst through. When you ride under the aspens their leaves shake like a million little golden bells. Far off and faint and dying away you hear the bugling of the elk. There is a stillness soft as the whispering of the grass. Dawn is a crystal held between brackets of sapphire; noon is the crystal with a light behind it; dusk is the crystal hiding a star.

The remembrance of beauty, the beauty of a thing, or of personal relationships, or of a country, has always seemed to me perhaps the chief end of life; at least, the only end that obviously justifies life. The present cannot be held; it slips through our grasping fingers; becomes immediately the past. The future may neither be beautiful nor worth remembering; certainly its beauty will be accompanied by ugliness and tragedy; but what has happened is ours and cannot be taken away from us, and the mind, like the gauze screen through which gold is run, transmutes in retrospect almost everything into loveliness. Remembrance is the one sure immortality we know. So long as the memory of a man remains he is never really dead. Nor does this lend to present negligence, for if we believe the theory, we will do our best with both the present and the future, since they are the stuff out of which memory is made.

And I can claim some memories. Even if my present and future add no more to what I have, I have had much. For moments I have been 'a brother of the sun,' and I have watched the moon rise, and I have heard the wind come from long distances, and I have lain down on the earth and felt its breath, and I have known people for short spaces intimately—I have seen the eye of the camera open for an instant before it closed again.

Crowds are the enemies of man and God. To steer your way through a crowd requires too many reactions, and too many of these reactions are automatic and need no thought. The man who lives in a crowd shaves himself automatically, and drives a car into town automatically, and does most of his business automatically and returns to a night of automatic card-playing and the automatic loving of his wife, or somebody else's wife. In the end he dies automatically and is buried automatically. The narrow, limpid continuity of reflection is missing. The thin lane whose blank, untroubled walls permit you to see at the other end some shadow of whatever god you are hunting is not there. In order to know any sort of god, or yourself, you must live part of your time like quick-silver in a vacuum. If you do not, your spiritual temperature will neither rise nor lower.

The grave-robbers of literature and the weary people who believe in them are not to be blamed. How can they see the necessity for any sort of a god when their instant necessity is to step out of the way of a motor-car; or how can they see the necessity for any sort of a woman, except physically, when they have never known what a woman's companionship in loneliness is? How can they respect their own race and think it more than a chemical formula if they have only seen it jostling and drinking and slobbering and thieving and begetting? Even democracy, if you have been fortunate enough to watch it actually in operation, seems, if not the final political philosophy, at least the best form of government as yet discovered; certainly the highest step yet reached. But democracy is over when crowds step in. It is done for, ended. I, however, have lived in a sparsely settled country and I have seen democracy, and like that other almost non-existent system, Christianity, it is admirable if real.

I have seen democracy articulated. When I first came into the valley no man could starve to death, and no man need be out of work, and no door was locked at night, and all men were hospitable and ingenuous, and they thought slowly and carefully, and they rendered assistance. Now the valley is a trifle more crowded, and a man can easily starve to death, and the question of labor and capital has entered in, and a few steal, and money is charged for meals because so many come for them . . . . What is it all about, when there are so few things a man needs, and everything else is merely a curtain between him and reality? It is not the devil who makes temptations, but man who makes his own and then invents the devil as a scapegoat.

What the world desires and what it struggles for is vividness. And all around and through the world is vividness the world cannot lay its hands upon. Sin is boredom. Prohibitions are the follies of reformers who do not know that no keenly interested man desires to waste his time; illegitimacy is the result of a baffled reaching out for vividness; wars are not fought well by vivid men living vividly. The man who is interested in life goes to war with a great yawn of indignation and is dismayed by the childish dullness of war as compared to his own vivid normal existence. It is appalling to hear men and women speak of the last war as if it had been to them a release. Release from what? From work, from love, from reflection?

But, like all men who have lived in the Far West, I have seen vividness and I know it, and no matter how much my latter years may take me into crowded places I will carry the memories of vividness with me. I know that life can be as sharp as a knife and as sweet as mint with river water on it, and as enveloping as the shadows flung out across a plain by the edge of a deep forest. How can it be otherwise when music, too, can touch this sharpness and sweetness, and a book, and exercise, and friends—if they have time—and dear pretty women—if they also have time?

In winter towards evening the mists rise from the river in iridescent coils, pale green and dark green, and scarlet and violet and silver gray and, the early sun setting behind the great snowfields, the mountains, from their tips to the blanket of the pines, turn blood-red, a sacrificial red, and, this fading, a small cold star comes out and the sky is held with a clear pallor as keen and tautly tremulous as the unheard notes of the upper scale. But the real night is thick with a purple sky that hangs close, and with stars, immense and brilliant, that drop down until they almost much the rooftrees.

In summer the hills are warm and lavender by day, and by night they are warm, thin silhouettes against a sky as remote as the tracery of a cathedral tower, and water under the moon runs in irrigating ditches like generous silver too warm to harden into shape. In the rows of vegetable-gardens the growing things are magical and un-real, and the breath of the dry forests meets the breath of the damp swamps and fields.

In autumn the ducks go by etched against the blacks and crimsons of the sunset; and in spring the first round shining pebble that shows beneath the snow is a discovery and a continent in itself.

I do not know. I have said that the old West is still there, and so it is, and I have said that in many places it will continue to exist, and that is true, also, but I am afraid for my own country unless some help is given it—some wise direction. It is too beautiful and now too famous. Sometimes I dream of it unhappily. And when my blood stirs in my dreams I think that somewhere the blood of my uncle and my great-grandfather must be stirring, too.

Other Books by Sastrugi Press

2024 Total Eclipse State Series by Aaron Linsdau

Sastrugi Press has published state-specific guides for the 2024 total eclipse crossing over the United States. Check the Sastrugi Press website for the available state eclipse books: www.sastrugipress.com/eclipse

50 Wildlife Hotspots by Moose Henderson

Find out where to find animals and photograph them in Grand Teton National Park from a professional wildlife photographer. This unique guide shares the secret locations with the best chance at spotting wildlife.

A Small Pile of Feathers by Gerry Spence

Gerry Spence reveals his spiritual, loving, and sometimes humorous sides, depicted in his devotion to family and preserving the wild places he writes of as though they were inscribed on his own bones and in his own blood.

Antarctic Tears by Aaron Linsdau

What would make someone give up a high-paying career to ski alone across Antarctica to the South Pole? This inspirational true story will make readers both cheer and cry. Fighting skin-freezing temperatures, infections, and emotional breakdown, Jackson Hole native Aaron Linsdau exposes the harsh realities of being on an expedition.

Cache Creek by Susan Marsh

Five minutes from the hubbub of Jackson's town square, Cache Creek offers the chance for hikers to immerse themselves in wild nature. It is a popular hiking, biking, and cross-country ski area on the outskirts of Jackson, Wyoming.

Cloudshade by Lori Howe, Ph.D.

The poems of Cloudshade breathe with the vivid, fragrant essence of life in every season on America's high plains. Extraordinarily relatable, the poems of Cloudshade swing wide a door to life in the West, both for lovers of poetry and for those who don't normally read poems.

Journeys to the Edge by Randall Peeters, Ph.D.

What is it like to climb Mount Everest? It requires dreaming big and creating a personal vision to climb the mountains in your life. Randall Peeters shares his successes and failures and provides the reader with some directly applicable guidelines on how to create a life vision.

Lost at Windy Corner by Aaron Linsdau

Windy Corner on Denali has claimed lives, fingers, and toes. What would make someone brave lethal weather, crevasses, and slick ice to attempt to summit North America's highest mountain? The author shares the lessons Denali teaches on managing goals and risks. Apply the message to build resilience and overcome adversity.

Prevailing Westerlies by Ed Lavino

With clarity and intensity, Lavino's photographs express a longing for the natural world and hope for its future. An intimacy with the Rocky Mountain West born of long familiarity and close observation is evident. These beautiful black and white images are timeless, yet decidedly modern.

Roaming the Wild by Grover Ratliff

Experience the landscape and wildlife photography of Grover Ratliff in this unique volume. Jackson Hole is home to some of the most iconic landscapes in North America. In this land of harsh winters and short summers, wildlife survives and thrives. People from all around the world travel here to savor the rare vistas.

Sleeping Dogs Don't Lie by Michael McCoy

A young Native American boy is taken from his home after tragedy strikes, grows up in middle America, and through his first real adult summer searches for Wyoming artifacts, falls in with the subversive Dog Soldiers Resurrected, and attempts single-handedly to solve the murder of his treasured coworker.

So I Said by Gerry Spence

The collected sayings of Gerry Spence provokes readers into thinking about their own vision of the world. As a lawyer with decades of experience in defending the defenseless, he's fought against giants. His insights provide a grander vision of how the nearly invisible world of the justice system in *So I Said*.

Voices at Twilight by Lori Howe, Ph.D.

Voices at Twilight is a guide takes readers on a visual tour of twelve past and present Wyoming ghost towns. Contained within are travel directions, GPS coordinates, and tips for intrepid readers.

Visit Sastrugi Press on the web at www.sastrugipress.com to purchase the above titles in bulk. They are also available from your local bookstore or online retailers in print, e-book, or audiobook form.

Thank you for choosing Sastrugi Press.

www.sastrugipress.com

"Turn the Page Loose"